THE SEXUAL LIFE OF THE CHILD BY DR. ALBERT MOLL

ISBN-13:

978-1533374042

ISBN-10:

153337404X

THE SEXUAL LIFE OF THE CHILD BY DR. ALBERT MOLL

Edited by
Mark Guy Valerius Tyson

Cover design & internal design by Mark Guy Valerius Tyson

www.markguyvaleriustyson.com
www.mgvt.co.uk

ALSO AVAILABLE FROM MGVT

CONTENTS

Exhibitionism--Skatophilia--Hermaphroditism.

Family Tendencies--Abnormal Nervous System--Race--Climate--Position in Life--Town and Country--Modern Civilisation--Importance of Congenital Predisposition--Seduction--Local Stimulation--Chemical Stimuli--Psychical Stimuli.

Diagnostic Difficulties--Recognition by means of Observation--Erroneous Diagnoses of Masturbation--The Value of Physical Signs--Value of a Confidant--Misleading Statements and Conduct on the part of Children.

Non-Sexual Erections--Non-Sexual Manipulations--Sucking Movements--Nail-Biting--Imitativeness--Impossibility of any Definite Demarcation of Sexual Feelings.

The Sexual Life and Morbid Hereditary Predisposition--Hygienic Dangers--The Dangers of Masturbation in General--Of Masturbation in the Child--Masturbation without Ejaculation--Exaggerated Views to be Avoided--Amatory Passion and Suicide--Freud's Theory--Infectious Diseases.

Ethical Dangers--Masturbation and Ethics--Social Dangers--Social Degradation of Girls--Seduction of Girls--Forensic Importance xvof the Sexual Life--Children's Evidence--Circumstances affecting Culpability--Penal Responsibility of Children--Intellectual Dangers--Sexuality and Altruism.

Sexual Perversions and the Choice of a Profession--Punishments and Masochism--Curiosity of Children--Sexuality and Art--The Question of the Offspring.

Importance of Tardy Sexual Development.

Pædophilia Erotica--Other Sexual Offences against Children--Sexual Acts Performed on Children--Significance of each Acts to the Child--Artificial Production of Sexual Perversions--False Accusations--Statistics of Accusations by Children--Reasons for Protecting Children----Injuries effected on Children by the Law--Responsibility of Pædophiles.

Exhibitionism--Sadism--Newspaper Advertisement.

IX.　Sexual Education 224

Limits of Educability--General Hygiene--Custom and Morality--Inculcation of the Sentiments of Shame and Disgust--Influence upon these Sentiments of Habit and Example--Morality and Nakedness--Excessive Sentiments of Shame and Disgust--The Nude in Art--Morality in Fanatics--Erotic Books and Pictures.

Co-Education of the Sexes--Children's Balls--Diversion of the Sexual Impulse--Religious Education--The Bible--The Confessional--Hypnotism--Psycho-Analysis--Counteraction of Psychical Contagion.

Sexual Enlightenment--General Educational Interests--Hygienic Reasons for Enlightenment--The Dangers of Venereal Infection--Of Masturbation--Ethical Reasons--Forensic Reasons--Social Reasons--Age at which Enlightenment is Desirable--Place of Enlightenment; School or Home--The School Physician--Importance of the Mother--Individualisation--Mode of Enlightenment.--Reasons urged against Enlightenment--Need that the Instructor should be an Enlightened Person--Exaggerated Views regarding the Importance of Sexual Enlightenment.

Physical Hygienic Measures--Stimulation by Means of the Bed--Local Stimulation--Mechanical Measures--Hydrotherapeutic Measures--Dirt--Sport and Games--Féré's Method.

Pedagogy and Sexual Perversions--Dangers from Pædophiles--Necessity for Heterosexual Influences--Dangers of Corporal Punishment--The Right of the Teacher to Inflict Punishment--Conclusion.

FOR ALL SEEKERS OF THE TRUTH

INTRODUCTION

Dr. Moll is a gifted physician of long experience whose work with those problems of medicine and hygiene which demand scientific acquaintance with human nature has made him well known to experts in these fields. In this book he has undertaken to describe the origin and development, in childhood and youth, of the acts and feelings due to sex; to explain the forces by which sex-responses are directed and misdirected; and to judge the wisdom of existing and proposed methods of preventing the degradation of a child's sexual life.

This difficult task is carried out, as it should be, with dignity and frankness. In spite of the best intentions, a scientific book on sex-psychology is likely to appear, at least in spots, to gratify a low curiosity; but in Dr. Moll's book there is no such taint. Popular books on sex-hygiene, on the other hand, are likely to suffer from a pardonable but harmful delicacy whereby the facts of anatomy, physiology, and psychology which are necessary to make their principles comprehensible and useful, are omitted, veiled, or even distorted. Dr. Moll honours his readers by a frankness which may seem brutal to some of them. It is necessary.

With dignity and frankness Dr. Moll combines notable good sense. In the case of any exciting movement in advance of traditional custom, the forerunners are likely to combine a certain one-sidedness and lack of balance with their really valuable progressive ideas. The greater sagacity and critical power are more often found amongst the men of science who avoid public discussion of exciting social or moral reforms, and are suspicious of startling and revolutionary doctrines or practices. It is therefore fortunate that a book on the sexual life during childhood should have been written by a man of critical, matter-of-fact mind, of long experience as a medical specialist, and of wide scholarship, who has no private interest in any exciting psychological doctrine or educational panacea.

The translation of this book will be welcomed by men and women from many different professions, but alike in the need of preparation to guide the sex-life of boys and girls and to meet emergencies caused by its corruption by weakness within or attack from without. Of the clergymen in this country who are in real touch with the lives of their charges, there is hardly a one who does not, every so often, have to minister to a mind whose moral and religious distress depends on an unfortunate sex history. Conscientious and observant teachers realize, in a dim way, that they cannot do justice to even the purely intellectual needs of pupils without understanding the natural history of those instinctive impulses, which, concealed and falsified as they are under our traditional taboos, nevertheless retain enormous potency. The facts, so clearly shown in the present volume, that the life of sex begins long before its obvious manifestations at puberty, and that the direction of its vaguer and less differentiated habits in these earlier years is as important as its hygiene at the more noticeable climax of the early 'teens, increase the teacher's responsibility. Moreover, there is probably not a teacher of ten years' standing who has not faced—or by ignorance neglected—some emergency where moderate insight into the laws whereby the vague instincts of sex are turned into healthy and unhealthy habits, and form right and wrong attitudes, could have rescued a boy or girl from years of wretched anxiety, or degraded conduct, or both.

The social worker, still more emphatically, knows his or her need of a surer equipment for the wise direction of the life of sex in childhood and its protection from the abominable suggestions of those who are themselves sexually diseased or depraved. The casual questioning of medical or legal friends, reminiscences of vague references in the Bible or classic literature, and the miscellaneous experiences which life itself throws in one's way, are hopelessly inadequate.

The conscientious practitioner of medicine, too, will gladly add to the scanty, though accurate, knowledge of the sex-instinct and its pathology which is all that even the best medical course can compass, the facts presented by a specialist in this field. The easiest way for those parents who accept the responsibility for rational guidance of their children in matters of sex-behavior to discharge this responsibility is by the aid of the family physician. For the physician in such cases to gain the child's confidence, understand his individual dangers and possible false attitudes, and give more than perfunctory general counsel, knowledge of the psychology of sex-behavior, as well as its physiology, is necessary. In general, also, modern medical practice must look after the prevention of bad habits and unnecessary anxieties in respect to the sex-life as well as their cure; and the science of preventive medicine in this field receives a substantial contribution from this summary of the sex-life of childhood.

There are now many men and women who are dissatisfied with doing for their children merely what outgrown customs decree, who are willing to give time and study, as well as money and affection, in their service, and who are eager to see or hear or read anything pertinent to their welfare. For many such parents, if they are of the scientific, matter-of-fact type, Dr. Moll's book may prove the means of answering many troublesome questions and of prompting to a wiser co-operation with church, school, and the medical profession in safeguarding their own—and, we may hope, all other—children against blunders and contaminations.

One word of caution is perhaps necessary for those readers who are unused to descriptions of symptoms of diseases, abnormalities, and defects. Such readers are likely to interpret perfectly ordinary facts as the symptoms which they have been studying. So the medical student at the beginning of his reading, fears appendicitis when he has slight indigestion, and sees incipient tuberculosis in every household! So the embryonic psychologist finds 'degenerates' in every crowd of boys, 'hypnotic suggestion' in every popular preacher, and 'aphasia' in any friend who forgets names and faces! Dr. Moll gives more protection against such exaggerated inferences than is commonly given in books on pathology, but many of his readers will do well to be on their guard lest they interpret perfectly innocent behavior as a symptom of abnormality. The mischief done by our present ignorance and neglect of important features of sex-behavior should be prevented without the incidence of mischief from exaggerated expectations and unwise meddling.

It would be evasive to shirk mention of the fact that many of the most devoted servants of health and morals object to public discussion of the facts of sex. They discard enlightenment about sex as relatively unimportant because a clean ancestry, decency in the family and neighborhood, and noble needs in friendship, love, and marriage must, in any case, be the main roots of healthy direction and ideal restraint of the sex-instinct. Or they fear enlightenment as a possible stimulus to undesirable imagination and experimentation. Or they dislike, even abhor, it as esthetically repulsive—shocking to an unreasoned but cherished craving for silence about these things—a craving which the customs of our land and time have made an unwritten law of society.

Of the first of these three attitudes, it may be said briefly that the relative unimportance of enlightenment is a fact, but no argument against it. Modesty, austerity, and clean living on the part of parents will counterbalance much negligence in direct guidance or protection. But the former need be in no wise lessened by improving the latter. Of the second, I dare affirm that if the men and women in America should stop whatever they are doing for an evening and read this book, there would be less harmful imagination as a result than from the occupations which its reading would replace. Of all the causes of sexual disorder, the reading of scientific books by reputable men is surely the least! The third—

that is, the esthetic—repulsion toward publicity in respect to the natural history of sex, I will not pretend to judge. Only we must not strain at gnats and swallow camels. It is no sign of true esthetic orix moral sensitiveness for a person to be shocked by 'Ghosts,' 'Mrs. Warren's Profession,' or 'The Sexual Life of the Child,' who finds pleasant diversion in the treatment of sex-behavior in the ordinary novel, newspaper, or play.

On the whole, the gain from giving earnest men and women the facts they need, seems likely to outweigh by much the harm done to such light minds as will be misled, or to such sentimental minds as will be wounded, by enlightenment about sex. No harm will be done to those men and women whose interest in the welfare of children makes them eager to face every problem that it involves, and whose faith in the ideal possibilities of love between the sexes is too well-grounded to be disturbed by the facts of its natural history.

EDWARD L. THORNDIKE.

May, 1912.

PREFACE

The number of books and essays dealing with sexual topics published during recent years is by no means small; but although some of the works in question have added considerably to our knowledge, the advance of sexual science as a whole has not been proportionate to the extent of these contributions. The reason is that insufficient attention has been paid to special problems; and the majority of writers have either repeated what has already been said by another, in identical or equivalent words, or else they have published comprehensive treatises on the sexual life, which may, perhaps, be of interest to the laity, but do not in any way enrich our science. Further advances in our knowledge of the sexual life can be effected only by the investigation of special problems. Such work is, indeed, laborious; but that it is also fruitful, has been clearly shown, not only in the first instance by von Krafft-Ebing, but more recently, above all, by Havelock Ellis, whose special studies have contributed more to the advance of sexual science than the work of dozens of other writers.

The recognition of the need for specialised investigations has led me, in this province of scientific work as in other departments, to devote myself to the elucidation of certain definite problems. For several reasons I determined to study the sexual life of the child. In the first place, I believe that an advance in our knowledge of the sexual life of the child will indirectly enrich our knowledge also of the sexual life of the adult. In order to understand the sexual life, the gradual development of that life must be recognised, and for this purpose it is essential that we should study the sexual life of the child. Moreover, the modern movement in favour of the sexual enlightenment of young persons renders indispensable the possession of precise knowledge of the sexuality of thexii child; and such knowledge is no less necessary to all instructors of youth, especially to those to whom the psychical life of children is a matter of concern. Judges and magistrates also, as we shall see in the seventh chapter, are very greatly interested in this matter: it is, in fact, hardly open to question that erroneous legal decisions and the unjust condemnation of reputed criminals can only be avoided by giving our judicial authorities the opportunity of obtaining sound knowledge concerning the sexual life of children in all its modes of manifestation. By all these considerations I have been induced to study the problem of the sexuality of children from the most widely different points of view. Although other writers, such as Freud, Bell, and Kötscher, have contributed certain data towards the solution of these questions, no comprehensive study of the subject has hitherto been attempted. My material does not consist only of the reports of patients. In addition, in order to avoid a one-sided dependence upon pathological considerations, I have accepted with greater confidence the reports concerning the sexual life of children which I have received from healthy individuals, both men and women. I take this opportunity of tendering my most heartfelt thanks to all those who have assisted me in this manner.

ALBERT MOLL.

CHAPTER I

INTRODUCTORY AND HISTORICAL

To speak of "the sexual life of the child" seems at first sight to involve a contradiction in terms. It is generally assumed that the sexual life first awakens at the on-coming of puberty (the attainment of sexual maturity of manhood or womanhood); the on-coming of puberty is regarded as the termination of childhood; in fact the term child is usually defined as the human being from the time of birth to the on-coming of puberty. But this contradiction is apparent merely, and depends on the assumption that the on-coming of puberty is indicated by certain outward signs (more especially the first menstruation and the first seminal emission), insufficient attention being paid to the long period of development which usually precedes these occurrences. And yet, during this period of preliminary development, the occurrence of certain manifestations of the sexual life is plainly demonstrable.

The period of childhood is subdivided into several sub-epochs, but the delimitation and nomenclature of these varies so much with different investigators, that to avoid misunderstanding I must first define the subdivisions which I myself propose to employ. If we regard the beginning of the fifteenth year as the termination of childhood, we may divide childhood into two equal periods, the first extending from birth to the completion of the seventh year, the second from the beginning of the eighth to the end of the fourteenth year. I shall in this work designate these two periods as the first and the second period of childhood respectively. In the first period of childhood, the first year of life may be further distinguished as the period of infancy. The first and second periods of childhood comprise childhood in the narrower sense of the term. The years that immediately follow the beginning of the fifteenth year I shall denote as the period of youth. Inasmuch as the symptoms of this latter come to differ from those of childhood proper, not abruptly, but gradually, the first years, at least, of youth will often come under our consideration, and I shall speak of this period of life as the third period of childhood. Although childhood in the narrower sense comprises the first and second periods only, childhood in the wider sense includes also the third period. It is hardly possible that any misunderstanding can arise if the reader will bear in mind that whenever I speak of childhood without qualification, I allude only to the period of life before the beginning of the fifteenth year. For all these periods of childhood, first, second, and third, I shall for practical convenience when speaking of males use the word boy, and when speaking of females, the word girl.

The use of this terminology must not be regarded as implying that the distinctions indicated correspond in any way to fixed natural lines of demarcation; on the contrary, individual variations are numerous and manifold. Not only does the rate of development differ in different races (in the Caucasian race, more especially, the age of puberty comes comparatively late, so that among the members of this race childhood is prolonged); but further, within the limits of one and the same race, notable differences occur. More than all have we to take into account the differences between the sexes, childhood terminating earlier in the female sex than in the male—among our own people [the Germans] this difference is commonly estimated at as much as two years. In addition, in this respect, there are marked differences between different classes of the population, a matter to which we shall return in Chapter VI.

It is also necessary to point out here in what sense I employ the term puberty (nubility, sexual ripeness, or maturity), and the associated terms, nubile and sexually mature. Much confusion exists in respect of the application of these terms. Some use puberty to denote a period of time, others, a point of time, and in various other ways the word is differently used by different authors. Similarly as regards the term nubile; some consider an individual to be nubile as soon as he or she is competent for procreation, others speak of anyone as nubile only when the development of the sexual life is completed. Obviously, these two notions are very different; for instance, a girl of thirteen who has begun to menstruate may be competent for the act of procreation, and yet her sexual development may still be far from complete. The confusion as regards the use of the substantive puberty is no less perplexing. One writer uses it to denote the time at which procreative capacity begins, and believes he is right in assuming that in the male this time is indicated by the occurrence of the first involuntary sexual orgasm. I may point out in passing that there is a confusion here between procreative capacity and competence for sexual intercourse, for as a rule the first seminal emissions contain no spermatozoa. But, apart from such confusions, the term puberty is used in various senses. Thus, a second writer denotes by puberty the point of time at which the sexual development is completed; a third means by puberty the period which elapses between the occurrence of the first involuntary orgasm and the completion of sexual development; a fourth uses the word to denote the entire period of life during which procreative capacity endures; and finally, a fifth includes under the notion of puberty the whole course of life after the completion of sexual development. In this work I shall mean by puberty the period of life between the completion of sexual development and the extinction of the sexual life. The period during which the state of puberty is being attained will be spoken of as the period of puberal development, and I shall therefore speak of the beginning and the end of the puberal development. The terms nubility, sexual maturity, nubile, and sexually mature, will be used with a similar signification. As regards the puberal development, let me at the outset draw attention to the fact that it takes place very gradually; and further, as we shall see, that it begins much earlier than is commonly believed. In the young girl, from the date of the first menstruation to the time at which she has become fitted for marriage, the average lapse of time is assumed by Ribbing to be two years. This is a fair estimate, but it does not correspond to the totality of the period of the puberal development. If we estimate that period from its true beginning its duration greatly exceeds two years, for the first indications of the puberal development are manifest in the girl long before the first menstruation, and in the boy long before the first discharge of semen. The approach of puberty is indicated by numerous symptoms, some of which are psychical and some physical in character. In perfectly healthy children, as will be shown in the sequel, individual symptoms may make their appearance as early as the age of seven or eight, and further symptoms successively appear during succeeding years, until the puberal development is completed.

What methods are available for the study of the sexual life of the child? Three methods have to be considered: first, the observation of children; secondly, experiment; and thirdly, reports made by individuals regarding their own experiences. As regards the last mentioned, we must distinguish clearly between accounts reproduced from memory long after the incidents to which they relate, and accounts given by children of their state at the time of narration. But both varieties of clinical history are defective. The child is often incompetent to describe his sensations—think, for instance, of the processes of the earliest years of life. Even when the child is able to make reports, a sense of shame will often interfere with the truthfulness of his account. Whilst as regards the memory-pictures of adults, recourse to this method often fails us because the experiences are so remote as to have been largely, if not entirely, forgotten. The autobiographies of sexually perverse individuals have drawn my attention to the fallacious nature of memory. Its records are uncertain, but that especially is recorded which has aroused interest. Not only the interest felt in the experiences at the time determines what shall be recorded, but also the interest felt later when reviving these experiences in memory. Childish experiences are very readily forgotten, either if they were uninteresting at the time, or if subsequently they have become uninteresting. During childhood, a homosexual woman has experienced sexual feeling, directed now towards boys, now towards girls. Later in life, when the homosexuality has developed fully, the memory of the inclination towards boys fades away, and her homosexual sentiments only are remembered. As a result, we often find that the homosexual woman—and the converse is equally true of the homosexual man—declares at first, when inquiries are made, that she has never experienced any inclination for members of the other sex; whereas, at any rate in a large proportion of cases, a stricter examination of her memory, or the reports of other individuals, will reveal beyond dispute that in childhood heterosexual inclinations were not lacking.

A further defect of memory has been made manifest to me by the study of perversions. Processes which in childhood were entirely devoid of any sexual tinge, but which later became associated with sex-feelings, very readily acquire false sexual associations also when they are revived in memory. Consider, for instance, the case of a homosexual man. He remembers that, as a small boy, he was very fond of sitting on his uncle's knees, and he believes that the pleasure he formerly experienced was tinged by sexual feeling. In reality this was by no means the case. His uncle took the boy on his knee in order to tell him a story. Possibly, also, the riding movements which the uncle imitated by jogging his knees up and down gave the child pleasure, which, however, was entirely devoid of any admixture of sexual feeling. But in the consciousness of the full-grown man, in whom homosexual feeling has later undergone full development, all this becomes distorted. The non-sexual motives are forgotten; he believes that even in early childhood he had homosexual inclinations, and that for this reason it gave him pleasure to ride on his uncle's knees.

Nor is observation in any way adapted to furnish us with a clear picture of the sexual life of the child. So little can be directly observed, that in the absence of reports much would remain entirely unknown. From the moment when the children gain a consciousness, however obscure, of the nature of sexual processes, they almost invariably endeavour to conceal their knowledge as much as possible, so that we shall discover its existence only by a rare chance. None the less, the results of direct observation are often important; sometimes because we are able to watch children when they are unaware of our attention, and sometimes because they do not as yet fully understand the nature of the processes under observation, and for this reason are less secretive.

The third method, that of experiment, is available to us only in the form of castration. I need not dilate on the inadequacy of this application of the experimental method, even apart from the fact that it subserves our purposes almost exclusively in respect of the male sex—for in the case of young girls, castration (oöphorectomy) is almost entirely unknown.

Thus we see that all our methods of investigation exhibit extensive lacunæ, and further, that they are all in many respects fallacious; we shall therefore endeavour to supplement each by the others, in order to arrive at results which shall be as free from error as possible. Thus guided, we learn that sexual incidents occur in childhood far more frequently than is usually supposed. So common are they, that they cannot possibly escape the notice of any practising physician or educationalist who pays attention to the question, provided, of course, that he enjoys the confidence of the parents. These latter have often been aware of such sexual manifestations in their children for a long time, but a false shame has prevented them from asking the advice of the physician. They have been afraid lest he should regard the child as intellectually or morally deficient, or as the offspring of a degenerate family. In addition, we have to take into account self-deception on the part of the parents, who, indeed, often deceive themselves willingly, saying to themselves that the matter is of no importance, and that the symptoms will disappear spontaneously.

Having given this brief account of the terminology to be employed and of the methods of investigation, I propose to sketch no less briefly the history of the subject.

Casual references to the sexual life of the child are to be found even in the older scientific literature. In the latter half of the eighteenth century, and at the beginning of the nineteenth, interest in the subject became more general. Two works, in especial, published almost simultaneously, attracted the attention of physicians and educationalists. One of these, Rousseau's Émile, discusses the proper conduct of parents and elders in relation to the awakening sexual life, and what they should do in order to delay that awakening as much as possible. The other, the celebrated work of Tissot, depicts the dangers of masturbation, but deals chiefly with persons who have attained sexual maturity. None the less, in consequence of this book, much attention was directed to the sexual life of the child. Earlier works on masturbation, such as that of Sarganeck, for instance, had not succeeded in arousing any enduring interest in this question. But Rousseau's and Tissot's books induced a large number of physicians and educationalists to occupy themselves in this province of study. Thus at this early day many authorities8 were led to advocate the sexual enlightenment of children, in order to guide them in the avoidance of the dangers of the sexual life. An excellent historical and critical study of this movement, written by Thalhofer, has recently been published. Among the educationalists who took part in it may be mentioned Basedow, Salzmann, Campe, and Niemeyer. The modern movement in favour of sexual enlightenment originated chiefly in the endeavour to prevent the diffusion of venereal diseases; but the earlier movement, occurring at a time when much less was known about venereal diseases, had a different aim. This was rather to prevent masturbation and other sexual excesses, on account of their direct effect upon the organism; an aim not neglected by the modern movement for sexual enlightenment, though subsidiary to the object of the prevention of the venereal diseases. Teachers of that day touched, of course, upon the subject of the sexual life of the child. But this was done cursorily, for when instruction was given on the sexual life, not the actual experience of children, but the sexual life of mature persons, was the subject of discourse. This must be said also of the works of those physicians who, like Hufeland in his Makrobiotik (written as a sequel to the work of Tissot), spoke of the dangers of masturbation.

A few of the numerous medical books dealing with the puberal development deserve mention in this place; for instance, Marro, La Pubertà (first edition, published in 1897), and Bacqué, La Puberté (Argenteuil, 1876). A number of recent works on masturbation have also touched on the topic of the sexual life of the child.

Apart from these recent special investigations, the older and the more recent medical and anthropological literature contains numerous observations which concern the subject of this book. More especially do we find reports of cases in which the external manifestations of sexual maturity appeared in very early childhood. Now we find an account of a girl menstruating at four years of age, now an account of a three-year-old boy who exhibited many of the external signs of sexual maturity. Even in the older, purely psychological works we find occasional references to the sexual life of the child—a fact that will surprise no one who is acquainted with the high development of the empirical psychology (Erfahrungspsychologie) of that day (1800). The Venus Urania of Ramdohr, for instance, a work on the psychology of love, emphasises the frequency of amatory sentiments in children.

In works dealing with the history of civilisation, we also encounter occasional references to our subject. Take, for instance, the knightly Code of Love (Liebeskodex), a work highly esteemed in the days of chivalry, and legendarily supposed to have originated in King Arthur's Court. Paragraph 6 of this Code runs: "A man shall not practise love until he is fully grown." According to Rudeck, from whom I quote this instance, the aim of the admonition was to protect the youth of the nobility from unwholesome consequences. Obviously, the love affairs of immature persons must have been the determining cause of any allusion to the matter. We may also draw attention in this connexion to many marriage laws, which show that the subject has come under consideration, either because they expressly sanction the marriages of children, or, conversely, because they forbid such unions. At the present day, among many peoples (as, for instance, the Hindus), child-marriages are frequent; and in many countries in which such marriages are now illegal, they were sanctioned in former ages. Many works on prostitution also touch on our chosen subject. Parent-Duchâtelet, in his great book, refers to girls who had become prostitutes at the ages of twelve or even ten years. I shall show later that in individual instances such early prostitution is directly dependent upon the sexuality of the children concerned. Many ethnological works also contribute to our knowledge of the sexual life of the child, describing, as they do, in certain races, the early awakening of sexual activity.

Remarkably little material do we find, however, in many works in which we might have expected to find a great deal. I refer to works on education and on the psychology of the child. In exceptional instances, indeed, as I have already indicated, the educationalists have taken part in the movement in favour of sexual enlightenment. But when we consider the enormous importance and great frequency of the sexual processes of the child, we are positively astounded at the manner in which this department of knowledge has been ignored by those who have written on the science and art of education, and by those psychologists who have occupied themselves in the study of the mind of the child. Has it been a false notion of morality by which these investigators have been withheld from the elucidation of the sexual life of the child? Or has the reason merely been their defective powers of observation? As a matter of fact, I suppose that both these causes have operated in producing this remarkable gap in our knowledge.

A certain amount of material is to be found in a number of books on zoology, and also in a few quite recent works on comparative psychology. Among works of the former class I mention especially that of Brehm, who has reported a considerable number of individual details; of books on comparative psychology, one of the most useful for our purposes is that of Groos, who gives us much valuable information regarding love-games of young animals.

I may also point out that in the autobiographies, biographies, memoirs, &c., of celebrated persons, we find much information regarding premature amatory sentiments. Goethe, in his Wahrheit und Dichtung, relates that as a boy of ten or so he fell in love with a young Frenchwoman, the sister of his friend Derones. Of Alfred de Musset, his brother and biographer, Paul Musset, records that at the early age of four he was passionately in love with a girl cousin. It is on record that Dante fell in love at the age of nine, Canova at five, and Alfieri at ten. Well known also is the story of Byron's love, at eight years of age, for Mary Duff. Möbius tells us of himself that when a boy of ten he was desperately enamoured of a young married woman. We are told of Napoleon I. that when a boy of nine he fell in love with his father's cousin, a handsome woman of thirty, then on a visit to his home, and that he caressed her in the most passionate manner. Belonging to an earlier day was Felix Platter, the celebrated Swiss physician of the sixteenth century, who tells us in his autobiography that when he was a child he loved to be kissed by a certain young married woman. In Un Coeur Simple, Flaubert describes the development of the love-sentiments. "For mankind there is so much love in life. At the age of four we love horses, the sun, flowers, shining weapons, uniforms; at ten we love a little girl, our playmate; at thirteen we love a buxom, full-necked woman. The first time I saw the two breasts of a woman, entirely unclothed, I almost fainted. Finally, at the age of fourteen or fifteen, we love a young girl, who is a little more to us than a sister and a little less than a mistress; and then, at sixteen, we love a woman once more, and marry her."

Most charmingly Hebbel describes his first experience of love, when but four years old. "It was in Susanna's dull schoolroom, also, that I learned the meaning of love; it was, indeed, in the very hour when I first entered it, at the age of four. First love! Who is there who will not smile as he reads these words? Who will fail to recall memories of some Anne or Margaret, who once seemed to him to wear a crown of stars, and to be clad in the blue of heaven and the gold of dawn; and now—but it would be malicious to depict the contrast! Who will fail to admit that it seemed to him then as if he passed on the wing through the garden of the earth, flitting from flower to flower, sipping from their honey-cups; passing too swiftly, indeed, to become intoxicated, but pausing long enough at each to inhale its divine perfume!... It was some time before I ventured to raise my eyes, for I felt that I was under inspection, and this embarrassed me. But at length I looked up, and my first glance fell upon a pale and slender girl who sat opposite me: her name was Emily, and she was the daughter of the parish-clerk. A passionate trembling seized me, the blood rushed to my heart; but a sentiment of shame was also intermingled with my first sensations, and I lowered my eyes to the ground once more, as rapidly as if I had caught sight of something horrible. From that moment Emily was ever in my thoughts; and the school, so greatly dreaded in anticipation, became a joy to me, because it was there only that I could see her. The Sundays and holidays which separated me from her were as greatly detested by me as in other circumstances they would have been greatly desired; one day when she stayed away from school, I felt utterly miserable. In imagination she was always before my eyes, wherever I went; when alone, I was never weary of repeating her name; above all, her black eyebrows and intensely red lips were ever before my eyes, whereas I do not remember that at this time her voice had made any impression on me, although later this became all-important."

In belletristic literature, also, we find occasional references to the love-sentiment in childhood. Groos refers to an instance which he thinks perhaps the most delicate known to him, and one in which the erotic element is but faintly emphasised, namely, Gottfried Keller's Romeo und Julia. "In a spot entirely covered with green undergrowth the girl stretched herself on her back, for she was tired, and began in a monotonous tone to sing a few words, repeating the same ones over and over again; the boy crouched close beside her, half inclined, he also, to stretch himself at full length on the ground, so lethargic did he feel. The sun shone into the girl's open mouth as she sang, lighting up her glistening white teeth, and gleaming on her full red lips. The boy caught sight of her teeth, and, holding the girl's head and eagerly examining her teeth, said, 'Tell me, how many teeth has one?' The girl paused for a moment, as if thinking the matter carefully over, but then answered at random, 'A hundred.' 'No!' he cried; 'thirty-two is the proper number; wait a moment, I'll count yours.' He counted them, but could not get the tale right to thirty-two, and so counted them again, and again, and again. The girl let him go on for some time, but as he did not come to an end of his eager counting, she suddenly interrupted him, and said, 'Now, let me count yours.' The boy lay down in his turn on the undergrowth; the girl leaned over him, with her arm round his head; he opened his mouth, and she began counting: 'One, two, seven, five, two, one,' for the little beauty did not yet know how to count. The boy corrected her, and explained to her how to count properly; so she, in her turn, attempted to count his teeth over and over again: and this game seemed to please them more than any they had played together that day. At last, however, the girl sank down on her youthful instructor's breast, and the two children fell asleep in the bright midday sunshine."

In erotic literature we also occasionally find descriptions belonging to our province, as, for instance, in the Satyricon of Petronius Arbiter. Indeed, a certain kind of erotic literature, more especially pornographic literature, selects this subject by preference. Thus, I may allude to the Anti-Justine of Rétif de la Bretonne. In a certain section of such literature, improper practices between children and their parents and other blood relatives play a part.

Recently, in connexion with two different fields of study, attention has been directed to the sexual life of the child. The first of these is concerned with the abnormal, and especially the perverse, manifestations of the sexual life, a study of which Westphal, and above all von Krafft-Ebing, have been the founders. The other is the modern movement in favour of the sexual enlightenment of children. As regards the latter, the literature to which it has given rise has not, indeed, contributed much, beyond a few casual references, in the way of positive material concerning the sexual life of the child. But none the less, it is this movement which has made it of prime importance that our subject should be carefully investigated. As regards studies of the abnormalities of the sexual impulse, under the name of paradoxical sexual impulse cases have been published in which that impulse manifested itself at an age of life in which it is normally non-existent—old age and childhood. Recent research has brought to light a large number of cases of this nature. Among those who have reported such cases, we must mention first of all von Krafft-Ebing, and in addition, Féré, Fuchs, Pélofi, and Lombroso.

In addition to these various works, others must be mentioned which have arisen mainly out of the recently awakened interest in the sexual life; for example, works on puberty, the psychology of love, and similar topics. In his Fisiologia del Amore (Physiology of Love), Mantegazza emphasises the love-manifestations of childhood. The same may be said of many other general works on the sexual life, and more especially, as previously mentioned, of works on prostitution. Certain works on offences against morality have also enriched our knowledge in this province.

It might at first sight appear from what has been said that the literature of the sexual life of the child was extremely voluminous, but this is not in reality the case. Almost always, this important question is handled in a casual or cursory manner. A thorough presentation of the subject has not, as far as my knowledge extends, hitherto been attempted. Freud rightly insists that even in all, or nearly all, the works on the psychology of the child, this important department is ignored. Quite recently, indeed, special works have appeared upon the sexual life of the child, among which I must first of all mention Freud's own contribution to the subject, forming part of his Drei Abhandlungen zur sexuellen Theorie (Three Essays on the Sexual Theory, Leipzig and Vienna, 1905). But what this writer describes as an indication of infantile sexuality, viz., certain sucking movements, has, in my opinion, nothing to do with the sexual life of the child—as little to do with sexuality as have the functions of the stomach or any other non-genital organ. A number of other processes occurring in childhood, which Freud and his followers have recently described as sexual in nature, and as playing a great part later in life in connexion with hysteria, neurasthenia, compulsion-neuroses, the anxiety-neurosis, and dementia præcox, have very little true relationship to the sexual life of the child. In any case, Freud has not systematically studied the individual manifestations of the sexual life of the child. I must also mention a small work by Kötscher, Das Erwachen des Geschlechtsbewusstseins und seine Anomalien The Awakening of the Consciousness of Sex and its Anomalies, Wiesbaden, 1907). Kötscher, however, does not give any detailed account of the sexual life of the child; he starts, rather, from the sexual life of the adult, and only as a supplement to his account of this does he give a few data regarding the awakening of the consciousness of sex. In the American Journal of Psychology, July 1902, we find an elaborate study of the sexual life of the child. In this paper, A

Preliminary Study of the Emotion of Love between the Sexes, the writer, Sanford Bell, devotes much attention to the love-sentiments in childhood. He discusses, indeed, only heterosexual, qualitatively normal inclinations, and his essay deals only with the psychological aspects of the question. The processes taking place in the genital organs do not come within the scope of the writer's observations, and, indeed, are outside the limits of his chosen theme. A great many other points connected with the question are also left untouched. None the less, the paper is full of matter. The same must be said of the works of the English investigator, Havelock Ellis, who is, in my opinion, the leader of all those at present engaged in the study of sexual psychology and pathology. Unfortunately his writings are not so well known in Germany as they deserve to be, the reason being that owing to their strictly scientific character they are not so noisily obtruded on the public notice as are certain other widely advertised and reputedly scientific works. In his various books, and above all in his six volumes entitled Studies in the Psychology of Sex (F. A. Davies Company, Philadelphia, Pa.), as a part of his general contributions to our knowledge of the sexual life, Havelock Ellis records numerous observations relating to the years of childhood; especially valuable in this connexion are the biographies given in the third volume of the above-mentioned Studies.

A valuable source of data for our field of inquiry exists in the form of unpublished diaries, autobiographies, and albums, which are not accessible to the general public. I have myself had the opportunity of studying a number of records of this nature, and have formed the opinion that a quantity of invaluable material lies hidden in these recesses. I may add that the records I have been able to use have not only related to living persons; in addition, I have been able to study a number of albums and diaries dating from an earlier day. These have remained unpublished, in part because they appeared to be of interest only to the families of the writers, and in part because many of them were in intention purely private memoranda, a written record for the sole use of the writer.

Speaking generally, however, this province of research has received but little scientific attention; and of comprehensive studies, intended to throw light on every aspect of the sexual life of the child, not a single one is known to me.

CHAPTER II

THE SEXUAL ORGANS—THE SEXUAL IMPULSE

A proper understanding of physiological functions is based upon anatomical knowledge of the organs concerned. For our purpose, therefore, a knowledge of the sexual organs of the child is essential. The proper course, in this instance, appears to be to start with an account of the adult organs, and then to describe the distinctive characteristics of the same organs in the child. Let us, then, begin with the organs of the adult man.

The membrum virile or penis is visible externally, and behind it is situated the scrotum. Within this latter are two ovoid structures, named testicles or testes. Each testicle is enveloped in a fibrous capsule, known as the tunica albuginea, from which fibrous septa pass into the interior of the organ, thus dividing it into a number of separate lobules. Each lobule is composed of seminiferous tubules, which are greatly convoluted and likewise branched, the branches being continuous with those of neighbouring tubules, both within the same lobule, and (by perforating the fibrous septa) in adjoining lobules. In the walls of the seminiferous tubules the spermatozoa are formed. The seminiferous tubules unite to form the efferent ducts (vasa efferentia), about a dozen in number for each testicle; immediately passing out of the testicle, these efferent ducts make up the epididymis, situated at the upper and back part of the testicle. After numerous convolutions, these unite at length on each side to form a single canal, which leaves the epididymis under the name of the vas deferens; this is the excretory duct of the testicle, conveying the secretion of that organ to the exterior. The vas deferens traverses the inguinal canal into the abdominal cavity, and therein passes downwards to the prostatic portion of the urethra (vide infra). The anterior portion only of the penis is visible externally, dependent in front of the scrotum; the posterior portion is concealed by the scrotum and the skin of the perineum. The terminal segment of the penis is formed by the glans, which is covered by the foreskin or prepuce. This last is sometimes artificially removed: either on ritual grounds, as, for instance, among the Jews; or for medical reasons, for example, when the preputial orifice is greatly constricted. At the anterior extremity of the glans penis is the orifice of the urethra (meatus). The urethra is a canal running through the entire length of the penis, opening by its proximal extremity into the urinary bladder, and serving for the passage of the urine from the bladder to the exterior of the body. The main substance of the penis is composed of three cavernous bodies, the paired corpora cavernosa penis, and the single corpus spongiosum, or corpus cavernosum urethræ. These consist of what is known as erectile tissue, a spongy mass within whose lacunar spaces a large quantity of blood can, in certain conditions, be retained. When this occurs, the penis becomes notably thicker and longer, and simultaneously hard and inflexible. This process is known as erection of the penis, and is requisite to render possible the introduction of the organ into the genital canal of the female.

The proximal segment of the urethra is surrounded by the prostate gland. The secretion of this gland is conveyed into the urethra by numerous short ducts, known as the prostatic ducts. Behind the prostate, at the base or fundus of bladder, are the paired seminal vesicles. The duct of the seminal vesicle joins the vas deferens of the same side (both functionally and embryologically the seminal vesicle is no more than a diverticulum of the vas deferens); passing on under the name of the common seminal or ejaculatory duct, the canal opens into the prostatic portion of the urethra (the orifices of the two common seminal ducts are in the folds of mucous membrane forming the right and left lateral margins of the prostatic utricle or uterus masculinus). These ducts convey the secretion of the testicles into the urethra along which canal it passes to the exterior. Behind the posterior part of the urethra, but distal to the prostate gland, are situate also the paired glands of Cowper, or suburethral glands, whose excretory ducts likewise open into the urethra. There are glands also in the walls of the seminal vesicles, the vasa deferentia, and the urethra; the urethral glands are commonly known as the glands of Littré.

As previously mentioned, it is in the testicles that the secretion necessary for the reproductive act is prepared. This secretion is evacuated during sexual intercourse, and also during masturbation and involuntary seminal emissions. The testicular secretion is a tenacious fluid. When examined microscopically, it is seen to contain countless spermatozoa, structures about 50 [Greek: m] (1/500 inch) in length, with a thick head and a long filiform tail. They represent the male reproductive cells, which during coitus are introduced into the interior of the female reproductive organs; a single spermatozoon unites with the ovum of the female to form the fertilised ovum. The spermatozoa are formed in the walls of the convoluted seminiferous tubules. The cells lining these tubules are of several different kinds (although in childhood they are not differentiated as they are after the puberal development has taken place). One variety of these cells, the spermatogonia, undergo an increase of size at puberty, and from these spermatogonia, after passing through several intermediate transitional stages, the spermatozoa are formed.

It was formerly believed that the sole function of the testicles was the production of the spermatozoa; recently, however, the opinion has gained ground that these organs have in addition another specific function, that of internal secretion. Whilst the spermatogonia become transformed into spermatozoa, other cellular structures of the testicle, more especially the interstitial cells, produce, it is assumed, the internal secretion of the gland. The constituents of this internal secretion, having been poured into the general circulation, are supposed to give rise to the specific masculine sexual development, and, in particular, to lead to the appearance of the secondary sexual characters. This matter will subsequently be discussed in detail, and here I shall merely add that perhaps none of the proper constituents of the internal secretion find their way into the external secretion of the testicle.

This external secretion of the testicles does, however, receive the admixture of a number of other secretions, to constitute the semen as actually discharged, viz., the secretion of the prostate gland, that of the seminal vesicles, Cowper's glands, and the glands of the vasa deferentia, and perhaps also that of the glands of Littré. The term semen is, indeed, often applied to the secretion of the testicles alone; but to avoid misunderstanding, Fürbringer recommends that only the mixed secretion, as actually discharged, should be spoken of as the semen, and that this term should never be employed to denote the testicular secretion alone.

In what has gone before, I have not only described the structure of the male sexual organs, but have alluded also in passing to their functions. These latter must, however, be described more fully. Let us begin with erection, which, as we saw, is due to distension of the penis with blood. How is this distension brought about? It results from stimulation of the erection centre. Until recently, it was supposed that this centre was situated in the lumbar enlargement of the spinal cord; but now, owing to the researches of L. R. Müller, it is believed to form part of the sympathetic plexuses of the pelvis. Stimulation of the centre leads to distension of the penis with blood, and thus to erection of that organ. The stimulation of the centre can be effected in either of two ways.

In the first place, by psychical processes. Thus, in a man, the sight of a woman exercises such a stimulus, the stimulation proceeding from the brain along the spinal cord to reach the centre. The psychical stimulus may also consist of reminiscences. In this way the memory of an attractive woman may be just as effective in causing erection as if she were actually visible at the moment; reading erotic literature may have the same result. When the sexual impulse is perverted, the ideas causing erection will naturally be themselves of a perverse character. Thus, in the homosexual male, erection occurs at the sight or remembrance of a man; in the fetichist, the idea of the fetich is operative—in the case of the body-linen fetichist, for instance, the idea of articles of underclothing.

In the second place, the activity of the erection centre can be aroused by physical stimuli. To this category belong masturbatory manipulations, stimulation of the glans penis and other parts of the genital organs. But other erogenic areas exist, the stimulation of which produces the same results. Among these areas, the buttocks must be particularly mentioned. But individual peculiarities play a great part in this connexion. Thus, in many persons, a slight stimulation of the nape of the neck, of the scalp, &c., has an erogenic effect. In all cases alike, the stimulus is conducted along the sensory nerves to the erection centre, and it is the stimulation of this centre which by reflex action leads to distension of the penis with blood and its consequent erection. The physical stimulus leading to erection may also result from some pathological process, such as inflammation of the penis or of the urethra. Finally, certain internal physiological processes may be the starting-point of the afferent physical stimuli leading to erection; for example, distension of the bladder, and also of the seminal vesicles, and of the seminiferous tubules of the testicle. In addition, it is probable that many of the processes of growth occurring in the reproductive glands act in a similar way. These internal stimuli all pass to the erection centre along the afferent (sensory) nerves, and induce erection by reflex action; and it is important to bear in mind that this effect may result without any direct affection of consciousness by the originating afferent impulses.

Although either kind of stimuli, psychical or physical, acting alone, may give rise to erection, experience shows that in most instances the two varieties co-operate in the production of this effect. Thus, in the sexually mature man, the accumulation of semen in the seminal vesicles gives rise, not only to excitement of the erection centre, but also to voluptuous ideas, and these latter, in their turn, further stimulate the erection centre.

Normally, during coitus, erection is followed by ejaculation. A special nerve centre for ejaculation is also supposed to exist; and the ejaculation centre, like the erection centre, was formerly believed to be situated in the lumbar enlargement of the spinal cord, but recent investigations have shown that it also most probably forms part of the sympathetic plexuses of the pelvis. This centre also may be stimulated either by psychical or by physical stimuli. In normal conditions, however, much more powerful stimuli are needed to cause ejaculation than those which are competent to give rise to erection. For this reason, erections often occur without leading to ejaculation, whereas in normal conditions ejaculation hardly ever occurs without erection. In fact, ejaculation in the absence of erection is almost peculiar to pathological states, and may occur, for instance, in many forms of impotence, in which the ejaculation centre still remains susceptible to stimulation, whilst the erection centre is exhausted. Whereas stimulation of the erection centre exercises its reflex influence through the vasomotor nerves, thus leading to distension of the penis with blood, the reflex impulses resulting from stimulation of the ejaculation centre are transmitted by the motor nerves to certain muscles—those, namely, whose contraction forcibly expels the accumulated semen. The contractions of the affected muscles occur rhythmically, the stimulation of the ejaculation centre giving rise to a series of contractions alternating with relaxations. True ejaculation, resulting from the activity of these muscles, must be distinguished from the appearance of a drop or two of fluid at the urethral meatus, which occasionally occurs at the outset of sexual excitement—the so-called urethrorrhoea ex libidine. This fluid runs out while the ejaculatory muscles are quiescent. It was formerly believed that it consisted of the secretion of the prostate gland; but Fürbringer, to whom we are indebted for the most valuable researches in this province, has shown that this view is erroneous. These drops are, he states, derived solely from the glands of Littré and the glands of Cowper (urethral and suburethral glands).

Sexual excitement is accompanied throughout by a sensation of pleasure, specifically known as voluptuous pleasure, the voluptuous sensation, or simply voluptuousness (in Latin, libido sexualis). Several stages of the voluptuous sensation must be distinguished: its onset; the equable voluptuous sensation; the voluptuous acme, coincident with the rhythmical contraction of the perineal muscles and the ejaculation of the semen; and, finally, the quite sudden diminution and cessation of the voluptuous sensation. Associated with the last stage we usually have a sense of satisfaction, and simultaneously a cessation of the sexual impulse; a sense of ease and calm ensues, and at the same time a feeling of fatigue. This voluptuous sensation localised in the genital organs must, of course, be distinguished from the general sense of pleasure produced in a man by the idea of, or by contact with, a woman in whom he is sexually interested.

Now let us pass on to the consideration of the reproductive organs in the female. The most conspicuous part of the external genital organs consists of two large folds, situated on either side of the median line, and known as the labia majora. Within these are two much smaller folds, the labia minora or nymphæ. In the median line, in the space between the labia minora, we see two apertures: the anterior of these is the urethral orifice (meatus), from which the comparatively short and almost straight urethra of the female passes upwards and backwards to the bladder; the posterior aperture is the vaginal orifice. The labia minora, divergent posteriorly, converge as they pass forwards like the limbs of a V; at the apex of the V is the clitoris; in shape and structure this resembles the penis of the male, but it is much smaller, and is solid, not being perforated by the urethra. It contains two corpora cavernosa, which unite to form the body of the organ, whilst the distal extremity is known as the glans, and is homologous to the glans penis. Posteriorly to the clitoris, and beneath the mucous membrane on either side, is an additional mass of erectile tissue, known as the vaginal bulb, or bulb of the vestibule. Just outside the vaginal orifice on either side are visible the orifices of the ducts of Bartholin's glands (known also as Duverney's glands); these are homologous with Cowper's glands in the male.

When we attempt to pass from the vaginal orifice to the internal reproductive organs, we find that in the virgin an obstacle exists, the hymen or maidenhead, consisting of a duplicature of the mucous membrane. It is very variable in form, but in the great majority of instances it diminishes the size of the vaginal inlet to such an extent as to render coitus impossible until the hymen has been torn. Through the vaginal orifice access is gained to the interior of the vagina, a tubular structure, but flattened from before backwards, so that in the quiescent state the anterior and posterior walls of the passage are in apposition. The uterus or womb is a muscular, pear-shaped organ, with an elongated central cavity, which opens into the upper part of the vagina. At the upper end of the cavity of the uterus are two small laterally placed apertures, which lead into the Fallopian tubes (or oviducts). These tubes pass outwards in a somewhat sinuous course towards the ovaries, the reproductive glands of the female, homologous with the testicles in the male, and situated on either side of the upper extremity of the uterus. The shape of the ovaries is somewhat ovoid. They contain a large number of vesicular structures, the ovarian follicles, the largest, ripe follicles being known as Graafian follicles, whilst the smaller, partially developed follicles are termed primitive ovarian follicles, or primitive Graafian follicles. In the interior of each follicle is an ovum. In the sexually mature woman, a Graafian follicle ripens at regular intervals of four weeks. When ripe, the follicle bursts, the ovum is expelled, and passes through the Fallopian tube into the interior of the uterus: here it is either fertilised by uniting with a spermatozoon derived from the male, in which case it proceeds to develop into an embryo; or else it remains unfertilised, in which case it is shortly expelled from the body.

In the uterus, as well as in the ovaries, an important change occurs at intervals of four weeks, characterised by an increased flow of blood to the organ, culminating in an actual outflow of blood from the vessels into the uterine cavity, and thence through the vagina to the exterior of the body; the whole process is known as menstruation, the monthly sickness or the (monthly) period. After the fertilisation of the ovum, during pregnancy, that is to say, menstruation usually ceases until after the birth of the child, and often until the completion of lactation.

I do not propose to discuss here the nature of the connexion between these periodic processes in the ovaries and the uterus, respectively—that is, between ovulation and menstruation. I shall, however, take this opportunity of stating that, as careful investigations have shown, the periodic processes in question are not limited to the uterus and the ovaries, but affect also the external genital organs, which become congested simultaneously with menstruation; and further, that the entire feminine organism is affected by an undulatory rhythm of nutrition, the rise and fall of which correspond to menstruation and to the intermenstrual interval, respectively.

I must now give some account of the peripheral processes occurring in the female genital organs in connexion with the sexual act. In part, they are completely analogous to those which take place in the male. I have already pointed out that in many respects the clitoris in the female corresponds to the penis in the male, In the clitoris, also, erection occurs, conditioned partly by psychical and partly by physical stimuli. The psychical stimuli consist of ideas relating to the male. The physical stimuli may, just as in the case of the other sex, vary in their nature. Thus, the condition of the reproductive glands may act as a physical stimulus to erection; also the touching of certain regions of the body, especially the clitoris, the labia minora, or other erogenic zones. Under the influence of such stimuli, the venus plexuses making up the vaginal bulbs also become distended with blood. In fact, speaking generally, sexual excitement is characterised by a vigorous flow of blood to the genital organs. During coitus, in woman, as in man, a process of ejaculation normally occurs, taking the form of rhythmical muscular contractions, affecting not only the perineal muscles, but also the muscular investment of the vagina, and occasionally, perhaps, the uterus itself. These muscular contractions also favour the expulsion of a secretion, but this secretion does not contain the reproductive cells of the female, and consists merely of a mixture of indifferent secretions—the secretion of Bartholin's glands, that of the uterine mucous membrane, and that of the mucous glands of the vagina and vulva. In the woman also, even at the outset of the sexual act, a secretion from the local glands takes place, whereby the genital region is moistened prior to the actual orgasm. We have as yet no precise knowledge as to which glands are concerned in the production of this phenomenon, which is homologous to the urethrorrhæa ex libidine of the male. In woman, as in man, the curve of voluptuousness exhibits four phases: an ascending limb, the equable voluptuous sensation, the acme, and the rapid decline. There are, however, in this respect, certain differences between man and woman, to which von Krafft-Ebing drew attention, and whose existence was confirmed by Otto Alder. Whereas in the male the curve of voluptuousness both rises and falls with extreme abruptness, in the female both the onset and the decline of voluptuous sensation are slower and more gradual. There is an additional difference between man and woman. In woman very often voluptuous pleasure is entirely lacking; certainly such absence is far commoner in women than in men—a condition of affairs which must on no account be confused with absence of the sexual impulse. Even when the sexual impulse is perfectly normal, the entire voluptuous curve with its acme may be wanting. In such cases, the after-sense of complete satisfaction, which occurs more especially when ejaculation has been associated with an extremity of voluptuous pleasure, it is commonly also lacking. Finally, it is necessary to add that in woman, as in man, the reproductive glands appear to have a duplex function—such is, at least, the belief to which recent investigations more and more definitely point. The ovaries, that is to say, do not only produce ova; they also, like the testicles, furnish an internal secretion, and the absorption and distribution of this secretion by the blood are supposed to cause the development of the secondary sexual characters in woman.

Having now concluded our account of the structure and functions of the productive organs of adults, let us turn to consider the differences between these organs and those of children. In the child, the testicles are considerably smaller; smaller also are the penis and the other genital organs. In the adult, the root of the penis is surrounded by the pubic hair; this hair is absent in the child. The most important distinctive characteristic, however, lies in the fact that in the child the morphological elements upon which the capacity for procreation depends, namely, the spermatozoa, are not yet present in the testicles. The spermatozoa first make their appearance during that year of life which is usually regarded as the year of the puberal development. The microscopical appearances of the testicle, of which an account has previously been given, thus naturally differ according as the specimen under examination has been taken from a child or from an adult. As regards the other glands considered to form part of the genital organs, some of these secrete even in childhood. This matter will be subsequently discussed in some detail.

In the female sex, also, there are notable differences in the condition of the genital organs between the adult and the child. In the first place, the relative sizes of the various organs differ greatly. But other differences are also noticeable, not dependent, however, on differences in age, but on whether there has or has not been experience of sexual intercourse, and on whether pregnancy and parturition have occurred. When we compare a female child with an adult woman, the first obvious difference is in the shape of the external genital organs. In the child, the vulva is placed much higher and more to the front, so that it is distinctly visible even when the thighs are in close apposition. In the child, also, the labia majora are less developed, for as womanhood approaches a great deposit of fat takes place in these structures. Again, in the child, the outer surfaces of the labia majora and that part of the skin of the abdomen just in front of the labia (the mons veneris) are as hairless as the rest of the body, whereas in the adult woman these regions are covered with the pubic hair. According to Marthe Francillon, to whom we are indebted for an elaborate study of puberty in the female sex, during the puberal development changes occur also in the clitoris. The genital corpuscles of Krause and the corpuscles of Finger (Wollustkörperchen), the terminals of the nerves passing to the erectile tissue of the clitoris, undergo at this time a marked increase in size. The clitoris itself, hitherto comparatively small, now attains a length of three to four centimetres (1.2 to 1.6 inch), in the quiescent state, and of four and a half to five centimetres (1.8 to

2 inches) when erect. In the virgin also, as previously mentioned, the hymen is present, a structure of very variable form. After defloration its remnants persist in the form of small prominences around the margin of the vaginal inlet (carunculæ myrtiformes). But, quite independently of defloration, in the child the vaginal orifice is much smaller than in the riper girl. The uterus undergoes remarkable changes. In the foetus, during the latter part of intra-uterine life, this organ grows very rapidly; but immediately after birth its growth is arrested, so that in a girl of nine it is little larger than in the new-born infant. During the period of puberal development, however, the growth of the organ is once more extremely rapid. Its shape also changes at this time. In the child, the uterus is longer in proportion to its thickness; in childhood, too, the comparative length of the cervix in relation to that of the body of the organ is much greater than in the adult woman. We need only allude in passing to the fact that later in life marked changes occur in the uterus as a result of pregnancy and parturition. The hyperæmia and the bleeding that take place periodically during menstruation lead to certain changes in the mucous surface of the uterus. Ovulation, which in the sexually mature woman recurs at four-weekly intervals, also gives rise to certain permanent changes in the ovaries. The site of each ruptured Graafian follicle becomes cicatrised, and in consequence of the formation of these little scars, the ovary no longer retains the smoothness of surface which was characteristic of the organ in childhood. From birth onwards the ovaries gradually increase in size, but the growth is disproportionate in different diameters. Thus, for instance, during the eighth year of life, growth is chiefly in thickness, so that the ratio between the length and the thickness becomes less than before. The structure of the ovaries also varies at different ages. In a girl of three years, the primitive ovarian follicles number about 400,000; at the age of eight it is estimated that their number has been reduced to about 36,000. Certainly the majority of the primitive follicles come to nothing. True Graafian follicles, of which an account has already been given, are not usually formed prior to the beginning of the puberal development; occasionally, however, they are formed in the ovaries of immature girls.

Let us now pass to the consideration of the sexual impulse. We learn from personal observation that two entirely distinct processes participate in this impulse. In the first place, we have the physical processes that take place in the genital organs; these are in part unperceived, but in part they affect consciousness in the form of common sensations, or as ordinary tactile and other similar sensations. In the second place, we have those higher psychical processes by means of which man is attracted to woman, and woman to man. In our actual experience of the normal sexual life, both these groups of processes do, as a matter of fact, work in unison; but not only is it possible for us to distinguish them analytically; it is, in addition, possible in many instances to observe them in action clinically isolated each from the other. A long while ago I utilised this distinction for the analysis of the sexual impulse, describing the impulse in so far as it was confined to the peripheral organs as the detumescence-impulse (from detumescere, to decrease in size), and in so far as it takes the form of processes tending towards bodily and mental approximation to another individual, as the contrectation-impulse (from contrectare to touch, or to think about). The distinction will become clearer to our minds if we familiarise ourselves first with cases in which either process occurs independently of the other. The detumescence-impulse is sometimes the sole manifestation of the sexual impulse. Certain idiots practise masturbation as a physical act, because sensations proceeding from the genital organs impel them to do so, precisely as itching of an area of the skin impels us to scratch. They masturbate without thinking of another person, and they feel no impulsion whatever towards sexual contact with another person. Analogous phenomena may be witnessed in the animal world also, in connexion with the masturbatory acts of monkeys, bulls, and stallions. When a stallion kicks its genital organs again and again with its hind-foot, and repeats the action until ejaculation ensues, we are hardly justified in assuming that the animal has the idea of a mare before its mind. We must rather suppose that we have to do with a local physical stimulus, to which the stallion reacts in the manner above described. The other component, also, of the sexual impulse, the contrectation-impulse, manifests itself, occasionally, at any rate, in isolation. Certain boys, long before the appearance of any signs of the puberal development, are impelled towards physical contact with members of the other sex, to kiss them, to think of them, although these boys may exhibit no tendency whatever to masturbate, or to manipulate their genital organs It often happens, indeed, that such a boy is himself greatly astonished to find, some day, that these ideas are reflected to the genital organs, giving rise to erection; or, when he is embracing a girl, to experience erection and ejaculation. In the sexually mature normal man, the detumescence-impulse and the contrectation-impulse act in unison, and hence he is impelled towards intimate contact with the woman, and is ultimately driven to effect detumescence by the practice of coitus. Nevertheless, we must hold fast to the idea that in the normal adult man the sexual processes may also be theoretically analysed into these two components.

This is true also of woman, in whom the processes in the genital organs are equally separable from those which impel to contact with a member of the other sex. But in woman, the processes in the genital organs do not culminate in the ejection of the reproductive cells, that is, of the ovum, but, as we have seen, in the ejaculation of indifferent secretions. In the woman, also, the detumescence impulse is occasionally met with in isolation—for example, in many female idiots. In the animal world, too, we encounter it as an isolated phenomenon. Certain mares, when rutting, rub their hind quarters against some object in their stalls. The contrectation-impulse may also manifest itself in isolation in woman. It is then directed towards the male, but is not in any way associated with the wish for a definite sexual act. Most commonly, however, in woman also the two components of the sexual impulse are united, and from this union results the impulsion towards coitus. But to this extent the conditions in woman are apt to differ from those in man, inasmuch as, in the former, voluptuous sensations are more often in abeyance; or in woman voluptuous pleasure may not arise during coitus, but may be produced in some other way, as, for instance, by a masturbatory act.

The sexual impulse, and indeed either of its components, may be excited either by bodily or by mental stimuli; but we must always bear in mind the fact that in normal adults, both male and female, the two components are so intimately associated that they can as a rule be separated only by artificial analysis. The nature and mode of operation of the stimuli need not be further discussed, since enough has been said about the matter in our description of erection. Nor is it necessary in this place to deal with such differences as may exist between the psychosexual life of the child and that of the adult, since this matter will be fully considered in the fourth chapter. In this chapter my aim has merely been to give a general description of the sexual impulse.

Here I need allude to one more point only, a knowledge of which is indispensable for the understanding of the sexual life of the child, namely, the connexion between the central processes and the peripheral voluptuous sensation. Let us ask, in the first place, by what means the voluptuous sensation, the voluptuous acme, and the sense of satisfaction, are produced. Various factors are here operative. A homosexual man, in heterosexual coitus, by keeping present to his imagination the idea of coitus with a man, may succeed in obtaining erection and ejaculation; but he does not experience the voluptuous acme, nor does he feel the sense of satisfaction. Notwithstanding the fact that the peripheral processes occur in normal fashion, the sense of satisfaction remains in abeyance; because the act is in his case inadequate, the sexual act in which he is engaged lacks harmonious relationship to his sexual impulse. But the same homosexual man, embracing a man with whom he is in full sympathy, will experience alike the voluptuous acme and the sense of satisfaction. Mutatis mutandis, the like is true of woman. Many cases which have been regarded as instances of sexual anæsthesia would appear in quite another light if the woman concerned were to have intercourse with a sexually sympathetic man. I have myself known cases in which women were able to experience the voluptuous acme in intercourse with men whom they earnestly loved, whilst in intercourse with men to whom they were indifferent, the voluptuous sensation and the sense of satisfaction were wanting, even though in some of these cases the peripheral processes culminated in ejaculation. Such a physically complete sexual act, without voluptuous acme or sense of satisfaction, may occur when the woman, having intercourse with a man whom she does not love, pictures in imagination that she is having intercourse with her lover. Unquestionably, the psychical processes are of the greatest importance in contributing to the occurrence of the voluptuous sensation and the sense of satisfaction. On the other hand, of course, certain peripheral conditions must also be fulfilled if the voluptuous acme is to ensue. Among these conditions may be mentioned a certain anatomical state of the skin and the nerves concerned. Experience also shows that in the adult the voluptuous acme coincides with the act of ejaculation. Ejaculation is effected by the rhythmical contraction of certain definite muscles, and Otto Adler believes that it is these contractions which are principally effective in producing the voluptuous acme, and that actual ejaculation is not indispensable. He believes, that is, that the voluptuous acme may occur in the absence of any discharge of actual secretion.

In any case, let us hold fast to the fact that in the adult, for the occurrence of the voluptuous acme and of the sense of full satisfaction, certain central processes are, in general, indispensable.

CHAPTER III

SEXUAL DIFFERENTIATION IN CHILDHOOD

In the previous chapter, I have described the differences between the reproductive organs of men and women, and between those of adults and children, respectively. Man and woman are, however, distinguished one from the other, not only by differences in their reproductive organs, but by other qualities as well, some of these being bodily, others mental. Such distinctive characters are spoken of as secondary sexual characters, in contradistinction to the primary sexual characters, the reproductive organs. Our terminology would, perhaps, be more exact if we were to regard the reproductive glands alone, the testicles and the ovaries, as primary sexual characters; including the rest of the genital organs among the secondary sexual characters. Havelock Ellis distinguishes, in addition to the primary and secondary sexual characters (as commonly defined), tertiary sexual characters, by which he denotes those differences between the sexes which do not attract our attention when we compare individual members of the two sexes, but which become noticeable when we compare the average male with the average female type. Among such tertiary sexual characters may be mentioned the comparatively flatter skull, the greater size and activity of the thyroid gland, and the lesser corpuscular richness of the blood, in women. Especially distinct are the secondary sexual characters in respect of general bodily structure. The form of the skeleton is different in the two sexes. Thus, in woman the pelvis is wider and shallower than in man. In the hair also there are notable differences: in woman the hair of the head tends to grow much longer, and woman is much less liable than man to premature baldness; the beard, on the other hand, is a masculine peculiarity. In woman the breasts attain a much greater development. The larynx is in man more prominent and longer; in woman it is wider and shallower. Woman's skin is more delicate than man's. And so on.

Now what have we to say regarding these sexual differences in the case of children? During the age which we have defined as the first period of childhood, except in the matter of the genital organs, we can detect hardly any important bodily characters distinguishing the sexes. Still, even at this early age some differences have been recorded. Thus, the average weight of new-born girls is less than that of new-born boys, the figures given by Stratz being, for boys, 3500 grams (7.7 lbs.); for girls, 3250 grams (7.15 lbs.). According to a very large number of measurements, the mean length of the new-born girl is somewhat less than that of the new-born boy, the difference amounting to nearly 1 cm. (2/5ths inch). Craniometric records, taken at the end of the first period of childhood, exhibit differences between the sexes; in general, the measurements show that the girl's head is smaller than the boy's in respect both of length and breadth. Further, dynamometric records, taken from children six years of age, have shown that the grasp in girls is less powerful than in boys. But if we except such differences as these, which relate rather to averages than to individuals, and which, moreover, are for the most part demonstrable only during the latter part of the first period of childhood, we find that, apart from the reproductive organs, very little difference between the sexes can be detected during the first years of life. Many investigators have been unable to confirm the assertion that even in the first year of life the hips are more powerfully developed in girls than in boys. Fehling, however, declares that as early as the fifth month of intra-uterine life, sexual differences manifest themselves in the formation of the pelvis. However this may be, it is beyond question that during the earlier years of the first period of childhood the differences between the sexes are comparatively trifling. But towards the end of this period, sexual differentiation becomes more marked. According to Stratz, it is at this time that the characteristic form of the lower half of the body develops. The thighs and the hips of the young girl exhibit a somewhat more marked deposit of fat than is seen in the boy of the same age. To a lesser extent the same is true of the calves. It is often assumed that even in very early childhood the sexes can be distinguished by the formation of the face. The girl's face is said to be rounder and fuller than the boy's; the expression of countenance in the former, to be more bashful and modest. Stratz, however, urges in opposition to this view, with justice, in my opinion, that we have here to do only with the effects of individual educational influences, or perhaps with individual variations, from which no general conclusions can safely be drawn.

During the second period of childhood sexual differences become much more distinct. Before considering these differences, I must say a few words regarding the growth of the child, since in this particular there exists a notable distinction between the sexes. Careful measurements have shown that during certain years of childhood growth occurs especially in height, whereas in other years the main increase is in girth. For this reason, it is customary to follow Bartels in his subdivision of each of the two periods of childhood into two subperiods. The age from one to four years is the first period of growth in girth; from the beginning of the fifth to the completion of the seventh year is the first period of growth in height; from the beginning of the eighth to the completion of the tenth year is the second period of growth in girth; and from the beginning of the eleventh to the completion of the fourteenth year is the second period of growth in height. During these periods there are certain differences in respect of growth between boys and girls. Although in general the growth in height of the boy exceeds that of the girl, there is a certain period during which the average height of girls is greater than that of boys. From the beginning of the eleventh year onwards, the girl grows in height so much more rapidly than the boy, that from this age until the beginning of the fifteenth year the average height of girls exceeds that of boys, although at all other ages the reverse is the case. In our consideration of the differences between the sexes, these differences in respect of growth must not be overlooked.

In addition to these, other important differences between the sexes manifest themselves during the second period of childhood. In the first place, it is an established fact that in the girl the secondary sexual characters make their appearance earlier than in the boy, the boy remaining longer in the comparatively neutral condition of childhood. We have seen that in the girl, at the end of the first period of childhood, the lower half of the body begins to resemble that of the woman in type. During the second period of childhood, this peculiarity becomes more marked; the pelvis and the hips widen, the thighs and the buttocks become more and more rounded; the enduring feminine characteristics in these respects are acquired. More gradually, the feminine development of the upper half of the body succeeds that of the lower; the transition from the lower jaw to the neck become less abrupt, and the face becomes fuller. The sexual difference in the growth of the hair also manifests itself in childhood. Whether cut or uncut, the girl's hair tends to grow longer than the boy's. Later, the typical development of the breasts occurs. As early as the beginning of the second period of childhood, the surface of the areola mammæ may become slightly raised; but the typical deposit of fat, leading to the hemispherical prominence of the breast, does not begin until towards the close of the second period of childhood. Even later than this is the growth of the axillary and pubic hair. Various answers are given to the question as to the relation in time between the appearance of menstruation and the development of the sexual characters just described. Unquestionably there are great differences in this respect. Whereas Axel Key declared that the secondary sexual characters appeared before the first menstruation, according to C. H. Stratz this is true only of girls belonging to the lower classes; whilst according to his own observations on girls belonging to the upper classes of society, the first menstruation precedes the development of the breasts and the growth of the pubic and axillary hair.

Concerning a number of sexual differences, during childhood, authors are not agreed. As regards the type of breathing, for instance, in the adult man, the abdominal type prevails; that is, the respiratory exchange of gases is effected chiefly by movements of the diaphragm and the abdominal muscles: whereas in the adult woman the respiration is costal, the respiratory exchange being effected chiefly by movements of the thorax. How unsettled our views are in respect of the types of respiration in children is well displayed by the collection of opinions given by Havelock Ellis. According to Boerhaave, sexual differences in the type of respiration were manifest even in very small children; but his observations have not been confirmed by others. Thus, Sibson states that the characteristic costal type of respiration begins in girls at the age of ten, for which reason some observers have assumed that the wearing of the corset is the cause of its appearance; others, however, among whom Hutchinson may be mentioned, deny this alleged causal connexion, stating that they have observed costal respiration in young girls who have never worn any constricting garments. Unquestionably, sexual differences in the type of respiration become apparent in the later years of childhood.

I have already pointed out that in girls the secondary sexual characters begin to make their appearance at an earlier age than in boys. In the onset of sexual differentiation, the boy thus plays a more passive part than the girl, inasmuch as he retains longer the childish type. None the less, in the boy also certain secondary sexual characters begin to develop comparatively early. Thus, in the second period of childhood, the boy's shoulders often become wider, his muscles stronger, than those of the girl. Since at the same period there occurs in girls the greater deposit of fat previously described, marked differences result in the external contours of the respective bodies. The boy's body is therefore much more angular and knobby, far less softly rounded, than that of the girl. Towards the end of the second period of childhood, an additional sexual character makes its appearance in the male sex, namely, the voice breaks. The chief remaining differences, the growth of the beard and the pubic hair, and the development of the characteristically masculine larynx, usually manifest themselves after the close of the second period of childhood—that is to say, during the period of youth.

As children become physically differentiated in respect of sex, so also does a mental differentiation ensue. Authorities are not agreed as to whether mental sexual differentiation exists in the very earliest years of life. Many assume its existence, and profess to have observed sexual differences even in the movements of quite small children. On the other hand, it is urged that the alleged differences are made up out of chance, auto-suggestion on the part of the observer, and the results of education. There is, however, general agreement as to the fact that during the second period of childhood mental differences become apparent between the sexes. Such differences are observed in the matter of occupation, of games, of movements, and numerous other details. Since man is to play the active part in life, boys rejoice especially in rough outdoor games. Girls, on the other hand, prefer such games as correspond to their future occupations. Hence their inclination to mother smaller children, and to play with dolls. Watch how a little girl takes care of her doll, washes it, dresses and undresses it. When only six or seven years of age, she is often an excellent nurse. As Padberg pictures her, she sits at the bedside of her sick brother or sister, resembling as she does so an angel in human form. Her need to occupy herself in such activities is often so great, that she pretends that her doll is ill. Chamisso, in his poem Das kleine Mädchen und die Puppe (The Little Girl and her Doll), describes this relationship between the child and her doll, one whose nature is fully understood only by a mother:—

"Wie Du mit den kleinen Kindern,
Will ich alles mit ihr tun,
Und sie soll in ihrer Wiege
Neben meinem Bette ruhn.

Schläft sie, werd' ich von ihr träumen,

Schreit sie auf, erwach' ich gleich,—
Mein himmlisch gute Mutter,
O, wie bin ich dock so reich!"

"All you do for your children,
For my Doll I do instead,
And in her little cradle
She lies beside my bed.
When she sleeps, I dream about her,
When she cries, I wake up too.
My own, dear, darling Mother,
I'm just as rich as you!"

Once I saw a little girl of seven running up and down the room, carrying all kinds of things as fast as she could to her doll. When I asked her what was the matter, she told me that her doll had the measles, and she was taking care of her. In all kinds of ways, we see the little girl occupying herself in the activities and inclinations of her future existence. She practises housework; she has a little kitchen, in which she cooks for herself and her doll. She is fond of needlework. The care of her own person, and more especially its adornment, are not forgotten. I remember seeing a girl of three who kept on interrupting her elders' conversation by crying out "New clothes!" and would not keep quiet until these latter had been duly admired. The love of self-adornment is almost peculiar to female children; boys, on the other hand, prefer rough outdoor games, in which their muscles are actively employed, robber-games, soldier-games, and the like. And whereas, in early childhood, both sexes are fond of very noisy games, the fondness for these disappears earlier in girls than in boys.

Differences between the sexes have been established also by means of experimental psychology, based upon the examination of a very large number of instances. Although it must be admitted that some of the acquirements of this school are still open to dispute, the data of these collective investigations must not be ignored. Berthold Hartmann has studied the childish circle of thought, by means of a series of experiments which are commonly spoken of as the Annaberg experiments. Schoolboys to the number of 660 and schoolgirls to the number of 652, at ages between 5¾ and 6¾ years, were subjected to examination. It was very remarkable to see how in respect of certain ideas, such as those of the triangle, cube, and circle, the girls greatly excelled the boys; whereas in respect of animals, minerals and social ideas, the boys were better informed than the girls. Characteristic of the differences between the sexes, according to Meumann, from whom I take these details, and some of those that follow, is the fact that the idea of "marriage" was known to only 70 boys, as compared to 227 girls; whilst the idea of "infant baptism" was known to 180 boys as compared to 220 girls. The idea of "pleasure" was also much better understood by girls than by boys. Examination of the memory has also established the existence of differences between the sexes in childhood. In boys the memory for objects appears to be at first the best developed; to this succeeds the memory for words with a visual content: in the case of girls, the reverse of this was observed. In respect of numerous details, however, the authorities conflict. According to Lobsien, boys have a better memory for numbers, words, and sounds. The same investigator informs us that in girls the visual memory is distinctly better than it is in boys, this indicating that girls' memory for objects is also better; but Netschajeff, on the other hand, maintains that boys have a better memory for objects perceptible by the senses. It is interesting to note that certain variations have been shown to exist at different ages. During the first years of school-life, boys' memories are in general better than girls', this advantage persisting up to the age of ten; from this time onwards until the end of the years spent in primary schools, girls excel boys in the matter of memory, but especially at ages of eleven, twelve, thirteen, and fourteen. Later than this, the boys become equal to the girls, and still later surpass them. Very striking is the fact, one upon which a very large number of investigators are agreed, that girls have a superior knowledge of colours. Experimental investigations made by means of Holmgren's test have shown that the superiority of girls in this respect is remarkable, and these experiments are confirmed by other lines of study.

There are additional psychological data relating to the differences between the sexes in childhood. I may recall Stern's investigations concerning the psychology of evidence, which showed that girls were much more inaccurate than boys. I may also refer, on the other hand, in relation to sexual differentiation, to the experiences obtained by Hans Gross by means of observations on practical life, although his results are not entirely free from certain sources of fallacy, and moreover have been disputed by other observers as not generally applicable. Hans Gross, however, found a notable difference between boys and girls, of which I shall later give a detailed description. Here, I shall merely quote the comprehensive summary given in his Criminal Psychology: "My results show that the boy who has passed his first years of childhood is, if well trained, the best observer and witness that can possibly be found, because he watches with interest all that goes on around him, stores it impartially in his memory, and reproduces it faithfully; whereas the girl of like age is often an untrustworthy, and even a dangerous witness. She is inevitably this when, after traversing the stages of talent, ardour, reverie, romanticism, and enthusiasm, she has passed into a condition of Weltschmerz, tinged with tedium vitæ. This emotional mental atmosphere is entered at an earlier age than is commonly imagined; and when such a girl's own personal interests are in any way affected by the occurrences under examination, we are never secure from gross exaggeration and misstatement. Petty larceny becomes robbery with violence; a trifling incivility, a serious assault; a harmless pleasantry, an interesting proposal for elopement; and the foolish prattle of children becomes a dangerous conspiracy."

I shall subsequently discuss in detail a psychical difference which is the most important of all those connected with the sexual life, namely, the direction of the sexual impulse, which attracts the man to the woman, and the woman to the man. We shall see to what a considerable degree this phenomenon manifests itself even in childhood.

It has been widely assumed that these psychical differences between the sexes result from education, and are not inborn. To avoid misunderstanding, we must, in our consideration of this question of education, distinguish between two distinct classes of phenomena, those which are individual and those which have existed for a number of generations. The sexually differentiated qualities in any individual may be regarded as inborn, and yet we may admit that the differentiation was originally the result of education, if we suppose that in earlier generations in either sex certain qualities were developed, and that gradually, by monosexual inheritance, the differences became confirmed, until finally they became inborn. Others, however, assume that the psychical characteristics by which the sexes are differentiated result solely from individual differences in education. Stern believes that in the case of one differential character, at least, he can prove that for many centuries there has been no difference between the sexes in the matter of education; this character is the capacity for drawing. Kerschensteiner has studied the development of this gift, and considers that his results have established beyond dispute that girls are greatly inferior in this respect to boys of like age. Stern points out that there can be no question here of cultivation leading to a sexual differentiation of faculty, since there is no attempt at a general and systematic teaching of draughtsmanship to the members of one sex to the exclusion of members of the other.

Without further discussing the question, to what extent in earlier generations there has been any cultivation of psychical differences, I believe that we are justified in asserting that at the present time the sexual differentiation manifested in respect of quite a number of psychical qualities is the result of direct inheritance. It would be quite wrong to assume that all these differences arise in each individual in consequence of education. It does, indeed, appear to me to be true that inherited tendencies may be increased or diminished by individual education; and further, that when the inherited tendency is not a very powerful one, it may in this way even be suppressed. Observations on animals which exhibit sexual differentiation very early in life, also support the notion of the inherited character of certain tendencies; for instance, the movements of male animals often differ from those of the females of the same species.

We must not forget the frequent intimate association between structure and function. This well-proved connexion would lead us a priori, from the more powerful muscular development of boys, to infer the different inclinations of the two sexes. Rough outdoor games and wrestling thus correspond to the physical constitution of the boy. So, also, it is by no means improbable that the little girl, whose pelvis and hips have already begun to indicate by their development their adaptation for the supreme functions of the sexually mature woman, should experience obscurely a certain impulsion towards her predestined maternal occupation, and that her inclinations and amusements should in this way be determined. Many, indeed, and above all the extreme advocates of women's rights, prefer to maintain that such sexually differentiated inclinations result solely from differences in individual education: if the boy has no enduring taste for dolls and cooking, this is because his mother and others have told him, perhaps with mockery, that such amusements are unsuited to a boy; whilst in a similar way the girl is dissuaded from the rough sports of boyhood. Such an assumption is the expression of that general psychological and educational tendency, which ascribes to the activity of the will an overwhelmingly powerful influence upon the development of the organs subserving the intellect, and secondarily also upon that of the other organs of the body. By the influence of the will, it is supposed by this school, certain association-tracts in the brain are developed; or at least certain tracts hitherto functionally inactive are rendered functionally active. We cannot dispute the fact that in such a way the activity of the will may, within certain limits, be effective, especially in cases in which the inherited tendency thus counteracted is comparatively weak; but only within certain limits. Thus we can understand how it is that in some cases, by means of education, a child is impressed with characteristics normally foreign to its sex; qualities and tendencies are thus developed which ordinarily appear only in a child of the opposite sex. But even though we must admit that the activity of the individual may operate in this way, none the less are we compelled to assume that certain tendencies are inborn. The failure of innumerable attempts to counteract such inborn tendencies by means of education throws a strong light upon the limitations of the activity of the individual will; and the same must be said of a large number of other experiences.

It is, moreover, established beyond dispute that in certain cases, in consequence of an inborn predisposition, contrary sexual inclinations make their appearance, and that these represent a divergency from the proper sexual characters. It is with these mental sexual differential characters just as it is with the physical secondary sexual characters, any of which may, on occasion, make their appearance in the wrong sex, or may be wanting in the right one. We know that there exist women with beards, masculine larynges, and a masculine type of thorax; and, on the other hand, men with feminine mammæ, feminine larynges, and a feminine type of pelvis. Because we meet with such atypical instances, we are not therefore justified in inferring that it is by a mere arbitrary sport of nature that in the woman a great mammary development is normally associated with the development of the ovaries, and that in man the growth of the beard is associated with the development of the testicles. But just as in these respects there are certain exceptions, whose origin we are not always in a position to explain, so also are there exceptional sexual associations in respect of the secondary psychical sexual characters. Thus it comes to pass that many women exhibit masculine tendencies, and many men exhibit feminine tendencies. Unquestionably, the fact that psychical qualities, just as much as physical characters, may occasionally make their appearance in the wrong sex, does not invalidate the general truth of the statement that sexually differentiated psychical tendencies are inborn.

Occasionally, indeed, even in late childhood, this psychical differentiation is still but little marked. We must also bear in mind the fact that in many instances the bodily development of the girl— apart, of course, from the actual reproductive organs—differs but little, even during the second period of childhood, from that of the boy; and that in such cases the specific differentiation makes its first appearance later than is usual. We find boys also who have entered upon the period of youth without exhibiting any trace of downy growth upon the upper lip or the chin; in some, the first definite growth of hair on the face may not occur until several years later. I remember also that I have seen boys in whom during the period of puberal development an enlargement of the mammæ took place, going so far that it was possible by pressure on the glands to expel fluid from the mammillary ducts; at a more advanced age, however, this mammary growth was arrested, and subsequently atrophy ensued.

But all these observations notwithstanding, the fact remains well established that even in childhood notable sexual differences make their appearance. Other observations, too, confirm this notion of sexual differentiation—for example, pathological experiences.

There are some diseases to which women are especially liable, others which occur by preference in men. To some extent, indeed, this is explained by the special exposure of one sex or the other to certain noxious influences. The neuroses that appear as the sequelæ of injuries are especially common in the male sex, because the occupations of men expose them more than women to injuries of all kinds. Of such cases, of course, we do not speak here. But there are some unquestionably hereditary morbid tendencies which manifest themselves by preference in one sex or the other, and such sexual predisposition shows itself even in childhood. I propose to give instances of this; some quoted from Möbius, some from other authors, and some taken from my own personal experience.

Chlorosis is a disease of feminine youth, but very often makes its appearance in childhood, especially towards the end of the second period of childhood, at this earlier age, also, attacking girls in preference to boys. Hæmophilia, on the other hand, and also certain hereditary forms of muscular atrophy, occur chiefly in males, and this in early childhood. Diabetes is principally a disease of adults, but occasionally it is met with in children also; among adults, there is a considerable preponderance of males affected with this disease when diabetes occurs in childhood, the disease also exhibits a preference for the male sex, although at this time the peculiar sex-incidence is less marked than in later life. Congenital defects of the heart are commoner in boys, the proportion obtained from a very large number of cases of this kind being 61.6 boys: 38.4 girls. Chorea (St. Vitus's dance) affects girls more often than boys, the ratio in this case being 2.5 girls: 1 boy. In the case of whooping cough, we find that two girls suffer for every one boy. As regards circumscribed facial atrophy, which usually begins during childhood, a preponderance of the disease in the female sex is also noticeable. Hysteria was formerly regarded as a typically feminine disease, and although this view has now been shown to be erroneous, the fact remains that girls and women are far more often affected than boys and men. As regards hysteria in childhood, Bruns states that the ratio of girls affected is to boys affected as 2:1. It is interesting to note that in the earlier years of childhood, prior, that is to say, to the age of nine years or thereabouts, no marked difference exists in the sex incidence of hysteria, the cases being distributed in the proportion, 55 per cent. girls, 45 per cent. boys; but after the age of nine, the proportion of girls affected with hysteria increases, while that of boys diminishes. Eulenburg, indeed, records 17 cases of hysteria, affecting children at ages nine to fourteen years; of these nine were boys, and eight girls. Clopatt, on the other hand, collected from the literature of the subject cases of hysteria in young children, 96 being boys, and 176 girls. Typhoid is commoner in males; and Möbius lays stress on the fact, which he regards as especially striking, that the difference in the sex-incidence of this disease is manifest even in childhood. As regards colour-blindness, there is a notable preponderance among males, and since we here have to do with a congenital affection, this preponderance is as marked among children as among adults. Many defects of speech also exhibit a notable difference in their sex-incidence. Hermann Gutzmann has shown that in the case of stammerers we find 71 per cent. boys and 29 per cent. girls. I take this opportunity of referring briefly to the fact that, as Max Marcuse reports, certain diseases of the skin exhibit sexual differentiation of type even during childhood. The disseminated cutaneous gangrene of children is far more frequent in girls than it is in boys; Broker, among twelve cases, found ten girls. Alopecia areata, on the other hand, affects both sexes with equal frequency, but affects them at different ages. Whereas during the first years of life girls are more frequently attacked; when the age of twenty is passed, the relation between the sexes in this respect are reversed.

Criminological experiences appear also to confirm the notion of an inherited sexual differentiation, in children as well as in adults.

According to various statistics, embracing not only the period of childhood, but including as well the period of youth, we learn that girls constitute one-fifth only of the total number of youthful criminals. A number of different explanations have been offered to account for this disproportion. Thus, for instance, attention has been drawn to the fact that a girl's physical weakness renders her incapable of attempting violent assaults upon the person, and this would suffice to explain why it is that girls so rarely commit such crimes. In the case of offences for which bodily strength is less requisite, such as fraud, theft, &c., the number of youthful female offenders is proportionately larger, although here also they are less numerous than males of corresponding age charged with the like offences. It has been asserted that in the law courts girls find more sympathy than boys, and that for this reason the former receive milder sentences than the latter; hence it results that in appearance merely the criminality of girls is less than that of boys. Others, again, refer the differences in respect of criminality between the youthful members of the two sexes to the influences of education and general environment. Morrison, however, maintains that all these influences combined are yet insufficient to account for the great disproportion between the sexes, and insists that there exists in youth as well as in adult life a specific sexual differentiation, based, for the most part, upon biological differences of a mental and physical character. I have referred to these criminological data for the sake of completeness, but I feel it necessary to add that their importance in relation to our subject of study is comparatively trifling, since most of the cases in question are offences committed by persons who can no longer properly be regarded as children.

As we have seen, during childhood, and especially during the second period of childhood, there exists a larger number of sexual differences both mental and physical. Some of these are obviously discernible when we compare isolated individuals; others only become apparent when we institute a statistical comparison. And when such differences appear in childhood, we find that they are quantitatively less extensive than the sexual differences of adults. For the sexual life is in the child less developed than it is in the adult. We shall learn that in the matter of the sexual impulse, the child exhibits an imperfect differentiation. A similarly imperfect differentiation is found in childhood in respect of a number of other qualities. Thus, there are many diseases which later in life manifest a sexual differentiation, but in childhood are undifferentiated. We observe a similar age-distinction in respect of suicide, which occurs in Europe far more frequently in men than in women, the ratio among suicides being three or four men to one woman. Among child-suicides there is far less disproportion between the sexes. According to Havelock Ellis, indeed, the suicidal tendency makes its appearance in girls at an earlier age than in boys.

Such a marked differentiation as there is between the adult man and the adult woman certainly does not exist in childhood. Similarly in respect of many other qualities, alike bodily and mental, in respect of many inclinations and numerous activities, we find that in childhood sexual differentiation is less marked than it is in adult life. None the less, we have learned in this chapter, a number of sexual differences can be shown to exist even in childhood; and as regards many other differences, though they are not yet apparent, we are nevertheless compelled to assume that they already exist potentially in the organs of the child.

CHAPTER IV

SYMPTOMATOLOGY

The data recorded in the preceding chapter suffice to show that the activity of the sexual life begins in childhood, for the secondary sexual characters and the other sexual peculiarities which manifest themselves thus early in life are dependent upon sex. We shall now proceed to the systematic description of the direct manifestations of the sexual life, and we can most usefully begin with the genital organs.

Erections occur during childhood; they have been observed even in infancy. They sometimes result from external stimuli, especially of a pathological nature, such as a strictured prepuce, or inflammatory states of the penis. Occasionally in the child, as normally in the adult male, distension of the bladder with urine leads to erection of the penis. Although in these cases the erection is not induced by sexual processes, it is nevertheless not devoid of significance in relation to the sexual life. The sensations in the genital organs to which the pathological stimuli give rise are further increased by the erection, and the child's attention is therefore increasingly drawn to his sexual organs. His attention may, of course, be directed to his genital organs by such stimuli as those we have described, even though these latter do not lead to the occurrence of erection. By such sensations, the child is very readily induced to manipulate his genital organs. Just as the little child soon learns to scratch other itching regions of the skin, so also he learns to scratch his genital organs when these are the seat of an itching eruption, or when in any other way irritating sensations arise in this region. Pflüger and Preyer have made investigations regarding the itching-reflex (Kitzelreflexe), and although in many respects their results are divergent, yet one point is clearly established by both, namely, that within a few months after birth a distinct itching-reflex is in operation, inasmuch as the child endeavours to scratch itching areas. Thus, by itching of the genital organs, a child is readily led to practise masturbation; and this is not necessarily effected by the hands, but sometimes by the feet, or by rubbing the thighs against one another, this last being generally done when the child is in the sitting posture. When erections occur in the child, we cannot always trace them to external stimuli, for in many cases they are due to stimuli of other kinds. Erection may, in fact, result from internal stimuli, connected with the development of the genital organs, and more especially that of the testicles. Moreover, such developmental stimuli may induce the child to manipulate the genital organs, and thus give rise to masturbation, without in the first instance causing erection. It appears that such stimuli leading to the practice of masturbation occur, during the first years of childhood, chiefly, if not exclusively, in children with morbid hereditary predisposition.

Such processes as these, viz., inflammatory stimuli originating in the external genital organs, or developmental stimuli proceeding from the testicles, may lead to the practice of masturbation without having directly affected the child's consciousness. Just as in the pithed frog, if we stimulate one foot with acetic acid, the other foot scratches the irritated area, so a child may, with his hands or in some other way, scratch itching regions of the body, and, above all, of the external genital organs, without its being necessary for us to assume that he is fully conscious of what he is doing. Further, as we have already pointed out, such masturbation may or may not be preceded by a reflex erection. And just as the boy soon learns that itching is relieved by scratching, so also he learns that by means of artificial stimulation he may induce sensations of a voluptuous character. It is the same with the little girl, in whom sensations occur in the genital organs, due in some cases to developmental, and in others to pathological stimuli (skin eruptions are an instance of the latter kind), and these lead to manipulations of the genital organs.

In contradistinction to the cases just described, in which the child has learned spontaneously to practise artificial stimulation of his genital organs, are the cases in which seduction by others is the cause of masturbation. Nurses sometimes touch, stroke, and stimulate the external genital organs of the children entrusted to their care—boys and girls alike—either to keep them quiet, or for the gratification of their own lustful feelings. In this way the child, who in the case of all agreeable sensations has a natural desire for their repetition, is gradually led to imitate the manipulations which have given rise to the voluptuous sensations, and is thus seduced to the practice of masturbation.

In the preceding passages I have spoken of all kinds of mechanical stimulation of the genital organs, and also of erections occurring in small children. I now pass on to consider ejaculation. Whereas during normal intercourse in the sexually mature man and woman a fluid secretion is expelled, nothing of the kind is possible in children, at least such is the general opinion. Frequently, indeed, as regards the male sex, the end of childhood, properly speaking, is supposed to be indicated by the first ejaculation of semen. Matters are, however, by no means so simple as this. We have seen that the testicular secretion, the most important constituent of the semen, consists, as Fürbringer has pointed out, almost entirely of spermatozoa. But how is it in the case of children? The spermatozoa may be first formed at very varying ages. According to the investigations of Mantegazza, they rarely make their appearance earlier than the eighteenth year of life. Fürbringer does not unconditionally accept this view; but he has himself, as he has personally informed me, examined boys at ages of fifteen to sixteen in whom the ejaculation was entirely devoid of spermatozoa. But, on the other hand, he has found spermatozoa in the semen of a boy aged only twelve or thirteen years. I have myself examined the emissions of boys in a considerable number of cases, and have repeatedly found that, even in the case of boys of sixteen, the ejaculated secretions contained no spermatozoa. The reports of other investigators also show that as regards this point very wide individual variations occur. Hofmann has contributed some data to this discussion. A case published by Klose, in which pregnancy is alleged to have resulted from intercourse with a boy aged nine years, is, indeed, regarded by Hofmann as probably apocryphal. But he had personal knowledge of a case in which a woman was impregnated by a boy fourteen years of age. He assumes that when a boy's general development is advanced (masculine habit of body, large penis, &c.), his reproductive capacity will also make its appearance at an earlier age. But he has met with exceptions to this generalisation. Thus, in the post-mortem examination of the body of a boy aged fourteen, whose physique was still quite infantile, he found well-developed spermatozoa both in the testicles and in the seminal vesicles. In the case of two boys aged fifteen years, in whom the genital organs were powerfully developed, he found in one abundant spermatozoa, but in the other none at all. In two other boys, also fifteen years of age, in whom the pubic hair had not yet appeared, spermatozoa were present. They were absent, again, in a young man of eighteen years. Similar variations were found by Haberda. Thus, for example, in two boys aged fifteen and seventeen years, respectively, he found no spermatozoa, notwithstanding the fact that in both the pubic hair had grown. On the other hand, in a boy aged 13¾ years, with an abundance of pubic hair, numerous well-developed spermatozoa were present. Haberda is of opinion that, speaking generally, the first formation of the spermatozoa is associated with the appearance of the other indications of puberty. The earliest authenticated age at which spermotozoa have been known to appear is 13½ years; they have been found at this age by two separate investigators, one in Paris, the other in Berlin. Notwithstanding the fact that, as we have seen, such extensive variations occur, we are justified in making the general statement that in the case of children in our own country no spermatozoa are developed; if exceptions ever occur, they can relate only to the last year or year and a half of the second period of childhood.

We must now proceed to ask whether it is possible for ejaculation to occur in children at a time of life when the formation of spermatozoa in the testicles has not yet begun; this question must be answered with an unconditional affirmative. We have seen that the secretions of several other glands intermingle with the secretion of the testicles. These glands are the following: the prostate gland, the glands of the vesiculæ seminales and the vasa deferentia, the glands of Cowper, and the glands of Littré. It is certain that these glands begin to secrete at different times, and, above all, that some of them begin to secrete before spermatozoa have appeared in the testicles. Hence it is rightly believed that the capacity for coitus (potentia coeundi) develops much earlier than the capacity for procreation (potentia generandi)—a fact which was well known to Zacchias. Quae enim hanc juventutem vel præcedunt ætates, vel sequuntur aut plane semen non effundunt aut certe infoecundum aut male foecundum effundunt. Strassmann considers that in our climate the capacity for procreation begins at the earliest at the end of the fifteenth year, and the capacity for coitus at the end of the thirteenth year. In a number of cases in which in children I found stains on the underclothing, or in some other way obtained specimens of the ejaculated fluid, the results of the examination for spermatozoa were entirely negative. In a case which came under my notice a long time ago, that of a child seven years of age, I had assumed that the fluid with which the underclothing was stained was produced by inflammatory irritation of the urethra consequent upon masturbation. Subsequent experience, however, in conjunction with the observations of other investigators, has led me to the firm conviction that even in our climate we do not need to invoke the idea of such inflammatory irritation of the urethra in order to account for the ejaculation of fluid by children—at any rate when these are approaching the end of the second period of childhood. In the case of twelve-year-old boys, I believe that such ejaculations of fluid occur in quite a large number of cases. One instance, which did not come under my own observation, but was communicated to me by one of our best-known educationalists, relates to a boy only ten years of age. This boy, endeavouring to climb over a fence, repeatedly slipped back; while thus engaged, he experienced his first seminal emission. In this way he then masturbated several times.

Let us now consider whence the ejaculated fluid can be derived prior to the age at which it comes to contain spermatozoa. In the first place, it is possible that the testicles themselves, before they begin to form the spermatozoa, may yet furnish an indifferent secretion, although in the adult the secretion of the testicles consists chiefly of the spermatozoa. We have also to consider the glands previously enumerated, whose secretions normally form constituents of the semen. We possess, however, hardly any trustworthy information regarding the time at which the glands of the vasa deferentia begin to secrete. The glands of Cowper, as Henle showed many years ago, begin to secrete within a few weeks after birth. He believed that these glands secreted continuously, but that the secretion was retained for a time in the ducts, and was discharged intermittently with the urine. For this reason he believed that the glands of Cowper did not form a part of the reproductive system. Subsequent investigations, however, have led us to believe that the secretion of Cowper's glands is one of the constituents of the semen. Another constituent is the secretion of the glands of Littré, and these glands also perhaps begin to secrete at a much earlier age than the testicles. We may regard it as certain that the seminal vesicles may contain secretion before any spermatozoa are formed in the testicles. As regards the prostate gland, it is supposed that this first begins to secrete at the commencement of the age of puberal development or even later. According to the data collected by Frisch, the prostate gland, comparatively small in childhood, first begins to grow quickly at the epoch of the puberal development. During childhood, the gland tissue is comparatively scanty, although it already contains concretions. Only during the puberal development does the prostate gland attain its full size; according to the researches of Englisch, who observed 1282 instances, this does not occur until after the full development of the testicles. Beyond question we are justified, from the information at our disposal, in concluding that the prostate gland begins to secrete comparatively late. But, on the other hand, it is equally clear that certain glands whose secretion in the adult forms part of the semen, begin to secrete long before any spermatozoa have been formed in the testicles, and may in this way give rise to the formation of a semen incapable of fertilising the ovum.

In respect of the extrusion of the fluid, we have to recognise two different ways in which this is effected: first, ejaculation, due to a rhythmical expulsive movement; and secondly, the urethrorrhoea ex libidine met with in adults, of which an account was given in the second chapter. In my own investigations on the subject, I have been able to learn nothing regarding the occurrence in children of any urethrorrhoea ex libidine; and my information relates only to the true ejaculation of a fluid, I have seen a few cases in which such ejaculation occurred in boys at the early age of twelve years, although this is quite exceptional, and, as already mentioned, in such cases the ejaculated fluid contains no spermatozoa.

In the case of women, what has been said of the glands of Cowper applies equally to the glands of Bartholin, the homologues of the former both as regards significance and development. The glands of Bartholin also begin to secrete in sexually immature girls, and even in children. It must be added that when ejaculation occurs in sexually immature girls, the products of other glands are probably intermingled with the secretion of the glands of Bartholin (mucous glands of the uterus, of the cervix uteri, the vagina, the vulva, and perhaps also of the urethra).

I have distinguished the simple outflow of secretion from its forcible expulsion—from true ejaculation. This latter demands the rhythmical activity of certain muscles, such as takes place during coitus. The question arises, whether such muscular activity can occur before any fluid has been formed capable of being ejaculated. When I compare what is published in the literature of the subject with what I have myself observed in this connexion, I regard the following points as definitely established. There are certain cases, and these in young persons of both sexes, in which typical rhythmical muscular contractions take place in the child, although no ejaculated fluid is discoverable. It remains doubtful, however, whether a small quantity of secretion, overlooked by the observer, and perhaps not even recognisable, may not, after all, be ejaculated. I consider it probable that this is so. Moreover, we must not forget that the rhythmical muscular contractions, which in the adult effect ejaculation, are able to expel the fluid from the urethra only when this fluid is present in sufficient quantity. When the quantity is minimal the fluid is retained for a time in that passage, owing to the frictional resistance of the urethra, and is perhaps not expelled until the next act of micturition. Some may, of course, object to denote such a process by the word ejaculation; but I myself see no reason why the term should not be extended to include the rhythmical muscular contraction both in the child and the adult, even in cases in which there is not sufficient fluid secretion in the urethra for this to be visibly extruded by these contractions.

What have we to say regarding the voluptuous sensation in children? It is extremely difficult to form clear ideas about this matter, for the sources of fallacy previously described are here markedly in operation; above all, in the case of little children, the voluptuous sensation, purely subjective in character, is extraordinarily difficult to recognise objectively. This much, however, may be said. It appears to me to be beyond question that in childhood, and even in very early childhood, a sensation may sometimes be excited of the same kind as the voluptuous sensation of adult life. None the less, we must be careful not to assume too readily, in any particular case, that such a sensation has actually been experienced. Certain oscillatory movements on the part of infants and other small children have frequently been regarded as an indication of the practice of masturbation, and of the occurrence of voluptuous sensations; but in my opinion that view is to a large extent erroneous. Such movements may be no more than the expression of a general sense of well-being, without having anything whatever to do with the sexual life or with the specific voluptuous sensation. Doubtless the voluptuous sensation may be experienced by very small children, and even by infants. When we see a child lying with moist, widely-opened eyes, and exhibiting all the other signs of sexual excitement, such as we are accustomed to observe in adults, we are justified in assuming that the child is experiencing a voluptuous sensation. But what is usually wanting in such cases, at any rate in young children, is the voluptuous acme which in adults occurs in association with the act of ejaculation. Cases have also been occasionally reported to me in which, even in infancy, a voluptuous acme has occurred; and still more frequently I have been told this in respect of somewhat older children, for example, at ages of seven or eight years. I believe, however, that this voluptuous acme is, at any rate in children, much less common than the equable voluptuous sensation which can be aroused by all kinds of manipulations and stimulations of the peripheral genital organs, and more especially of the glans, the penis, the clitoris, and the labia minora. The older the child, the more frequently is the voluptuous acme attained; in our own

62

climate, during the last years of the second period of childhood, this occurs comparatively often; the voluptuous acme does not last so long as in sexually mature individuals, but is in other respects described in identical terms. It is experienced simultaneously with the occurrence of the rhythmical muscular contractions which have previously been described. It is possible, as I suggested before, that in such cases the ejaculation of a certain quantity of glandular secretion always occurs, although, as I have also explained, this secretion may sometimes be too small in quantity to be actually expelled from the urethra by the muscular extractions. This point is, however, still obscure. But it may be regarded as definitely established that the equable voluptuous sensation, and more particularly the voluptuous acme, may occur at an age at which, at any rate, secretion does not yet exist in sufficient quantity to be expelled from the urethra, and the existence of such secretion is therefore not unequivocally manifested. In exceptional, and doubtless pathological instances, and above all in cases in which, owing to the practice of masturbation, there has been excessive stimulation, instead of the voluptuous acme, a painful sensation may be experienced. In general, however, in children, just as in adults, the voluptuous acme is associated with a sense of satisfaction, and with the subsidence of the previously existing sexual excitement. This much is beyond question, that the voluptuous acme and the sense of satisfaction associated therewith make their appearance subsequent to the development of erection and the equable voluptuous sensation in the genital organs. Mutatis mutandis, this is equally true of both sexes.

In other respects, however, the voluptuous sensation and the voluptuous acme exhibit in the child an important difference from the same phenomena in the adult, to which we shall have to return later. To sum up, we may regard it as certain that erections often appear many years before the end of the second period of childhood; not infrequently, indeed, in the beginning of the second period of childhood, and even earlier. These erections may very early in life be associated with an equable voluptuous sensation, allied to the sensations of itching or tickling. The voluptuous acme and ejaculation do not make their appearance until later. These statements apply, in the first place, to boys. The conditions in girls appear, however, to be analogous. But here we must be most cautious in drawing conclusions, for the reason that the sexual life of the girl is still much more obscure to us than that of the boy; this difference in our knowledge of the sexes is no less marked in the case of children than it is in respect of the adult man and woman.

Hitherto we have occupied ourselves with the description of the peripheral sexual organs, and of the processes of detumescence. We must now pass on to the second group of sexual phenomena, the processes of contrectation. Even in childhood, these processes play an important part; indeed, they generally manifest themselves at an earlier age than the processes of detumescence. But first, let me briefly summarise Max Dessoir's account of the stages of the sexual impulse—stages in which the contrectation impulse is alone concerned. In its development, three stages may be distinguished. One of these is the neutral stage, in earliest childhood, in which, speaking generally, the processes of contrectation are not yet to be observed, and during which the child does not feel attracted towards anyone in such a manner as to make it necessary for us to assume the occurrence of any psychosexual process. This stage is succeeded by the extremely important undifferentiated stage, to which Max Dessoir has drawn attention. Its principal characteristic is indicated in its name: the direction of the impulse is not yet completely differentiated. It oscillates to and fro, and depends upon the external objects which happen to be in the vicinity. This undifferentiated stage is of profound importance; and owing to the fact that its existence has been ignored in the study of sexual perversions, great confusion has arisen. During the undifferentiated period, it may happen that quite normal children exhibit homosexual excitement, whose importance is apt to be greatly over-estimated by their relatives and others. During the undifferentiated stage a boy may love one of his teachers or one of his friends, and yet in later life be perfectly normal; many a woman, again, who loves her husband ardently has earlier, during the undifferentiated period, passionately loved a school-fellow or a governess. On the other hand, during the undifferentiated stage a boy may exhibit an inclination towards someone of the opposite sex, the governess or the girl-friend of his sister, for instance; conversely, the girl may be attracted by a boy or a young man. This inclination, whether homosexual or heterosexual, often leads to bodily acts, to contact with the beloved person, embraces, and kisses, without the necessary occurrence of any manifestations on the part of the external genital organs, although such manifestations may at times ensue. The undifferentiated stage is followed by the third stage, in which the contrectation impulse becomes differentiated, so that in normal individuals the sexual impulse becomes unmistakably heterosexual. Normally, this differentiated stage endures until the time of the final extinction of the sexual impulse.

I do not believe that an undifferentiated stage occurs in every one without exception. On the other hand, I have absolutely no doubt that it occurs very frequently indeed—far more frequently than is commonly believed—and that it occurs in persons whose subsequent sexual development is perfectly normal. Moreover, during the undifferentiated stage, in addition to heterosexual and homosexual inclinations, perverse sentiments may make their appearance. Masochistic, sadistic, fetichistic excitations of all kinds are met with, and sexual inclination towards animals is by no means rare. As regards the last named, the inclination is directed especially towards the animals with which the child is most intimately associated, as, for instance, a dog, a cat, a bird, a horse, and the like. Again, during the period of undifferentiated sexual impulse all kinds of disordered ideas may become associated with that impulse; for instance, an impulse may arise to touch the saliva, or some other excretory product, of the beloved being, human or animal, as the case may be, and even to take such a product into the mouth. Many persons completely forget all these manifestations of the undifferentiated sexual impulse which have formed part of their own early experiences. The causes of such oblivion have been discussed in the first chapter.

Yet another reason may be mentioned for regarding a knowledge of the undifferentiated stage of the sexual impulse as of great importance. In works on the pathology of the sexual impulse we are frequently assured that in this or that specific instance the perversion was inborn, because perverse sensations have existed since the days of childhood. But the existence of the undifferentiated stage teaches us that we are not justified in inferring, from the mere fact of the primary occurrence of a "perverse" mode of sexual sensibility, that this perversion is congenital; for the primary direction of the contrectation impulse during the undifferentiated stage often depends to a considerably greater extent upon chance than upon an inherited predisposition.

The undifferentiated stage begins at very various ages. I have known instances in which it could be traced back to the fifth, year of life. I regard it as probable, however, that it may begin even earlier than this. But more commonly it begins somewhat later; not infrequently at the age of seven or eight, and very often at the age of nine or ten years. As previously mentioned, I do not maintain that an undifferentiated stage is of universal occurrence. When such a stage is absent, the symptoms of the differentiated sexual impulse often make their appearance at the age at which in other cases the undifferentiated stage of the impulse usually begins. In the case of a large number of men, inquiry will show that at the age of nine or ten they began to experience an inclination towards persons of the female sex; in a good many this occurs even at the age of eight, and in a few yet earlier; as regards women, mutatis mutandis, the same conditions obtain. In cases in which an undifferentiated stage is well marked, its duration is likewise very variable. In isolated instances it lasts until the age of twenty, or even a few years longer. Ordinarily, however, the differentiation of the impulse becomes manifest at an earlier age—between the ages of fifteen and seventeen years. Beyond question, in the great majority of cases, the "perverse" sentiments of childhood subsequently disappear spontaneously. But when I come to discuss sexual perversions in detail, I shall point out that this disappearance, in certain circumstances, fails to occur.

I take this opportunity of referring to a beautiful example of the undifferentiated sexual impulse which is found in Wilhelm Meisters Wanderjahren. In the twelfth chapter of the second book, Wilhelm describes "one of the earliest incidents of his youth":—"The elder of these boys, a year or two my own senior, the son of the fisherman, seemed to take no pleasure in this sport with flowers. This boy, by whom at his first appearance I had been greatly attracted, invited me to go with him to the river, a fairly wide stream which flowed past at a little distance. We sat side by side in a shady spot with our fishing-rods.... As we sat there quietly, leaning towards one another, he seemed to grow rather weary of our inaction, and he drew my attention to a flat stretch of gravel which extended from our feet beneath the surface of the water. This would be a fine place to bathe. At last, jumping to his feet, he cried out that the chance was too good to be missed, and almost before I realised his intention, he had stripped, and was in the water. Being a good swimmer, he soon left the shallows, swam across the stream, and then back again into the deep water near the bank on which I was sitting. My own mood was a strange one. Grasshoppers danced round about me, ants crawled to and fro, many-coloured beetles hung from the twigs, and brilliant dragon flies hovered in the air; my companion caught sight of a great crayfish, flashing merrily out from its hole beneath the roots overhanging the water, and cleverly eluding an attempt to seize it by darting back into its lair. The air was so warm and moist; in the sunshine one longed for the shade, and even in the coolness of the shade one longed for the still greater coolness of the water. Thus it was easy for him to entice me into the stream; his invitation, once or twice repeated, proved irresistible, notwithstanding my fear of a scolding from my parents, mingled with some dread of the unknown element. Soon I undressed upon the gravelly bank, and ventured gently into the water, not too far down the gradually shelving bank; here he let me wait awhile, swimming out himself across the stream; then he returned to my side, and as he left the water, standing upright, to dry himself in the bright sunshine, it seemed to me that my eyes must be dazzled by the power of the sun, so blindingly beautiful was the human form—far more beautiful than I had ever before imagined. He seemed to look at me with equal attention. Dressing quickly, we stood beside each other with all barriers broken down, our spirits were drawn closely together, and with ardent kisses we swore eternal friendship."

Groos rightly sees in this passage a delicate intimation of sexual sensibility. A little later we read how Wilhelm, having made an appointment with this boy to meet him one evening in the forest, encounters a young girl, a little younger than himself. "Spring flowers of all kinds were growing in the beautifully adorned fields, among the grass, and along the hedges. My companion was beautiful, blond, gentle; we walked trustingly side by side, each holding the other by the hand, and seeming to wish for nothing better in the world.... When, after the lapse of so many years, I look back upon my former state, it seems to me to have been a truly enviable one. Unexpectedly, in the same instant, I experienced the sentiments of friendship and of love; for as I unwillingly took leave of the beautiful child, I was consoled by the thought of explaining these ideas to my young boy-friend, by the prospect of confiding in him, and of rejoicing in his participation in these newly discovered sentiments."

The following description of the period of the undifferentiated sexual impulse has been placed at my disposal:—

Case 1.—X. is now thirty-four years of age, happily married, with several healthy children. He is himself a thoroughly healthy man, with normal impulses, and free from all bodily and mental abnormality. His description of the period of the undifferentiated sexual impulse may best be given in his own words. "At the age of nine, when I was still living in the country, and was being educated by a private tutor, a passionate affection for him took possession of me. Generally speaking, he was good-natured and indulgent, but was at times strict, I used my utmost endeavours to be near him as much as possible. I was happy when he touched me. Gradually this inclination increased; everything that he had touched, everything that he had warmed with his body, I also wished to touch. If he had drunk from a glass, I secretly drank from it myself, so that my lips might touch the very spot where his had rested. At the age of ten I began to attend the public school in the town, I sat beside a fellow-pupil who, like myself, came from the country. Soon I conceived a fondness for him. He was not only my playmate, I wished always that we should do our work together; whenever he had any other companion than myself, I was profoundly unhappy. Was this jealousy? I believe it was. When he left the school—it must have

been about a year after I had entered—I was at first very unhappy, but my fondness for him was soon replaced by a passion for his sister, a girl about twelve years of age. I had made her acquaintance through so often working with her brother, and through visiting his parents' house. She was a pretty girl. At first, after my friend had departed, I went to the house occasionally, in order to hear some news of him, and of his doings in the school abroad to which he had been sent. In the house that had been his home I had also an indefinite feeling that I was near him once again. But gradually my liking for his sister grew, and I was glad that her parents gave me renewed invitations to the house, especially for the Sundays. To be with this girl, to play with her, were to me an enduring source of delight; and I remember that at this time I even developed a taste for girlish amusements, which had hitherto been very disagreeable to me, and for which later also my antipathy returned. Simultaneously with this fondness for the girl, when I myself was about twelve years old I was attracted by one of the schoolmasters, a man who ruled his classes very strictly. My sentiments for this master were of exactly the same character as those with which my tutor had formerly inspired me, but the conditions of our intercourse were different, for I could see him only in school, and on very rare occasions out of school hours, whereas in the case of my tutor, who lived with us when I was at home, I could be with him as much as I desired. This fondness for my schoolmaster persisted simultaneously with the passion for the girl. When her brother came home for the holidays, I saw him for a few days only, for I also returned home for the holidays. Although I was by no means indifferent to him, my former passionate affection for him had entirely disappeared. My passion for his sister and for the schoolmaster lasted for a long time. I also fell in love with a somewhat elderly female cousin who chanced to visit our house. Growing older, I at length attained the age of puberty, and experienced definite erections; these occurred especially when I thought of my friend's sister; or when she touched me, as occasionally happened, without, I believe, any sexual feeling on her part. At this time also when erections had already begun, I still felt definitely attracted by my schoolmaster, and under the influence of this attraction erections occasionally occurred. Somewhat later came the time when I began to masturbate. I can no longer remember with certainty whether I was seduced to this practice by any of my school-fellows. We sometimes talked to one another about the matter. I continued at times to be influenced by the inclinations previously mentioned, viz., that for my schoolmaster, and that for my friend's sister. I experienced also transient passion for one of my school-fellows, who was remarkable for his pleasing and delicately girlish exterior. It was not until several years had elapsed, and the occurrence of seminal emissions had shown that I had attained some degree of sexual maturity, that all inclination towards the male sex disappeared, and the inclination towards the female sex persisted in isolation. When I left the town, in order to attend a different school, my fondness for my friend's sister passed away. I was then sixteen years of age; from this time onwards my sexual passion was exhibited exclusively towards members of the female sex."

Case 2.—This case provides us with another description of the undifferentiated sexual impulse. X. is thirty years of age. No morbid condition is demonstrable in him. He remembers that the first sentiments which he regards as sexual were experienced by him in the country. His home was in a town, but during the holidays he was sent to board in the country, in the house of a clergyman. He played much in the open air, and he still recalls quite distinctly the passion with which, first of all, he approached animals. "As if by an irresistible impulse I was attracted, now by a goat, now by a dog, sometimes even by a horse. No excitement of the genital organs was noticeable at this time, but I have no doubt whatever now that these inclinations were sexual in their nature. Not only did I touch the animals, but I embraced them and kissed them. The warmth and the odour proceeding from such an animal, which is now as a rule distasteful to me, was then a source of pleasure. When I left the country, I took these memories away with me, but gradually they faded and became faint. Next a fondness for one of my school-fellows became most marked, and this lasted for a long time. I know not how to describe the feeling I had for him otherwise than as an immeasurable, passionate love. I was unhappy when I sat above him in the class. Occasionally we sat side by side, but not always, since our places were determined by our performances in class. If I was sitting next above him, it was a joy to me to fail deliberately to answer a question, simply in order to enable him to take my place, and thus to give him pleasure. This relationship continued undisturbed for several years; we rose together from class to class and remained friends. Not until the beginning of the true puberal development did this fondness begin to wane. I began to learn dancing rather early, and in the dancing-class was a girl by whom I was now greatly attracted. She was of the same age as myself—fourteen years. As far as I can remember, my inclinations were now confined for a time to my boy companion and to this girl. At first my affection for the boy was the greater, but gradually my affection for the girl, who was healthy and vivacious in appearance, became stronger. Still, this passion was a fire of straw, for though, in the course of the next few years, my fondness for the boy gradually declined, whilst my affection for the girl grew stronger, yet later this girl was expelled from my circle of interests by others, my inclinations changing rapidly from one girl to another. Homosexual sentiments hardly existed any more. Very occasionally, indeed, even up to my twentieth year, a certain interest was aroused in me by any youth with a truly girlish, milk-white countenance. But subsequently this homosexual inclination disappeared entirely, and my heterosexual development was completed, so that I am now, I believe, in every respect a healthy male."

Case 3.—Next we have the case of a woman, now married and twenty-six years of age, in whom also the undifferentiated sexual impulse was clearly manifested. From the age of eight to the age of fifteen years she attended a day-school for girls, and subsequently, after receiving private tuition for a time, went to a boarding-school. "In my earlier years I can recall no feelings for my school-fellows beyond those of simple friendship. We kissed one another, but no more intimate contact took place. In these kisses, I was not aware of any sentiment exceeding pure friendship; and to-day when I thoroughly understand the nature of the kiss of erotic love, I do not believe that there was any erotic element intermingled with these first kisses. Such simple friendliness towards my fellow-schoolgirls persisted unaltered even after in my tenth year I first experienced a sentiment of enthusiastic devotion. This latter was inspired by an actress, a remarkably beautiful woman visiting our town—I lived then in a town of medium size—whose pictures were displayed in all the shop windows. Although I realised later that her talents were by no means of a high order, and notwithstanding the fact that I never saw her on the stage, I conceived for her an enthusiastic admiration. I tried from time to time, when I could do so without being observed, to catch a glimpse of her in the street; almost the only possible opportunity was when she was on her way to rehearsals. When the actress went away, her place in my heart was occupied by a schoolmaster of typically masculine appearance, with a full, fair beard. He gave us lessons in history, literature, and German. Nearly all the class were fascinated by him, and I by no means less than the others. This admiration lasted almost the whole of the remaining time during which I attended the school. When I went to the boarding-school, being now somewhat older, and regarded as almost a young woman, I was allowed to witness a representation of Faust. The part of Gretchen was played by an actress who is still of note to-day, and she made a most enduring impression on me. To my great delight I was unexpectedly presented to her, and she wrote a line or two in my album. Unfortunately, the headmistress would not allow us to go often to the theatre, a prohibition doubtless in part dependent on the high prices of the seats. But I still remember quite distinctly how I trembled with joy whenever I was allowed to go. I remember, too, that on one occasion, in which it had been arranged that I was to go to see a play in which this actress did not appear, I shammed illness in order to save up the price of the seat, go that I might use it on another occasion, on which I should be able to see her. This particular enthusiasm lasted as long as I remained at the boarding-school. When later I grew old enough to marry, and when with the approval of my parents a gentleman who appeared to love me (though, in fact, I think he was influenced rather by prudential motives) began to pay me his addresses, my fondness for the actress soon began to fade away. Even at the present day, however, I esteem this artiste very highly indeed, and the impression which she made on my imagination will never be entirely expunged from my memory. If I were to see her to-day, I should willingly kiss her hands, in thankfulness for the happy hours she has given me; but I do not believe that any erotic element now remains in my feeling for her. I may add that I do not love my husband passionately, although I love him well enough. Physical contact with the actress of whom I have spoken would not be positively repulsive to me, but such contact would, as far as I am concerned, be entirely devoid of sexual feeling, and the idea of sexual contact with a person of my own sex is very unpleasant to me; whereas in sexual intercourse with my husband I am perfectly normal." This patient does not belong to the class of sexually anæsthetic women; she feels the impulse towards sexual intercourse, and in intercourse she experiences normal enjoyment.

I shall now discuss some of the general phenomena of the contrectation impulse in the child. Sanford Bell has published cases in which as early as the age of two years psychosexual phenomena have been observed. But in many of Bell's cases a sexual basis for the feelings of attraction does not appear to have been adequately proved to exist. Unquestionably, however, sexual phenomena are more frequently observed in proportion as the child's age increases. Although in the case of children it is very difficult for others to arrive at certainty regarding the sexual or non-sexual character of certain manifestations, still, in the eighth year of life, the phenomena of the contrectation impulse become so frequent—I am referring here to personal observations—that at this time of life these phenomena must be regarded, not merely as not pathological, but further, as not even abnormal. The older the child becomes, the more are the phenomena of the contrectation impulse complicated by those of detumescence. The processes of contrectation, however, may continue to manifest themselves during the first years of the period of youth in complete isolation from any apparent changes in the genital organs. The manifestations of what is known as "calf-love" commonly occur quite independently of any thought of sexual contact.

Very various are the objects of this early attraction. Often a boy is attracted by a girl of about his own age; often, again, by a girl considerably older than himself. On the other hand, as has been previously shown, when the sexual attraction felt by the boy is exhibited towards one of his own sex, it may sometimes happen that the object of attraction is a boy of his own age, sometimes a man considerably older than himself. By no means rare are sexual inclinations on the part of boys towards their masters—in some cases a private tutor; in others, a schoolmaster. With girls similar variations are observed. A girl may love another girl of her own age, and this is extremely common in the case of girls at boarding-schools. But a boy, a friend of her brother's, may be the object of a girl's affection. Frequently, again, a girl may become attached to some one considerably older than herself, commonly a master or a governess. Persons playing some conspicuous part in life very readily inspire love: an artist, for instance; or an actress, about whom all the papers are writing, and of whom everyone is talking. In many cases, the personal appearance plays a considerable part in originating the attraction. At times, indeed, affection is inspired by individuals devoid of all personal charm. But, speaking generally, we shall find that to the child, no less than to the adult, in sexual relationships beauty is by no means indifferent. A pretty girl is more attractive to a boy than an ugly one. A handsome master will charm a girl much more than one who is ill-favoured or deformed. Other qualities besides beauty affect the issue. Effeminate boys or tomboyish girls are apt to be repulsive to other children; they are exposed to mockery and teasing of all kinds, and are very unlikely to give rise to erotic sentiments in their companions. It is by no means rare for the inclinations of children to be directed towards their own parents. In the case of many children who are fond of "getting into mother's bed," sexual sentiments lie at the root of the

73

desire. Moreover, it is occasionally asserted that sexual differentiation manifests itself in this connexion in very early childhood, the little boy preferring to cuddle his mother; the little girl, on the other hand, to be caressed by her father. In the chapter on diagnosis, I shall consider the distinction of such sexual inclinations from other sympathetic feelings manifested in childhood. It is a remarkable fact that the first sexual inclinations are very rarely directed towards a child's own brother or sister. I have, indeed, been able to observe a considerable number of such exceptional instances, both homosexual and heterosexual in character. But, I repeat, such cases are comparatively rare. We must not, of course, confuse with genuine sexual inclinations and acts, cases in which from curiosity alone brothers and sisters indulge together in obscene conversation and even improper practices. Unquestionably, the lack of sexual sympathy between brothers and sisters depends upon a deeply rooted psychological causation. Above all, in this connexion, we have to bear in mind the slight degree of influence each exercises on the senses of the other, precisely in consequence of the long-continued, comparatively unrestrained intercourse between them. Further, the conventional factors implanted in mankind from earliest childhood play their part. Many, perhaps, will see an additional cause in teleological considerations, aiming at the avoidance of in-and-in breeding.

Many lovers incline to the romantic transfiguration of the object of their affection, a process in which the imagination plays an important part; but for this to be possible, it is, of course, necessary that an age should have been attained at which the imagination is sufficiently active. The age at which the child has learned to delight in fairy-tales is here of importance; from the contents of such fairy-tales all kinds of ideas are transferred to the sexual sphere. Romantic embellishment plays a great part not merely in childhood, but also later in life; but in childhood, this tendency often exists to an extraordinary degree. The person whom a boy loves must be very highly placed; for example, during the period of the undifferentiated sexual impulse, he prefers a boy of the highest possible birth. Similarly, a young girl who loves a boy will invest him in imagination with every possible attribute of distinction and high rank. Often the love is directed towards a person of no concrete existence, or towards one who is unattainable. We may sometimes be in doubt whether we have to do with sexual love, or whether some other sentiment may not be in operation. For example, the devotion to some saint of either sex may overpower all other feelings. Where a child is enamoured of some definite individual, self-deception occurs just as it does in adults similarly situated. The faults of the beloved one are imaginatively transmuted into virtues, or any possible excuse is found for them. Is a boy attracted by a girl known to be habitually untruthful? Especially when himself unaware that his interest is sexual, he looks out for every merit she may possibly possess, in order that his fondness may be justified. Her untruthfulness is transfigured as caution and cleverness; her vanity becomes neatness; idleness is excused on the ground that she has to attend to more important duties; and the boy regards his interest in the girl as exclusively friendly in character, and as justified by her superlative excellences. Sometimes, in children no less than in adults, a sexual inclination masquerades as an educational interest. Thus, under the influence of sexual attraction, a girl becomes intimate with a boy endowed with various bad qualities and impulses, and endeavours to utilise this intimacy for the boy's advantage, in order that he may free himself of his faults as he grows to manhood. Such a girl may succeed in persuading herself that this motive is the exclusive cause of her interest in the boy. A similar combination of educational and sexual motives is, moreover, often encountered in the case of homosexual sentiments.

The child's sexual inclination may manifest itself in many different ways. It seeks every opportunity of seeing, of being in close proximity to, of touching, and of kissing the beloved person. Thus, many a boy takes part in the common sports, solely because the girl whom he loves is one of the players. Sanford Bell mentions numerous games in which children find pleasure chiefly for the reason that kissing plays a principal part in them. For kissing is one of the leading manifestations of sexual desire; and another is the wish for close proximity to and for embracing the beloved person. A mother who kept a close watch on her eight-year-old daughter told me that when in play a boy of ten pressed close up against the girl; they kissed one another somewhat passionately, and the boy broke out in the naïve utterance, "You don't know how fond I am of you; I do love you so." Not infrequently, indeed, children are really troublesome to adults in their desire for close physical contact. I have known instances in which young women or girls have been intolerably annoyed by boys eight or nine years of age, who have continually followed them about and pressed up against them; this has gone on for a long time without those concerned recognising the sexual foundation of such conduct. Love on the part of children almost invariably gives rise to the desire for physical contact of some kind. Of course, other manifestations also occur. Besides the contemplation of the beloved person, contemplation of his or her picture plays a notable part. A sexual motive occasionally underlies the wrestling so common among boys—in such cases it is the manifestation of a desire for intimate physical contact with the beloved boy. According to Sanford Bell, a boy and a girl may also wrestle with one another with the same end in view of attaining intimate contact; and he states that children lift one another with the same object. Moreover, children are induced to wrestle by sexual motives of a somewhat different character; the wish is operative to be overcome by, or, it may be, to overcome, the beloved boy. Herein we see displayed very clearly those sexual feelings known to us in adults under the names of masochism and sadism; the same feelings are occasionally observed also in childhood; in some cases as manifestations of the undifferentiated sexual impulse, in others as manifestations of developing sexual perversions.

The more intensely passionate the love of the child, the more fantastical is its conduct. The child sometimes endeavours to imitate the beloved person in every detail, often with the most ridiculous results. A boy's mode of dress, even, may be influenced by his love for a girl, and still more by his love for another boy. The child tries also to imitate the movements of the beloved person, and in walking to tread in the same footsteps. The youthful knight seeks in every possible way to become pleasing to the girl of his choice, and to exhibit to her every attention in his power. He does all this, not merely in imitation of the conduct of grown-up persons, but for the gratification of his own impulses. Sometimes we are able to observe the changes of mood that occur in the child when the loved one is present or absent. The boy bubbles over with joy when the girl he loves draws near; sorrow and depression overwhelm him when the hour of parting is at hand. All kinds of fetichistic sentiments are also met with even in childhood. Every object belonging to the loved one is covered with passionate kisses; and everything which has been touched by the beloved, has been endowed for the child-lover with a quite exceptional value. "Those lovely girls whom kindly or cruel Nature has predestined to awaken desire and to call forth sighs at every footstep they take, are often unaware that among the crowd of their admirers are numbered boys also, who have hardly outgrown the age of childhood, who kiss in secret every flower which their beloved has let fall, who are happy if they have been able to steal like thieves into the room in which the fair one has slept, who kiss the carpet where her foot has pressed, to whom she is the most wonderful creature in the universe. And when a young woman allows a boy to sit on the ground beside her, resting his head on her knee, when her fingers play lightly among his curls, how rarely does she know that his heart is beating furiously under her caressing touch; when he throws back his curly head, and she sees that his face is reddened, she does not know that this is not simply on account of the heat of the fire, but that he is glowing from the effect of an internal fire whose nature is a mystery even to himself—the fire of Love."

Children have also ample experience of jealousy. A boy is tortured by its pangs when he sees his much-loved friend conversing with another. A girl of ten may suffer from sleepless nights when the governess she loves has spoken affectionately to another girl. A child may wait for hours before the door or in the neighbourhood of the beloved person, simply to snatch a glance in passing. Speaking generally, it appears to me that children are jealous of adults to a less extent than they are jealous of children of their own age.

Very frequently even in childhood sexuality gives rise to enduring imaginative sexual activity. There results that which Hufeland in his Makrobiotik terms psychical onanism, viz., the imaginative contemplation of a train of lascivious and voluptuous ideas. In many instances there even results a poetical treatment of the sexual topic.

Among children, love-letters also play their part. Sometimes, indeed, their contents is so harmless that the sexual motive remains unsuspected; but in other cases, the child's sentiments are clearly displayed, even when the whole character of the letter is extremely naïve. Sometimes the letter appears out of harmony with the child's conduct in other respects. For example, I have seen cases in which, though in conversation children spoke to one another in an impassioned manner as "darling" and "my dear love," no such expressions were used by them in their letters. Verses are also composed by comparatively youthful lovers. As we should expect, such verses are commonly deficient in the matter of artistic technique. A lady who, when twelve years of age, had been enamoured of her governess, copied for me from her album the following verses:—

"Es gibt nichts schöneres auf der Welt,

Als wenn einem ein Wesen besonders gefällt;

Und fühlt man sich gezogen hin

Zu einer süssen Lehrerin,

Das ist ein Glück.
Und liebt man sie so inniglich,
Dann fürchtet wohl gar sehr man sich
Vorm Abschiedtag..."

"Of all things sweet beneath the sun,
The sweetest is to love but one;
And when the object of one's fondness
Is one's darling governess,
Supreme the joy.
And if one love her so intensely,
Then, of course, one dreads immensely
The day of parting...."
In this style the poem continues for some time, and occasionally we come to verses showing that jealousy was felt:—

"O! Du Pauline sei kein Dieb,

Raub' mir nicht Fräulein ——'s Lieb'.

Die Eifersucht, die quält mich sehr
Und noch mit jedem Tage mehr.
Sie sucht mich heim selbst in der Nacht.
O Liebe, Du hast dies vollbracht."

"Pauline, you my anger move,

Stealing my Miss ——'s love.

From jealousy I've no release;
Day by day my pangs increase;
I've jealous thoughts too in the night.
Love, I suffer from thy might."

Many of the accompaniments of love may make their appearance the very first time the passion awakens, such as the desire to please and to astonish the object of affection, whether by mental or by bodily excellence, A schoolmaster, of whom a child is enamoured, will frequently find that this child is more obedient and more diligent than all the others, the child endeavouring in every possible way to inspire a reciprocal admiration. I remember a girl who during her first years at school was extremely idle. Although by no means lacking in intelligence, all the efforts spent on her failed to bring about a proper advance. All at once she became most industrious; no task was too hard for her, and everyone wondered at the sudden change, until after a time the enigma was explained. The child, having conceived a great fondness for her schoolmistress, wished to please the latter by attention to her lessons. In addition, she was jealous; afraid lest the mistress should prefer some other girl. In many instances, where a child's behaviour is puzzling, such a solution of the riddle will become apparent when it is looked for. Boys, again, endeavour by feats of strength to make the greatest possible impression upon the girls of their choice, in gymnastic exercises, for example, in athletic sports, and games. Coquetry also occasionally manifests itself very early in life. Girls try to please boys by their dress, and in similar ways. In boys also similar phenomena may often be observed.

Vanity, too, plays an important part, and this all the more because a child often wishes to appear older than his years, and despises childish ways. If a boy loves a girl several years older than himself, his sensitive pride will suffer if, as usually happens in such cases, the girl treats him as a child. Goethe, who at the age of ten was inspired by such a passion, describes it in Wahrheit und Dichtung. "Young Derones introduced me to his sister, who was a few years older than myself, a very agreeable girl, well-grown, regularly formed, a brunette, with black hair and eyes. Her whole expression was quiet, and even sad. I tried to please her in every possible way, but could not succeed in attracting her attention. Young girls are apt to regard themselves as greatly in advance of boys a little younger than themselves, and whilst they look up to young men, they assume the manners of an aunt towards any boy who makes them the object of his first love."

The sense of shame makes its appearance in childhood. Havelock Ellis and others indeed deny this, pointing out how readily shyness is mistaken for the sense of shame. The error is common enough, but it certainly does not apply to all cases, for even in childhood we often enough encounter distinct manifestations of the sexual sense of shame. I shall not here discuss the question to what extent this sense is innate and to what extent acquired, since the matter will come up for consideration in later part of this book. Unquestionably, during childhood, the sense of shame in respect of certain processes may be awakened by means of imitation and education. Thus we may observe that many children, boys as well as girls, are greatly distressed, at any rate during the second period of childhood, at having to undress in the presence of others, and especially in the presence of persons of the opposite sex. It is interesting to learn that many homosexuals declare that even during childhood they felt ashamed when they were compelled to undress before someone of their own sex, whereas in the presence of a person of the opposite sex they were comparatively unashamed.

Sanford Bell is of opinion that girl-children, although in them as in boys the sense of shame awakens comparatively early, are yet more aggressive than boys. I have not myself been able to observe any such difference. In the earlier years of childhood I have been unable to detect any notable difference in this respect between the sexes; but during the latter part of the second period of childhood, boys are unquestionably more active. In general, the girl-child, when in love, displays far less coyness and reserve than the young woman. In this respect the difference between children and adults is most marked. A girl of eleven, for example, will not make any difficulties about the exchange of love-letters with the boy she loves, or about appointments for secret meetings; whereas the young woman, at any rate when well-behaved and well brought up, is cautious in such matters. But none the less, I cannot admit that girls are more free in their behaviour in these respects than boys. We must not forget that many typical sexual differences do not develop until later in life, for this reason, if we observe in respect of the sense of shame that girls seem somewhat defective, we must contrast their condition with that which will subsequently develop as age advances, and not expect to find prematurely in the girl a keener sense of shame than is exhibited by the boy.

Sanford Bell believes that at a certain period during childhood, namely, between eight and twelve years of age, manifestations of love are less noticeable than either earlier or later. He alleges as the reason of this that at this particular age the child tends to conceal its fondness from others, and perhaps even from the person beloved; hence it is difficult during these years to observe the phenomena. According to this view, the difference is apparent merely, and depends only upon greater secretiveness. It may, indeed, be regarded as proved that in the course of development, especially in the case of boys, there are certain years during which children are less inclined to seek the company of those of the opposite sex than either before or afterwards. This occurs especially during the period of hobbledehoyhood, during which boys take pleasure above all in rough sports. It has, indeed, been suggested that this phenomenon has a teleological significance, that nature is here pursuing a quite definite aim, to minimise by means of sexual antipathy the danger attendant on the awakening of the sexual impulse. We must not, however, over-value this self-help of the part of nature [if it exists], since, if boys and girls avoid one another, the perverse activities of the undifferentiated sexual impulse may very readily appear in place of the suppressed heterosexual manifestations.

In the child, the moods of the amatory sentiment are exceedingly variable. To-day, the love may be romantic in character; to-morrow, on the other hand, rather sensual. To-day, a girl is enamoured of some friend of her father's; to-morrow, she is in love with some little friend of her brother's, or with one of her schoolmasters. A little later, a member of her own sex becomes the object of passion, a girl-friend of her own, or some actress of note. In general, especially, too, when the stage of the undifferentiated impulse has not been well-marked, we notice that as the years pass the inclination gradually comes to relate to older persons. Since the period of childhood embraces a comparatively small number of years, it is naturally not easy to establish this point with mathematical precision; but I have been led to form such an opinion by questioning a large number of persons of either sex. In this respect we sometimes observe that which, in the Satyricon of Petronius, Quartilla said long ago, when young Giton is united to the seven-year-old Pannychis. In free phraseology, Quartilla assures us that she has no remembrance of ever having been a virgin. "When I was a child, I made use of children for this purpose; as I became older, bigger boys served my turn; and thus, from stage to stage, I attained my present age."

Thus we can explain how it sometimes happens that a fondness conceived in childhood may endure on into adult life, and may even culminate in marriage. In large towns, indeed, such an occurrence is comparatively rare, but in small towns and in the country, quite a number of instances have been brought to my notice. As children, the two have grown up together. Their reciprocal fondness originated long prior to the formation of any conscious sexual sentiments; subsequently, when such sentiments have arisen, and the sexual impulse has awakened, it is natural that sexual relations should often ensue. Since in the country (in contrast with large towns, in which prostitution is commonly rampant) premarital sexual intercourse is comparatively frequent, we can readily understand that such a relationship as has been described will often culminate in marriage, for in the country marriage is far less often prevented by the occurrence of pre-marital intercourse than it is in large towns.

On the whole, however, the amatory manifestations of childhood are of brief duration. Separation at first gives rise to spiritual pain, but this is as a rule soon forgotten; similarly when the beloved one is snatched away by death, the child's grief is not enduring. Commonly such painful emotions speedily pass away; and whether the parting is due to death or to other causes, a new passion is apt shortly to replace the old. In exceptional cases, however, the death of the beloved one, or separation otherwise effected, may, even in the child lead to suicide or to severe nervous disturbances.

Hitherto I have spoken of the processes of detumescence and contrectation as isolated manifestations. As regards the relationships between these respective processes, there are various possibilities. In the first place, one may exist when the other is absent, that is to say, the phenomena of detumescence or the phenomena of contrectation may appear in isolation. Secondly, the two processes may be in complete association each with the other. A boy of thirteen years feels the impulse to draw near to a girl, and to kiss her; when this close contact takes place, erection ensues. Of all the cases known to me, the earliest age at which such a phenomenon occurred is given in a case published by Féré.

Two cousins, boy and girl, were playmates from the time they were both about three years old. They played at being man and wife; and when they were not actually together, the boy's imagination was occupied with the subject. He thought continually about it, and when he was in bed at night erection occurred, accompanied by an agreeable sensation. He went to sleep, and dreamed that other persons got into bed with him and touched him. Among these persons was the little girl, his cousin. Such dreams recurred very frequently; the girl, moreover, was constantly in his waking thoughts. As he grew older, his fondness persisted; but when at the age of seventeen he made up his mind to tell his cousin of his love for her, she became engaged to someone else. Consequently he suffered from severe nervous shock.

In the third place, the two processes, contrectation and detumescence, may occur simultaneously, without the detumescence being associated with the object of the contrectation impulse. Thus cases occur in which boys experience organic sensations in the genital organs leading them to masturbate, and at the same time love someone; and yet when in the company of, and even when embracing the beloved, such a boy will not experience any specific sensations in the genital organs, nor will any impulse arise towards sexual contact with the beloved person.

When the two processes are associated in such a manner that proximity to the object of the contrectation impulse arouses the phenomena of detumescence, sexual acts between the two persons are very likely to result—provided, of course, that the affection is reciprocal. In this way many of the sexual acts effected between children originate; and the same is true of those in which children at times very readily lend themselves to the gratification of the sexual passion of adults. We learn from experience that in such cases attempts at actual intercourse may be made by children, usually accompanied by erection, but in most cases without ejaculation. I append a brief report of one case which came under my own observation.

Case 4.—X., twenty-one years of age, apparently sprung from a healthy family, and at least free from hereditary taint, declares that his first experience of sexual sensations occurred at the early age of five or six years; at this age he became enamoured of a servant girl, who caressed him very frequently, and pressed her genital organs against his body. Later, when eight or nine years old, he fell in love with a girl of about the same age, and made attempts at coitus. He remembers quite distinctly that he then had erections, and also a kind of voluptuous sensation, but no ejaculation. After continuing this practice for a considerable time, he became aware, being very religiously brought up, that he was behaving very wrongly. He therefore gave up all attempts at sexual congress, and lived quite chastely until he attained the age of nineteen. Throughout this time he neither masturbated, nor endeavoured to effect coitus, nor practised any kind of sexual act. At the age of nineteen, however, the sexual impulse becoming very powerful, he began to masturbate, and has continued to do so up to the present time—- once, twice, thrice, or even four times weekly. Once he did not masturbate for as long as three months, but this was the only prolonged continent interval. He experiences a normal impulse towards members of the other sex. Prostitutes are repulsive to him; he is attracted chiefly by girls of exceptional intelligence. He feels quite certain that to kiss and embrace such a girl would be very pleasurable to him, although he is not aware of any definite impulse towards coitus. Masturbation has always been practised by him as a purely physical act, unaccompanied, that is to say, by any imaginative ideas.

In most cases, the complete association of the processes of detumescence and contrectation, such as occurs in the impulse towards coitus, first takes place at a somewhat later age. This is so even when the sensory element, which constitutes a part also of the contrectation impulse, has been already clearly manifested. The contrectation impulse does not consist solely in this, that the boy experiences a purely spiritual love for the girl; it may rather happen that certain definite sexual bodily peculiarities in a woman attract him. When such a boy one day unexpectedly sees a girl's breasts, this may exercise on him a powerful stimulus. Similarly, I have known instances in which, in the absence of any evidence of definite seduction, a woman's genital organs have excited a very young boy, without arousing any idea in his mind of contact between his own genitals and those of the woman. Conversely, on many girls, masculine attributes, and especially the male genital organs, sometimes exert a stimulating influence. But in these cases also, the complete fusion of the processes of detumescence and contrectation occurs very gradually. Sometimes the boy himself is greatly astonished to discover that close contact with a person whom he loves leads to erection and even ejaculation. At the outset the impulse is much less definite than it is in adults. It is by gradual stages only that the sense of indefinite longing develops into the impulse towards sexual union in coitus; at first the imagination contemplates pictures of a quite indefinite character.

Although, as we have seen, the processes both of detumescence and of contrectation may manifest themselves primarily in childhood as associated conscious sensations, by far the most common event is for the processes of contrectation to appear separately, before those of detumescence. From an inquiry relating to eighty-six heterosexual men, who to the best of my belief were sexually normal, I ascertained that in more than 75 per cent., the feelings of contrectation appeared first, and not until after this had happened was the boy's consciousness attracted by sensations in the genital organs. This appears rather remarkable, inasmuch as we must assume that in the phylogeny of our species the processes of detumescence appeared earlier. Originally, in the earlier ancestral types, reproduction was effected by fission or gemmation (simple division or budding), without any necessity for conjugation with another individual of the species; and reproduction by gemmation corresponds to the processes of detumescence, to the ejaculation of the spermatozoa by the male. But although in most individuals the processes of detumescence make their appearance in consciousness only in a secondary manner, it does not follow that in the actual course of development they are also secondary. They do not, indeed, enter so early the sphere of conscious impulses, but there is a considerable amount of evidence to show that important processes are going on in the external genital organs long before consciousness is directly affected by these processes—consider, for example, the consequences of early castration.

Case 5.—This is a typical example of the primary awakening of the contrectation impulse, and the secondary superposition of the phenomena of detumescence. The patient is a man thirty-two years of age, somewhat neurasthenic, but, as far as I could ascertain, free from any other morbid manifestations. "At the age of seven I went to school; at first to a private school, in which little boys and girls were co-educated. In our playtime also the sexes were not separated; the girls came as friends to my house, and I visited them at theirs. Soon I became especially intimate with one of the girls; we did our lessons together. Thus it went on until I was nine years old, when I went to a school for boys only. My friendship with the girl at the other school persisted, however; we met from time to time, and all the more readily because a friendship had sprung up between our respective parents; they used to make holiday journeys together, and we children went with them. From the time when we were first at school together, this girl had always been more dear to me than the others, I do not know what it was in her by which I was particularly charmed. Was it that her general appearance seemed sympathetic to me; was it her abundant fair hair, her clear blue eyes, or her frank and natural manner? I do not know. But I remember quite distinctly that this same girl was a favourite with the other boys also, that they preferred to play with her, to have her as their companion. But it was to me that the girl, and perhaps her parents also, gave the preference. There was never any impropriety in our mutual relations; indeed, it is probable that I loved her too much for anything of the kind to be possible. Every night, before I went to sleep, I prayed to God to watch over this girl. As I have said before, my fondness was reciprocated; we often spoke to one another about our love, and of our dreams of the happy days to come, when we should be grown up, and should become man and wife. This was quite a settled matter; we had arranged every detail, how the wedding should be conducted, and whom we should invite to the ceremony. With this girl I shared all my possessions, although before I knew her I had been considered close-fisted. I was often angry when in games with the other girls she failed to win. In a word I can truthfully declare that I have hardly ever since loved so fondly and so sincerely as I did then. When I went to the boys' school, it was no longer possible for us to be together as much as before. Thus it came to pass, that the less we saw of one another, the less were my thoughts occupied with this girl. But I cannot remember that my fondness for her was ever replaced by a similar passion for a boy, nor, speaking generally, can I recall having ever at any time had any kind of sexual inclination towards one of my own sex. I would not venture absolutely to deny that this ever occurred; but, bearing in mind what I have learned from you on several occasions, I have carefully taxed my memory, and can only repeat what I told you at first, that I remember nothing of the kind. Somewhat later, in my dreams, boys occasionally played a part, but I cannot recall that these dreams about boys had any sexual complexion. They were vague images of boys sympathetic to me, but these dreams were not accompanied by any excitement of the genital organs, or by any other sexual manifestation. When I was thirteen years of age, my parents and those of my girl-friend had taken us to spend the summer at a seaside resort. The girl and I played together on the seashore, and occasionally, though we were now somewhat old for such an amusement, we dug sand-castles. As small children we had from time to time embraced one another, but a kiss had been the most intimate contact we had experienced. One day we were

playing on the shore—I remember it very distinctly—and were rolling about together in the sand; thus occupied we came into close physical contact, and thereupon I had an erection. I remember too that the sensation of this was very agreeable. I cannot describe this agreeable feeling with precision, but there was no sense of sexual gratification, nor definite voluptuous sensation. From this time forward I always had the desire for close bodily contact with the girl. Moreover she was continually in my thoughts, and this to a much greater extent than formerly. It was my desire to gain a harmless pleasure by being always with her; it was impossible for me to imagine that we should ever be separated. I had naturally heard a great deal about marriage. With these and with similar thoughts I was occupied, but I cannot recall my thoughts in a more detailed manner. But to this day I remember very clearly my desire that the girl and I should never be separated from one another. We returned home, and in the ensuing winter, as in previous winters, we met at intervals. Naturally, physical contact was now much more difficult. One night I had a dream with seminal emission. Then, as for a long time before, I had been thinking a great deal about the girl; I dreamed of one of the scenes on the seashore which I have just described; it was in this dream that I had my first seminal emission. My fondness for the girl persisted. Only when she left the day-school in the town, and was sent away to a boarding-school, did my passion gradually abate. At first when she went away, I felt very unhappy and very lonely. My parents forced me to go out for walks with other boys and to play with them; I did so only with the greatest reluctance. Later, the girl did not disappear completely from my circle of acquaintances, but I lost all interest in her. From school I went to the university, having just before begun to masturbate. From the time I went to the university until the present day I have occasionally had intercourse with women, and my sexual development has been perfectly normal."

In so far as in what has gone before I have described the individual processes, there appear to be no important differences between the boy and the girl, over and above those dependent upon the different structure of the genital organs in the respective sexes. But one notable difference must now be indicated. Just as in adult life in the female sex sexual anæsthesia is very frequently observed, so that in coitus the specific voluptuous sensation is wanting, and indeed often enough the impulse to coitus itself is actually in abeyance (whereas in men the sexual impulse and sexual pleasure are very rarely absent), so also in the case of children a similar difference between the sexes is conspicuous. In female children the peripheral processes of the sexual impulse are, comparatively speaking, far less active than in the case of males. Thus it happens that, although in the girl the phenomena of the contrectation impulses are hardly, if at all, less conspicuous than they are in the boy, and appear at as early an age in the former as they do in the latter, yet in respect of detumescence there is an important distinction between girls and boys. A girl who has fallen in love with a boy will be greatly interested in all his doings, and will gladly embrace and even kiss him; but she will be far less disposed to proceed to actions in which the genital organs play a part than would a boy with a like affection for a girl. The same rule holds good when, in the undifferentiated stage of the sexual impulse, homosexual sentiments and practices ensue. In such cases, when girls are concerned, caresses of all kinds will follow, but the genital organs will in all probability not be involved; whereas in the case of an analogous fondness between two boys, manipulation of the genital organs is very likely to occur. Homosexual intimacies between girls are far more often platonic than similar intimacies between boys.

I have had occasion several times to allude to the practice of masturbation by children, and will now proceed to give a more detailed description. I have previously alluded to masturbation as a manifestation of the detumescence impulse. Much more frequently, however, it occurs in those in whom the phenomena of the contrectation impulse have also been previously manifested. Sometimes it is a purely organic act, the individual masturbating in the entire absence of any imaginative sexual ideas; but at other times the imagination plays a notable part in the process, alike in children and in adults. When an imaginative idea is concerned in the process of masturbation, it is the idea of the object of the contrectation impulse; that is to say, the boy when masturbating thinks now of a girl, now, again (and this especially during the undifferentiated stage of the sexual impulse), of a boy, or in many cases of an adult; in the cases of girls who masturbate similar relationships obtain, Just as during youth masturbation is more commonly practised in association with than without imaginative sexual ideas, so also is it in the case of children; and even though imaginative activity may often be in abeyance when the masturbatory act is begun, during the progress of the act the imagination usually comes into operation. None the less, masturbation of a purely mechanical kind, in which the imagination plays no part, is comparatively more common during childhood than it is during youth. The peripheral processes of the detumescence impulse and the central processes of the contrectation impulse are not at this early age so intimately associated as they are later in life. Even when the contrectation impulse is already awakened, as usually happens before the detumescence impulse becomes active, when the detumescence impulse finally manifests itself, its gratification by means of masturbation without any imaginative activity is comparatively common in children. In such cases artificial stimulation of the genital organs is effected quite independently of the longing for intimate physical contact with and the embraces of another individual.

In an earlier chapter I have explained that in the adult the voluptuous sensation is closely associated with the psychosexual perceptions, associated, that is to say, with the mode of the contrectation impulse; I stated that as a rule the voluptuous sensation was experienced to the full in those cases only in which the sexual act was one adequate to the contrectation impulse of the person concerned. But when the association between the processes of detumescence and those of contrectation has not yet occurred, the voluptuous sensation is independent of the contrectation impulse. This explains the fact that in the child both the peripheral voluptuous sensation, and also the voluptuous acme and the sense of satisfaction, are more frequently independent of the processes of contrectation than is the case in the adult Gradually the two groups of processes become associated with one another; and, as we have learned, this association frequently occurs even in childhood. In the latter case, the voluptuous acme and the subjective sense of satisfaction ensue only when the sexual act or the sexual idea is adequate. But we must always remember that in the child more often than in the adult the voluptuous acme and the sense of satisfaction occur independently of the processes of contrectation.

An ejaculation of fluid secretions does not invariably occur when masturbation is practised. Whereas in the adult masturbation ordinarily culminates in ejaculation, in the child this is not usually the case; at any rate, as regards many children the occurrence of ejaculation is not demonstrable. I refer in this connexion to what I have already stated. It is self-evident from what has been previously said that during the second period of childhood masturbation is more likely than during the first period to culminate in ejaculation.

The methods by which the artificial stimulation of the genital organs is effected are extremely variable. The commonest way to masturbate is with the hands, but this is by no means the invariable practice. All kinds of little artifices are employed, partly to render it possible to masturbate unobserved in the presence of others, and partly in order to increase the intensity of the stimulus. Boys sometimes manipulate their genital organs through their trouser pockets; some even make a hole in the pocket to enable them to masturbate more effectually. In other cases, children, especially girls, lean against some article of furniture—a chair or a table— apparently in a harmless manner, but really in such a way that pressure is exercised upon the genital organs, which are stimulated by pressure or friction. In some, strong mechanical stimulation is required; in others, weaker stimuli suffice, because the way has previously been sufficiently prepared by psychical processes. In female children frequently, but less often in males, masturbation is effected by rubbing the crossed thighs one against the other. We learn from many girls that they tie a knot in the nightgown or chemise, and masturbate by rubbing this against the genital organs. I must allude also to horseback riding, working the treadle of a sewing machine, cycling, the vibration of a carriage or railway train in motion; we must, however, be careful not to attach undue importance to these factors of masturbation, for in such cases much depends upon the individuality, and much also upon the external mechanical conditions—- as, for instance, on the construction of the saddle used in cycling and the like. In the case of the male genital organs, the glans penis is the most sensitive portion, and mechanical stimulation of this structure in especial is likely to induce the practice of masturbation; in the case of the female genital organs, on the other hand, it is the clitoris which is most sensitive, and of which, therefore, we have especially to think in this connexion. But there is a tendency to overestimate the proportion of cases in which stimulation of the glans penis, in the male, or the clitoris, in the female, is the exciting cause of masturbation. In a very large number of cases of masturbation, it is not the glans, but some other portion of the penis, which is the focus of stimulation. In girls, also, in numerous instances, masturbation is effected by stimulation of the labia minora, and I am inclined to believe that the importance of the labia minora is in this respect not inferior to that of the clitoris. In solitude, and above all in bed, masturbation can naturally be effected much more readily. Some little girls grasp a pillow between their legs in such a way as to give rise to a masturbatory stimulus. Others introduce cylindrical objects into the vagina, a practice much commoner among fully-grown girls than among children. Still, physicians are sometimes called on to remove such articles from the vaginæ of quite little girls. But it is an error to suppose that the hymen is frequently ruptured by practices of this kind; the rupture of the hymen is far too painful for it to be likely to be effected during masturbation.

Erogenic zones, that is to say, areas of the surface of the body whose stimulation gives rise, directly or indirectly, to voluptuous sensations, are met with often in early childhood. First of all we have those parts of the genital organs mentioned in the last paragraph; secondly, other regions of the body. Thus, in some individuals, stimulation of the anal and gluteal regions gives rise to voluptuous sensations. Freud maintains that voluntary retention of the fæces is utilised for this purpose, but this appears to me very doubtful. In many children, however, gentle scratching of the anal region or the buttocks, and also more powerful stimulation of the gluteal region, such as occurs in flagellation, are associated with sexual excitement. Some children, with this end in view, stimulate the anal region with the finger or with some instrument. Other erogenic zones are also at times found in children, but not often; whereas in adults such erogenic zones are numerous, but differ greatly in different individuals. In this connexion, I need merely allude to the production of voluptuous sensations by tickling the nape of the neck.

Attempts have often been made to determine the comparative frequency of masturbation in the two sexes. On one point at least all writers are agreed, viz., that of boys an overwhelming majority masturbate occasionally. The only point in dispute is whether there are any exceptions. For my own part, I am confident that exceptions exist. I have received direct information on the point from leading men of science, and from others whose absolute veracity I have never had any reason to doubt. Healthy men, endowed with a normal sexual impulse, are occasionally to be found who have never masturbated at all. I go further, and believe that such persons are by no means so rare as many authorities maintain. Nevertheless, as regards the male sex, differences of opinion are, after all, not very extensive, since it is only in relation to a minority that these differences exist. But when we pass to the question of the extent of masturbation among girls, the differences become more acute. On this point also I have endeavoured to obtain exact information by means of numerous inquiries, with the following results. Among girls, masturbation is less general than it is among boys. Among those who have never masturbated during girlhood, we find women who as adults have powerful sexual impulse. On the other hand, many girls who masturbate do so very often. I believe, indeed, that cases in which masturbation is performed twice or thrice in brief succession are relatively commoner among girls than they are among boys. As regards this point my own experience harmonises with that of Guttceit. On the other hand, Guttceit's assumption that almost all girls who attain the age of eighteen or twenty years without any opportunity for sexual intercourse practise masturbation conflicts with my own experience. I am acquainted with a number of women of a fairly ardent temperament who do not masturbate, although they have no opportunity for sexual intercourse. Moreover, this view is confirmed by the common experience regarding the relative sexual anæsthesia of women; it is an admitted fact that complete sexuality is in women far less readily awakened than it is in men.

I must take this opportunity of referring at some length to a matter which, though somewhat obscure, is none the less profoundly interesting. In many instances sexual excitement occurs in children as the result of a feeling of anxiety; in boys such anxiety may lead to ejaculation, with or without erection, and with more or less voluptuous sensation. A schoolboy informed me that he had had a seminal emission with a slight sense of voluptuous pleasure when in class he was in difficulties with a passage of unseen translation, and he was afraid he would be unable to finish the passage before the end of the lesson. Another reported to me a precisely similar experience; he was overcome with anxiety during a written examination, and had a seminal emission. A third had an ejaculation when, being detected in some offence against school discipline, he was sent for by the headmaster, and was afraid he would be expelled. Quite a number of similar cases have been reported to me of sexual excitement occurring in childhood as a sequel to anxiety. I have recorded the facts, and do not propose to discuss exhaustively the theoretical aspect of the matter. Perhaps the phenomenon is allied to masochism, since anxiety is to a certain extent painful. We may also, in this connexion, think of the seminal emissions sometimes observed in cases of suicidal hanging. Freud's theory may also be mentioned, that the anxiety-neurosis is referable to certain sexual processes; but we must not forget that Freud makes a similar assumption in the case of other neuroses as well. Stekel, one of Freud's pupils, in an elaborate monograph, also lays stress on the sexual factor of the anxiety-neurosis. In my own view, however, Freud's generalisation is too comprehensive; inasmuch as he symbolises all things in accordance with his own peculiar preconceptions, the concept sexual receives, in his hands, an undue extension. But I do not deny the occasional association of sexual excitement with a sense of anxiety. Certain boys would appear to have a peculiar predisposition to the occurrence of such processes; at any rate, several persons have told me that during childhood they had frequently had ejaculations as a result of feelings of anxiety. As a rule, however, each of these persons has had such an experience either once only, or but very few times. Two identical instances have been reported to me as occurring in girls—ejaculation with an indefinite voluptuous sensation as a sequel of anxiety. These girls were from thirteen to fourteen years of age. In one of the two, the phenomenon recurred several times; and even at the present day, when she is a fully-grown woman, she occasionally experiences ejaculation in connexion with a feeling of anxiety.

Case 6.—A student, twenty years of age, described his experiences to me in the following terms:—As regards his sexual development, he remembers that he was sixteen years of age when he first experienced sexual sensations. Before this time he had been told by other boys about sexual intercourse, masturbation, and many other things. He had, however, never masturbated, though he had once or twice attempted to do so. One day, when he was in the Upper Second Class, a mathematical problem was given out, and as he found a difficulty in solving it, he became anxious, all the more because his chances of promotion to a higher class were largely dependent on his success. When he had barely finished half the necessary calculations, the master announced that there were only ten minutes left, at the end of which time the exercise books would be collected. Thereupon his anxiety became extreme, and simultaneously he experienced his first seminal emission. He is unable to give a more detailed description of what occurred, and does not remember having had an erection; but, as he expresses it, the sensation was extremely pleasant. Subsequently, when in the First Class, the same experience recurred several times, that is to say, he had a seminal emission as a result of a similar feeling of anxiety. In other respects his sexual development was normal. Seminal dreams were accompanied by the idea of contact with a woman. On one occasion, however, he had a seminal emission during the night in association with a feeling of anxiety. He dreamed that he was being pursued by a mad dog, when suddenly he became, as it were, paralysed and unable to run a single step further. The consequent acute anxiety culminated in emission.

During sleep, sexually mature men and many sexually mature women have from time to time involuntary sexual orgasms; these occur chiefly in persons without opportunities for sexual intercourse, who do not practise masturbation. In such involuntary orgasms the male ejaculates semen, the female indifferent glandular secretions. As a rule, the ejaculation is accompanied not merely by a voluptuous sensation, but also by a psychical process corresponding with the mode of sexual sensibility of the person concerned. A normal man during the orgasm dreams that he is embracing a woman; a normal woman that she is embracing a man; a homosexual man dreams of the embraces of another man. The dream-ejaculation is distinguished from the waking act of intercourse to this extent, that in the former the ejaculation usually takes place during the preparatory stages to the act of intercourse—during kissing, physical contact, or the embrace—so that the dream stops short of complete sexual intercourse. But in other respects the dream ordinarily corresponds to the psychical processes of the waking state. The same correspondence exists as regards sexual dreams that do not culminate in ejaculation. Children also experience sexual dreams either with or without orgasm. In those who have never masturbated in the waking state, a sexual dream is commonly the cause of the first experience of ejaculation; and this occurs more often than is generally believed. More especially in the female sex I have come across many cases in which the orgasm made a primary appearance during sleep. In both sexes alike it is usual for psychosexual phenomena to manifest themselves before the erotic dream makes its appearance; a boy, for instance, will during his waking life have felt an attraction towards members of the other sex before he has begun to dream of embracing a girl. We must not, however, forget that, apart from those cases in which a dream beyond question first unveils to consciousness the psychosexual life, dreams are forgotten very rapidly indeed, especially when the memory is not stimulated by so vivid an occurrence as the sexual orgasm. Hence, even though it is true that the psychosexual life commonly appears to begin during the waking state, we must admit that it is quite likely that psychosexual dreams may have previously occurred and have been forgotten. Thus, in many individuals, sexual perversions make their first appearance in dreams. It has even been suggested that dreams may exercise a similar influence to that of post-hypnotic suggestion; that is to say, that a dream may be the actual originating cause of sexual perversion. This is a matter which I cannot discuss further, more especially in view of the fact that the whole idea is too hypothetical.

The earlier the age at which the child begins to ripen sexually, the earlier do sexual dreams and nocturnal ejaculations make their appearance. I have known of numerous instances in which children ten or eleven years of age have had sexual dreams; occasionally, even, I have been informed of the occurrence of such dreams in children of seven or eight years of age. In children, as in adults, the object which is sexually exciting in the waking state plays a leading part in the sexual dream. But in the sexual dreams of children the imagination is even more active than it is in the sexual dreams of adults. All kinds of perverse dreams may, in children, accompany the emission, even when the corresponding ideas have no erotic association in the waking state. Things of which the child has learned from fairy tales, stories of robbers, of imprisoned or enchanted princesses, princes, fettered slaves—all may play a part in the psychosexual processes of the dream-life. Anyone unaware of the fact that in the great majority of children this tendency disappears spontaneously in the course of the further development of the sexual life might too readily infer the existence of some morbid perversion. In such instances we must, indeed, bear in mind the possibility of sexual perversion, especially in view of the fact that sexually perverse adults are often able to trace back into childhood the memory of sexual dreams characteristic of their peculiar type of perversion. Occasionally the feelings of anxiety of which we have spoken above may, even in dreams, lead to the occurrence of involuntary ejaculations. Thus we are told of dreams of pursuit by robbers or by wild animals, or of dreams of missing a train the dreamer has been running to catch, in which ejaculations occur. In isolated cases the dreams of children which are associated with ejaculations may be quite indistinct; in such cases, just as sometimes in the sexual dreams of adults, it is impossible to recognise any definite relationship to the psychosexual feelings of the waking state. In this connexion no difference between the sexes can be shown to exist, except this, that, at any rate as far as my own experience goes, nocturnal ejaculations are much more often absent in girls than in boys. Occasionally, manual or other artificial stimulation of the genital organs is effected during sleep; I have myself known several instances of this, both in boys and in girls. In several cases, at least, there were satisfactory grounds for believing that we were not concerned with masturbation practised at night in the waking state, but all the indications pointed to the fact that the processes were carried on unconsciously during sleep.

In isolated cases I have had children watched throughout the night, in order to clear up this point, and my conclusion was thus confirmed that children do at times play with the genital organs during sleep.

A classical description of her first nocturnal orgasm is given by Madame Roland in her Mémoires Particuliers, written during the last months of her life in prison in Paris at the time of the Terror. She menstruated for the first time, she informs us, soon after she had been partially enlightened regarding sexual matters by her grandmother. Even before menstruation began, she had experienced sexual excitement in dreams. "I had sometimes been awakened from a deep sleep in a most remarkable manner. My imagination played no part in what occurred; it was occupied with far more serious matters, and my tender conscience was far too strictly on guard against the deliberate pursuit of pleasure for me to make any attempt to dwell in imagination on what I regarded as a forbidden province of thought. But an extraordinary outbreak awakened my senses from their quiet slumber, and, my constitution being a very vigorous one, a process whose nature and cause were equally unknown to me made its appearance spontaneously. The first result of this experience was the onset of great mental anguish; I had learned from my 'Philothea' that it was forbidden to enjoy any bodily pleasure, except in lawful wedlock; this teaching recurred to my mind; the sensations I had experienced could certainly be described as pleasurable; I had, therefore, committed a sin, and, indeed, a sin of the most shameful and grievous character, because it was the sin most of all displeasing to the Lamb without blemish and without spot. Great disturbance of mind, prayers and penances; how could I avoid a repetition of the offence? for I had not foreseen it in any way, but in the moment of the experience I had taken no trouble to prevent it. My watchfulness became extreme; I noticed that when lying in certain positions I was more exposed to the danger, and I avoided these positions with anxious conscientiousness. My uneasiness became so great that ultimately I came to wake up before the catastrophe. When unable to prevent it, I would jump out of bed, and, notwithstanding the cold of winter, stand bare-footed on the polished floor, crossing my arms, and praying earnestly to God to guard me from the snares of Satan." She goes on to describe her subsequent attempts to mortify the flesh by means of fasting.

I have hitherto described the individual sexual processes which are observed during childhood, I have already explained that in some, one process, in some, another process, is alone present, or, at any rate, preponderates. For instance, a girl may be sexually attracted towards a boy without the genital organs playing any conscious part in the attraction. But the converse may also occur. Moreover, the strength of the sexual feeling is subject to extensive individual variations. In some children the sexual impulse is so powerful that scandalous misconduct can hardly be avoided; on the other hand, we see cases in which the sexual impulse manifests itself at the normal age, but is so weak that it can scarcely be said to play any important part in the consciousness of the child. This is true of both components of the sexual impulse, of the phenomena of contrectation, no less than of those of detumescence. Formerly it was very generally believed that in sexually perverse persons the sexual sensations awakened unusually early in life. There is no foundation for this view. Normal sexual sensations can be detected very early in childhood. The existence of these was ignored, simply because the study of the normal was neglected for the study of the perverse. Moreover, the strength of the sexual sensations has no necessary association with the existence of perversions; these latter sometimes occur without being particularly strong. On the other hand, qualitatively normal sexual sensations may be associated with sexual hyperæsthesia, and they may attain a notable strength even during childhood.

In the third chapter I showed that in childhood the sexes are differentiated both physically and mentally, altogether apart from the genital organs and the sexual impulse; and I pointed out that games in particular afforded indications of mental sexual differentiation. Many games, indeed, may even be regarded as direct manifestations of the sexual impulse, and I must therefore now return to the consideration of this topic; but I shall confine myself to certain phenomena observable in the animal world, since the games of animals are, in this connexion, so much simpler than those of children. Play constitutes a major part of the activitioo of young animals; think, for instance, of a kitten playing with a hanging tassel or with a ball, of puppies chasing one another, and of young birds playing with fluttering wings. The games of young animals often exhibit the character of love-games, and are in that case sexually differentiated. Various authors, and especially Brehm, have recorded numerous examples of this; I give here a few instances, quoted from Groos. The young male, even before its testicles have developed, woos the female by movements, song, or other characteristic sounds. The female, also sexually immature, responds coquettishly to these advances of the male. Song, which Brehm regards as a sign of the awakening of love, makes its appearance at an age when the animal is still unfitted for the reproductive act.

"Young magpies (Corvus pica) address one another in September, and often in August and in October, in consecutive clucking notes, and in this way make exactly the same kind of noise that they are always heard making in early spring just before the pairing season. The young male green woodpecker (Picus viridicanus) sings in September as beautifully as in April, as I have myself heard more than once; the young great spotted woodpecker (Picus major) may even be heard at times in autumn, just as in spring, making his characteristic tapping sound as he explores hard branches in search of insects. Both varieties of creeper begin to sing before they have changed their youthful plumage; their song closely resembles that of the adult birds in spring, but the note is somewhat shorter and weaker. Similarly, both the German varieties of crossbill commonly begin to sing before losing the plumage characteristic of youth. Young house-sparrows and hedge-sparrows not only chatter and swear at one another like the full-grown birds at pairing time, but also like the latter the young birds distend their throats, let their wings droop, peck at one another, and in fact behave as exactly as they will next spring when fully grown. Young linnets also begin to sing before losing their youthful plumage, learn to sing well during the moulting season, and often continue to warble right on into the winter; in a mild winter young linnets will sing just as well as old ones. The young woodlark begins to sing as soon as its first moulting is nearly over, and not only does this when perching, but flies aloft like the adult bird in the spring-time, and soars for a long time, singing continually. Titmice all sing when still quite young, but more especially the large crested titmouse and the marsh titmouse; the notes of the young marsh titmouse are precisely similar to those with which in spring the adult bird sings to his mate; and as regards the crested titmouse, in October 1821, I observed a young male bird making advances of a most marked character to a young hen, whilst the hen drooped its wings and spread out its tail—in short, these two young birds were behaving exactly as do the full-grown birds before pairing in the spring. The young cock starling conducts itself precisely as if it wished to pair. At the beginning of September, as soon as moulting is completed, this bird returns to its birthplace, apparently in order to take possession of the nest. It perches on the tree-top, just like the full-grown bird in March, and sings almost for the whole morning. While still perching, it flaps its wings, quarrels with and chases other young starlings; sometimes it even creeps into the hollow tree or other hiding-place containing the nest in which it was hatched. The yellow wagtail sings while still in its youthful plumage, and the young birds chase one another about while in this condition; during and immediately after the first moulting, these birds produce peculiar trilling notes, identical with those with which in April the cock bird salutes his mate, and they may also be seen in the remarkable fluttering flight characteristic of many birds in the pairing season. The grey wood wren begins to sing before the first moulting, but sings more powerfully during and after moulting, right on into the month of October, singing like a full-grown bird. At the same time this bird twists the body from side to side, and moves the tail to and fro; it quarrels also with birds of its own species, and quarrels, too, with other birds, sometimes with birds as much as four times its own size. In August and September young mountain fowl and heath fowl utter love calls to each other, not, indeed, so loudly as those of the adult birds, nor in association with the characteristic movements of the body made by these latter in the spring-time, but still unmistakable love calls.... According to Hudson, many kinds of American woodpecker carry on a kind of duet, and they practise this artistic performance from the very earliest youth. On meeting, the male and female, standing close together, and facing each other, utter their clear ringing concert, one emitting loud single measured notes, while the notes of its fellow are rapid, rhythmical triplets; their voices have a joyous character, and seem to accord, thus producing a kind of harmony. This manner of singing is perhaps most perfect in the oven-bird (Furnarius), and it is very curious that the young birds, when only partially fledged, are constantly heard in the nest or oven apparently practising these duets in the intervals when the parents are absent; single measured notes, triplets, and long concluding trills are all repeated with wonderful fidelity, and in character these notes are utterly unlike the hunger cry, which is like that of other fledglings."

In such cases as those just enumerated, actual copulation is not effected; but animals still sexually immature may perform coitus-like acts, and Groos's work contains observations of these made by Seitz and others. Seitz saw an antelope six weeks old making copulatory movements. In young dogs such movements may often be observed, also in young stallions and young bulls.

The view that in such cases the movements are imitative merely is untenable, for young animals which have never had any opportunity of watching the physical manifestations of love in older ones, will nevertheless themselves exhibit such manifestations. At most it remains open to dispute whether in these cases it is still permissible to speak of love-games, as do Groos and others, or whether we should not rather speak simply of manifestations of the activity of the sexual impulse. But the dispute does not involve differences of opinion regarding matters of fact; it is purely terminological. For, in the first place, Groos himself, who regards the games of childhood as a form of training, suitable to the nature of the individual, for its subsequent activities, recognises that games are sexually differentiated. He believes that we have to do, not, as some think, with imitative processes, but with preliminary practice, subserving the purposes of self-development; and he considers that girls naturally turn to games adapted to train them for their subsequent profession of motherhood, whilst boys incline to games corresponding to their predestined activity as men. Even if we accept this theory of Groos, we are compelled to recognise a sexual element in the games of youthful animals. In addition, however, we must note the fact that Groos gives a wider extension to the concept of play than other writers, and that he regards as love-games processes which others might perhaps describe as sexual manifestations. According to Groos, caressing contact is to be regarded as playful when, in the serious intercourse between the sexes, such contact appears to be merely a preliminary activity rather than an end in itself. Here two cases are possible: in one the carrying out of the instinctive activity to its real end is prevented by incapacity or by ignorance; in the other, it is prevented by a deliberate exercise of will. The former occurs in children; the latter, often enough in adults. Whatever view we hold regarding this matter, the sexually differentiated love-games of young animals must be regarded as a manifestation of the sexual life. None the less, in sexually immature animals, just as in the case of children, sexual differentiation is not always so marked as it is in adults; and it may happen that the sexes may exchange their rôles. Cases observed by Seitz have been published by Groos and also by myself. I have myself watched a young cow which repeatedly attempted to mount another young cow; I have also on several occasions seen young bitches attempt to cover dogs. To this part of our subject belongs the observation of Exner, that when dogs are playing wildly with one another one hardly ever sees a bitch among them. But if an exception should occur, the bitch is usually a young one. In animals, sexual differentiation is not complete until sexual maturity is attained, and the same is true of the human species, although, as I have shown above, children already manifest sexual differentiation in their games, their inclinations, and their general conduct.

I have thought it desirable to refer to the play of animals in this place, as well as to treat of the subject in its direct relationship to the sexual impulse. What is true of play is true also of the other interests and inclinations of the child, many of which are also associated with the sexual life; these have been described earlier, so that here I need merely allude to the matter in passing.

Hitherto I have described the sexual life of the child in so far as it is the subject of direct observation or can be recalled to memory. But it was explained at the outset that there is still another way of gaining clear knowledge of the subject, namely, by experiment; and it was shown that castration may be regarded as such an experiment. Although the reproductive capacity of the male is not developed prior to the formation of spermatozoa in the testicles, nevertheless we learn from the effects of castration that the testicles exhibit important functional activity much earlier in life. This fact was long overlooked, and its importance is even to-day largely underestimated, because we have been accustomed to regard the provision of an external secretion as the only function of the testicle. But it is now firmly established that these glands exercise influence in other ways. We know that bodily and mental development are affected by the removal of the testicles; and that the influence is greater the earlier in life the castration takes place. A number of secondary sexual characters remain undeveloped. The beard does not grow; in many instances a thick panniculus adiposus is formed; there are changes in the growth of the bones; the voice remains a soprano; and the other reproductive organs are imperfectly developed, the penis and the prostate remaining comparatively small An early castration does not, of course, result in the obliteration of all differences between the male and the female; we must rather say that a part only of the typical differential characters of sex remain undeveloped. The earlier assumption, that the secretion of semen competent to effect fertilisation influenced the development of the secondary sexual characters, has of late been more and more generally abandoned. Many considerations tell against such a theory, more especially a comparison of the three following facts. First, if castration is not effected until after the formation of spermatozoa has already begun, the familiar results of this operation are either entirely wanting, or else appear to a small extent only, and are limited to a small number of the secondary sexual characters. Secondly, the results of castration are most marked when the operation is performed in early childhood. Thirdly, when castration is effected in the later years of childhood, but before the secretion of fertilising semen has taken place, the results are intermediate in degree, being much less marked than in the second class of cases, but more extensive than in the first. If the secretion of a fertilising semen were the principal factor in the development of the secondary sexual characters, we should expect the results of castration to be the same whether the operation were performed early in childhood or late so long as it was done before any spermatozoa had been formed.

The secondary sexual characters are, therefore, independent of the formation of spermatozoa, and the appearance of these characters must depend upon other processes, occurring much earlier in life. Thus, in persons who were castrated in the eighth or ninth year of life, we note the presence of definite secondary sexual characters, which are, indeed, less strongly developed than in normal persons, but which do not appear at all when the castration has been effected at a still earlier age. The varying views of different authors regarding the influence of castration in early life upon the development of the secondary sexual characters may readily be explained with reference to the individual differences that may be observed in the functional activity of the testicles in different males before the power of reproduction has been acquired. Just as in boys the capacity for reproduction, and in girls the function of menstruation, does not appear at a fixed and definite age, so also in the case of the other processes that come into being under the influence of the activity of the reproductive glands, we have to reckon with such individual differences. For this reason, in persons who have been castrated at the same age, the subsequent course of development may vary to some degree, notwithstanding the apparent identity of the determining factor in each case. In some, the pelvis, the beard, the voice, and the mental qualities, develop in normal fashion; in others, there is interference with the development of one or all of these characters. In certain cases, the bodily structure is influenced by castration at an age when the mental development is no longer affected. This explains the fact that many oriental eunuchs, in whom castration is commonly effected shortly before the seventh or eighth year of life, while they exhibit the bodily configuration characteristic of the eunuch, are nevertheless capable of experiencing heterosexual feelings, and even passionate love.

In Western countries we rarely have an opportunity of studying the full consequences of castration, for with us the operation is hardly ever performed so early in life as it is in the East; and the reports that are available concerning oriental and other foreign eunuchs are to a large extent untrustworthy. None the less, from such reports, and from accounts that have come down to us from earlier days in the West (more especially in the case of the boys who were formerly castrated in Italy for the preservation of the soprano voice), we obtain evidence amply sufficient to justify the statements made above. Even more convincing are observations made on the lower animals. For example, in horses which have been castrated at a very early age the sexual impulse remains undeveloped; but we have to contrast with this the fact that a certain number of geldings possess a well-marked sexual impulse, because in these animals, though they were gelded while still immature, the operation was performed too late. All these observations combine to justify the inference that long before spermatozoa capable of effecting fertilisation are formed in the testicles, changes occur in these glands which are of great importance in relation to the sexual life, both in the human species and in the lower animals.

We cannot speak so positively as to the truth of this in the case of the reproductive glands in women, the ovaries, because alike in the human female and in the females of the lower animals oöphorectomy is less commonly performed than is castration in the male. The literature of our subject contains few references to this matter. What little information we do possess, derived in part from travellers who have had opportunities for observation in extra-European countries, and in part from students of animal life, leads to the same conclusion as in the case of males, namely, that long before the age commonly regarded as the commencement of sexual maturity, important changes are going on in the reproductive glands.

No detailed discussion can be attempted here of the other observations there may be on record to show the existence of such sexual processes during childhood. We may merely refer, for example, to the results of the removal of one testicle before the commencement of puberty; this is followed by a compensatory hypertrophy of the other testicle—whereas removal of one testicle after the attainment of sexual maturity does not lead to any such hypertrophy of the remaining testicle, or if so, only in comparatively slight degree.

Although from the facts just stated it appears that, alike in human beings and in the lower animals, before the formation of the specific germ-cells and sperm-cells has begun in the reproductive glands of the respective sexes important processes take place in these glands, it still remains obscure what is the nature of these processes, and in what manner they influence the organism. One question complicating this problem, and one which is to-day frequently discussed, is the extent of the influence exercised by the reproductive glands on the development of the secondary sexual characters. I can here do little more than state the difficulty. Whereas it was formerly assumed that the reproductive glands exercised a direct determining influence in this direction, more recently another view has been put forward, among others by Halban. According to this theory, the stimulus proceeding from the glands is protective merely, not formative, nor directly stimulating the growth of organs. In the fertilised ovum, it is supposed, the rudiment of sex already exists, likewise the rudiment of the reproductive gland, and the rudiments of the appropriate sexual characters. That is to say, the development of the secondary sexual characters is not determined by the presence of the reproductive gland; but the sex of the reproductive gland and the associated sexual characters are already determined by some common cause at the moment of fertilisation. But this theoretical controversy has no very important bearing on the problem with which we are especially concerned; and the influence of the reproductive gland upon the development of the secondary sexual characters is admitted as fully by Halban as it is by other writers, the only difference between the two views lying in the dispute whether the influence of the glands is of a formative or a protective nature. The influence exercised by the reproductive glands on the development of the secondary sexual characters can be adequately discussed, even though the precise way in which that influence is exerted remains in dispute.

As to the general nature of the influence, two chief theories have to be considered, viz., the nervous theory and the chemical theory. According to the former, we must assume that a stimulus originates in the reproductive glands, the testicles in the male, and the ovaries in the female, and that these glands excite a kind of reflex action— that is, that the stimulus passes to the central nervous system, and thence is "reflected" to the periphery, where it promotes, either the growth of particular parts of the body, e.g. the beard, or the development of definite properties in certain organs, e.g. the characteristics of the male larynx or of the female mamma. It is possible that the reflected impulse stimulates trophic nerves. But it may be that in cases of early castration the state of affairs is similar to that which obtains when from earliest infancy one of the sense organs is wanting, as a result of which the corresponding portions of the central nervous system are found to undergo atrophy. On this assumption, the manifest arrest of the development of certain organs which results from castration is to be regarded as the sequel of a partial atrophy of certain portions of the brain. Of late, however, the chemical theory, that the results of castration are dependent on the lack of the internal secretion of the excised glands, has gained ground at the expense of the nervous theory. The reason for this change of view is that much which was unsuspected in former years has recently been learned about the chemical activities of other glands. It suffices to allude to the function of the thyroid body. According to this chemical theory, chemical substances are prepared in the reproductive glands, and these substances exert a specific influence in promoting the development of the secondary sexual characters. The same theory has been invoked to account for the alleged ill effects of sexual abstinence, it being suggested that the reabsorption of glandular products properly destined for excretion may give rise to toxic effects. If it be assumed that the testicles can secrete substances upon the influence of which the development of the secondary sexual characters depends, it is obvious that these substances have nothing to do with the spermatozoa, inasmuch as the testicles exert the influence under consideration at an age at which the formation of spermatozoa has not yet begun. The substances that act in this way must be of a different kind. As was pointed out earlier in this book, recent researches have shown that the testicles possess a twofold activity; and some French physicians even go so far as to say that the testicle is not a single gland, but two glands. They distinguish between the gland that prepares the spermatozoa and the interstitial gland. Whilst the formation of spermatozoa subserves the generative act, the function of the interstitial gland is to prepare substances which pass into the lymph or blood-stream, and give rise to the development of the secondary sexual characters. Thus, the effects of castration are due, on this theory, not to the absence of the formation of spermatozoa, but to the absence of the products of the interstitial glands. French investigators consider that the assumption that such an interstitial gland exists is justified by the results of experimental work.

Whichever theory we accept, the chemical or the nervous, both theories harmonise equally with the fact that in boys, before the formation of spermatozoa begins, processes occur in the testicles which powerfully influence the organism. Thus, we learn also from a study of the results of castration how active is the sexual life even in childhood, since thus early in life influences proceed from the reproductive glands whereby the development of the secondary sexual characters is markedly affected.

The principal sexual processes occurring in childhood have now been described. Although we have been forced to admit the fact that in the child sexual processes are much more extensive than has commonly been believed, we must, on the other hand, guard ourselves against the exaggerations of those who interpret everything in sexual terms. In the chapter on diagnosis it will be necessary to refer to these exaggerations once again.

As a rule, of course, the manifestations of the sexual life of the child increase from year to year, although not always by continuous gradations. Thus, in consequence of misdirection, sexual manifestations may arise in the child, and then, if these evil communications are cut off, such manifestations may cease. But, altogether apart from deliberate seduction, we may observe periods of more rapid and periods of less rapid sexual development, the causes of which may remain obscure. Individual cases vary to such an extent, that it is impossible to lay down a rule to which there are no exceptions. This applies equally to both components of the sexual impulse, to the phenomena of detumescence as well as to those of contrectation.

But although as we have seen, the development of the sexual life is not always by regular progression, yet on the whole the increasing intensity of sexual manifestations from the years of childhood to the termination of the period of the puberal development cannot be denied. Especially extensive are the changes occurring at the end of the second period of childhood. At this period we note more particularly the development of the outward signs of sexual maturity. In the boy, we observe the growth of the beard and the pubic hair, and a more rapid enlargement of the testicles and the other organs of reproduction. In the girl, the breasts and the pelvis assume the adult female type, and ovulation and menstruation begin. During this period, also, the mental changes are extremely marked, even though in many cases these changes may have begun considerably earlier. The internal organic changes make themselves felt also in the sphere of action. The years of adolescence in the male are characterised by an impulse to travel, to adventures, but in addition to all kinds of ideal efforts and to religious activity. The loftiest ethical ideas alternate with a self-conscious bumptiousness. A change of disposition manifests itself which is sharply contrasted with the behaviour at an earlier and a subsequent age. This is no less true of the girl. That which formerly was no more than a vague indication, now becomes a manifest quality. More and more does the feminine mode of feeling display itself. The "tom-boyishness" so often seen in girls during the second period of childhood disappears. The former tomboy has become one—

"In whose orbs a shadow lies
Like the dusk in evening skies,"

and we see her—

"Standing, with reluctant feet,
Where the brook and river meet,
Womanhood and childhood fleet!

"Gazing, with a timid glance,
On the brooklet's swift advance,
On the river's broad expanse!"

The considerations put forward in this chapter show us how necessary it was to explain the conception of puberty at the very outset of this work. If the period of the puberal development be understood to correspond to the development and ripening of the sexual life, we see that this development begins much earlier than is commonly assumed in books on the subject. Writers have been too ready to identify with this developmental period the appearance of certain external manifestations, more especially the growth of the pubic hair in both sexes, the development of the breasts in the female, and the breaking of the voice in the male; and the appearance of certain definite outward signs—in the girl, the first menstruation, and in the boy, the first ejaculation—has usually been regarded as marking a turning-point in this development. But neither in the boy is the occurrence of the first ejaculation a proof of capacity for reproduction, or a proof that the period of the puberal development is completed; nor in the girl is the occurrence of the first menstruation, which may long precede the establishment of the far more important function of ovulation, characteristic in either of these respects. Observations made on children, accounts given by children and memories of childhood, and the results of castration (and oöphorectomy), all combine to prove the occurrence of sexual processes during childhood, at least as early as the beginning of the second period of childhood. At this time of life, the psychosexual in especial often plays a great part. If, notwithstanding all these facts, anyone desires to associate the beginning or the end of the puberal development, as was formerly done, with the appearance of "the external signs of puberty," no one can prevent this usage. But the scientific investigator, the physician, the schoolmaster, and the parents, should all alike fully understand that such external processes comprise but a small part of all that constitutes pubescence. A straining of terminology may at times be permissible; but on no account must we allow currency to so disastrous an error as the belief that the sexual life of the child either begins or is completed with the appearance of these external signs. The sexual life of the child begins long before, and the puberal development is not completed till many years after, the appearance of these external signs, which by most people are erroneously regarded as typical of pubescence.

Although I have detailed a number of phenomena characteristic of the sexual life of the child, it must not be assumed that these phenomena are common to all cases, or that every individual symptom is invariably observed. As I have previously explained, numerous exceptions occur. In some instances, only one symptom is discernible; in others, another only. The commonest early manifestations of the sexual life in childhood are, as was said before, the psychosexual phenomena. Frequently, the individual symptoms are so faintly marked that they can be detected only by a very thorough and careful examination. I wish merely to insist upon the fact that during the years of childhood which are commonly regarded as asexual, manifestations of the sexual life can with care almost always be detected, although at times their detection is by no means easy.

In conclusion, however, it is necessary to point out that there are a certain number of children in whom up to the fourteenth year of life, and even later, manifestations of the sexual life are hardly discernible; but we have to remember that the results of castration prove, as has been shown above, that even when, in early life, the occurrence of sexual processes cannot be demonstrated, such processes are nevertheless going on. We meet with individuals in whom, even during the first years of youth, the development of the sexual life is extremely backward. There are boys of fifteen or sixteen who from time to time have an involuntary seminal emission, but who exhibit no other indications whatever of an active sexual life—neither masturbation, nor any discernible psychosexual processes. Nevertheless, in most cases of this kind, more careful observation will bring to light much, besides the occurrence of the involuntary seminal emissions, which points to an awakening of sexuality. Still, in some individuals, it is remarkable how long entire sexual innocence may persist. This is doubtless due in such cases, not to any specially rigorous natural virtue, but simply to the fact that in these cases sexual development is much slower than the average. Those concerned are thus devoid of all understanding of the sexual, just in the same way as persons born blind lack all understanding of colour. In most of the cases in which such retardation occurs, the sexual life subsequently becomes entirely normal, showing that the only abnormality was the exceptional delay in the occurrence of the various processes. I have myself seen a number of cases in which the development of the sexual life was delayed to such an extent that ejaculation during coitus was not effected until towards the end of the third decade of life, although erections, and even occasional nocturnal emissions, had occurred long before. I believe that cases of this kind are to a small extent only, if at all, the result of educational influences, and they are in no way dependent upon the so-called sexual neurasthenia; we are concerned simply with a retardation of development, dependent upon congenital predisposition.

CHAPTER V

PATHOLOGY

In the previous chapters I have from time to time mentioned some phenomenon of comparatively rare occurrence; but for the most part I have described those processes only which are regularly met with, which cannot be regarded as exceptional peculiarities, and therefore must not be considered to be pathological manifestations. It is true that much that has been described comes within the province of the pathological; for example, many of the active manifestations of the sexual impulse occurring during the first period of childhood. For practical reasons, however, such cases as this cannot always be dealt with as members of a distinct pathological group. On the other hand, it is necessary to give a separate consideration to the pathological aspect of our subject. Many of the cases which must be grouped as pathological occur in girls. Thus, we meet with cases in which menstruation becomes established at the age of eight, five, two, or even earlier. Carus reports the case of a woman whose medical history showed that she had begun to menstruate at the age of two years, and that she became pregnant for the first time when eight years old. In girls from ten to twelve years of age, pregnancy has many times been observed. A French physician had under observation a girl who when only three mouths old had well-developed breasts, and in whom only a little later the pubic and axillary hair grew and menstruation began. When twenty-seven months old, the child was again seen by the same physician, and at this time menstruation was proceeding regularly; the features had now lost the infantile type, and the body as a whole exhibited all the signs of premature development. A collection of cases made by Gebhard contains one case in which menstruation was established at birth; in quite a number of the cases menstruation began during the first year of life.

A case was reported from New Orleans in which menstruation began at the age of three months and continued regularly thereafter. This was a case of premature general growth; at the age of four years the girl was over 4 feet high, and her breasts were the size of a large orange. As a general rule, in these cases of premature development of the reproductive organs in girls, the great size of the breasts attracts especial attention. According to Kisch, these girls with precocious menstruation and premature sexual development very commonly exhibit also a comparatively high body-weight, great development of fat, and early dentition; they look older than their years, and their genital organs also develop very early, with hair on the pubes and in the axillæ; the labia majora and the breasts resemble those of full-grown women, and the pelvis also has the adult form. Commonly also the sexual impulse develops early, whilst in other respects the mental development lags behind the physical.

In the post-mortem room, corresponding conditions are occasionally found in the ovaries; and some writers express the opinion that such premature sexual development is commoner than would appear from the comparative rarity of reports on the subject. Unquestionably, examination of the ovaries of young girls not infrequently leads to the discovery of ripe ovarian follicles; in one case this happened in the body of a female infant born prematurely. In a girl five years of ago, fifteen follicles were counted in the ovaries. Liégeois, in post-mortem examinations, twice found mature ova in girls two years of age.

Similar cases of premature sexual development are occasionally seen also in boys. For example, Breschet, in the year 1820, reported the case of a boy three years of age who exhibited all the signs of puberty. His voice resembled that of a young man of sixteen to eighteen. The length of the flaccid penis was 9.6 cm. (3¾ inches), its diameter at the root was 7.2 cm. (2¾ inches); the length of the organ when erect was 13.5 cm. (5¼ inches). In the presence of girls or women the boy's penis became erect, his whole manner became more vivacious, and his hands were directed towards the genital organs of these females. Masturbation was never observed. The boy showed many additional signs of premature development. For instance, the central incisors of the upper jaw were cut at the age of three months. Breschet also quotes a case published by Mead, in which a boy had undergone the puberal development before the end of the first year of his life; when five years of age, he died of pulmonary consumption, attended with all the signs of old age. The same writer records another case, that of a boy five years of age, whose genital organs were fully developed, who had a well-grown beard, and exhibited, in short, all the (physical) characteristics of complete sexual maturity. In accordance with the theoretical views of that day, more especially as a result of the wide acceptance of the phrenological doctrines of Gall, it was generally believed that an exceptional development of the cerebellum (which was supposed by Gall to be the seat of the sexual impulse) was the determining cause of such premature awakening of the sexual impulse.

Contrasted with the cases just described, are those in which there is a retardation of the whole course of sexual development, so that the signs of sexual maturity are not manifested until an age greatly exceeding the average "age of puberty." In respect of one symptom or several, many individuals may remain throughout life in an infantile condition. This is occasionally seen, for example, in dwarfs. It would be of great interest, from this point of view, to make a careful study of the sexual behaviour of dwarfs. In this respect, dwarfs appear to vary greatly. These differences depend, in part, at least, upon the fact that many persons are classified as dwarfs who do not, strictly speaking, belong to this category. This statement applies more especially to those whose growth has been impaired by rickets; for, properly speaking, those only should be designated dwarfs who are, though small, generally well-proportioned; and the term should not be applied to those in whom the defective stature is consequent on rachitis or some similar disease. It appears doubtful, however, if the confusion of terms just mentioned explains all the observed differences in the sexuality of those commonly spoken of as "dwarfs." From data communicated to me concerning a fairly large community of dwarfs, living in a single place, and in whom the dwarfing appears to have no connexion with rickets, it would seem that in the case of true dwarfs there is considerable variation in sexual behaviour. This particular group of dwarfs constitute a society of persons living and working together. Although they are all living in close association, there seems to be a striking lack of warmth in their sexual relationships. Notwithstanding the fact that they have been living together for ten years, they still address one another formally as "Mr." and "Miss." In the case of the male dwarfs, with one exception all had fully developed genital organs; the exceptional instance was that of a member of the community then thirty years of age, in whom the genitals were rudimentary. All were endowed with normal sexual impulse, but this was directed towards persons of normal stature. In one of these dwarfs, an Italian, the genital organs remained undeveloped and hairless until he attained the age of twenty-eight; then these organs underwent the normal degree of growth, and at the same time pubic hair appeared. As already mentioned, the sexual inclinations of dwarfs appear as a rule to be directed towards fully grown persons, and I knew one dwarf twenty years of age who never missed an opportunity of pressing up against a certain very pretty young lady. These observations of my own regarding the sexual inclinations in dwarfs are confirmed by other cases recorded in the literature of the subject, although in isolated instances sexual attraction between a male and a female dwarf has been observed to eventuate in the birth of a child.

This is the place in which to refer to those cases of which a brief mention was made in the first chapter, to which von Krafft-Ebing has given the name of sexual paradoxy. Activity of the sexual impulse is sometimes observed at an age at which this impulse is normally quiescent. The term applies alike to cases in which the sexual impulse becomes active in early childhood, and to cases in which the impulse persists to an advanced age. Whilst the cases in which the phenomena of contrectation alone occurred have commonly been overlooked, considerable attention has been paid to those cases in which the sexual impulse manifests itself by peripheral changes, more especially by premature impulse towards masturbation or towards actual sexual congress with one of the other sex. It was shown, however, in the last chapter, that active manifestations of the sexual impulse during childhood are not always paradoxical. If we examine cases which have been published as coming under this latter category (I limit myself here to cases occurring in childhood, and am not speaking of sexual paradoxy in old age), we find that they are characterised more particularly by the strength with which the peripheral sexual impulse manifests itself. There is, in fact, a marked distinction between cases, according as we have to do with an occasional general sensation in the genital organs, or with masturbation to excess and with sexual assaults upon others. But we must not describe as sexual paradoxy all manifestations of the sexual life occurring in early childhood. A reference to the last chapter will show that the cases of sexual paradoxy, when accurately studied, differ from the normal rather quantitatively than qualitatively. During the first period of childhood, and more especially during the first few years of life, a case in which sexual activity in a child threatens the well-being of members of that child's social environment is so sharply differentiated from the normal that there can hardly arise even momentary hesitation regarding the paradoxical nature of the manifestation. On the other hand, we shall do well to follow von Krafft-Ebing in excluding from the category of sexual paradoxy those cases in which sexual excitement is caused solely by peripheral inflammatory stimuli, balanitis (inflammation of the glans penis), threadworms, and the like. These are not instances of sexual paradoxy, because the essential characteristic of the latter is that it originates centrally, even though its manifestations take a peripheral form.

I will now recount three cases which I regard as pathological in nature, and as examples of a paradoxical sexual impulse.

Case 7.—The girl X., six years of age, stated by the mother to be free from all morbid inheritance, produces the general impression of being a nervous subject. She is affected with facial muscular spasms, especially affecting the corners of the mouth, the eyelids, and the neck. Her mental development, as far as can be judged from my own observations and from the account given by the parents, is perfectly normal; but attention is at once attracted by the appearance of premature development. The mother states that in the second year of life, owing to the carelessness of a nursemaid, the child fell out of her cradle, without, however, sustaining any manifest injury. The mother does not think there is any reason to suppose that the child has ever been led astray in sexual matters. For the past two years or more, the mother has noticed that the child likes to press up against articles of furniture in such a way that her genital organs come into contact with narrow edges or corners; for example, the back of a chair, and especially a small portfolio-stand in the room. At first the child did this very often. Then the mother forbade it, and the father whipped her several times for doing it; since then it has been done more furtively, but the mother has none the less often seen it done. When the child is in bed she plays with the genital organs with her fingers. A definite orgasm occurs: there are spastic twitchings of the whole body, the eyes brighten, the respiratory rhythm changes; all these changes, occurring as they do in association with the artificial stimulation of the genital organs, combine to prove that we have not to do here with a simple spasmodic neurosis, but with the artificial induction of the sexual orgasm. The process is, moreover, confined to peripheral manifestations. The most careful observation failed to show the existence, in association with the sexual excitement, of any especially tender sentiments towards other individuals.

Case 8.—The boy Y. was brought to see me when he was eight and a half years of age. From the second year of life he had been noticed to be subject to masturbatory impulses, attended from the first with erection of the penis. The practice of masturbation increased to such a degree that before the boy was four years of age it was found necessary to keep him separate, as far as possible, from his brothers and sisters to save these latter from being corrupted by him. But notwithstanding this precaution, by the time he was five years old he had begun to make sexual attacks on a sister one year older than himself. He was cunning enough to arrange matters in such a way that he was alone with his sister, at times when the usual safeguards to keep him separate from the other children were suspended—for example, when his parents were away, and when his governess (who had been made fully acquainted with the circumstances) was keeping some assignation of her own. (All this was fully elucidated at a later date. The distressed parents were foolish enough to imagine that a child with inherited morbid predispositions of this character could be adequately safeguarded by means of hired help; they were painfully disillusioned when it appeared that the hired assistant, instead of watching the child, was pursuing her own pleasures—a point in which she merely imitated the parents, themselves earnest pleasure-seekers, deluding themselves with the belief that everything possible was being done for their child.) Although the parents had known all about the boy's habit of masturbation for many years past, it was only through a fortunate accident, and after the sexual malpractices with the sister had been going on for a long time, that these at length came to light. It appears that the boy had from time to time made sexual advances to other girls than his sister. One day, while playing with the little daughter belonging to a neighbouring family, he endeavoured to lead this child sexually astray. The little girl told her parents what had happened, and these latter consequently refused to allow her to play with Y. any more. This prohibition led Y.'s parents to inquire into the whole matter with great care. It was then discovered that for years past Y. had been engaged in sexual misconduct with his sister, his usual method being to play with her genital organs with his hands. In the girl, the frequent repetition of this act had given rise to abrasions and local inflammations.

The following case, the leading features of which are the early age at which seminal ejaculation occurred, and the marked hyperæsthesia of the sexual impulse, may also be regarded as an example of sexual paradoxy. This patient exhibits a number of different perverse modes of sexual sensibility, some of which have persisted to the present day.

Case 9.—Z., now thirty years of age, admits prolonged sexual excesses, and divides his sexual history into two periods: the first period extends from the age of seven to the age of twelve, before he had learned the use of alcohol; during the second period, from the age of thirteen to the age of thirty-years, his sexual excesses occurred under the influence of alcohol. He gives his own history in the following terms:—

"In very early childhood my imagination began to exercise itself pleasurably in the pictured contemplation of the bodies of naked girls. I can also remember distinctly that my dreams were chiefly concerned with images of this character. In the later years of childhood (nine to twelve years) I masturbated to great excess, often five to ten times daily, sometimes actually while in class at school. Seminal emission had already begun—I remember this quite distinctly at the age of ten, and perhaps even at the age of nine years—but the quantity of semen was very small. I found several schoolmates with similar inclinations to my own, and with these I practised mutual masturbation. When I was eleven years old I became acquainted with a boy somewhat younger than myself, and in this case the proposal for mutual masturbation came from his side. At that time the thought that there was anything wrong in the practice had never entered my mind; on the contrary, I was always on the lookout for boys who would join with me in mutual masturbation. Such were my sexual habits, until as a boy of thirteen I for the first time had complete sexual intercourse with a woman, a prostitute. Thenceforward, for a time, I had intercourse at intervals of from four to six weeks, continuing in the meanwhile daily masturbation. Subsequently I sought and found opportunities for intercourse with women, married and unmarried, about once a week, for money. These almost daily venereal excesses appeared to have no bad effects on my physical health; my diet was at the time abundant, if not superabundant. On the other hand, I lacked effective will-power to make a successful stand against the promptings of my bodily lusts; nor was I able, though not devoid of talent, to perform any arduous or enduring mental work. There ensued also at this early stage a great infirmity of purpose, from which I still suffer to this day. I would take up now one thing, now another, at first with fiery zeal, soon to cast it aside in favour of some new undertaking, to be abandoned with the like precipitation.

"Having command of abundant means, I now, at the age of fifteen, became enabled to gratify my sexual desires without restraint with dependents of the other sex; nor did any untoward physical consequences arise to impose limitations. After a time, ordinary sexual intercourse ceased to furnish adequate gratification; and I began to excite myself sexually by contact with special parts of the body, most often the breasts. But the woman must not, as had formerly been my desire, strip herself completely nude; for I found the most powerful sexual stimulus was now exerted by her white drawers. The display, intentional or unintentional, of this article of feminine attire sufficed to arouse in me sexual feelings. For this reason I now came to frequent the skating rink, in order to obtain a sexual stimulus from the glimpse of a woman's drawers when putting on her skates. But even when a girl was physically beautiful and elegantly dressed, if her drawers were not white but coloured, she produced in me no sexual appetite whatever.

"As a result of long-continued excesses, attempts at ordinary intercourse no longer evoked an adequate sexual stimulus, so that I now began the practice of cunnilinctus. It was when the woman herself became excited through the cunnilinctus, that I experienced the highest sexual gratification. In the intervals, when I had no opportunity for sexual intercourse, I would endeavour to secure sexual gratification by exposing my genital organs in the presence of females, or when passing them in the street—especially female children. I also sought every possible opportunity of watching female dependents engaged in the act of urination. This gave me especially great gratification if, when they were urinating, I could see their white underlinen. I also procured pornographic literature, and masturbated frequently while reading it."

The next period in this patient's history now begins. But I shall not recount his case further, since the subsequent episodes have no bearing on the questions with which we are especially concerned. It will suffice to remark that Z. now exhibits numerous neuropathic and psychopathic characteristics. But the various psychopathic symptoms, some of which are very severe, lie altogether outside our chosen field of study.

Paradoxical sexual impulse is observed also in the lower animals. Weston reports the case of a colt which when only six weeks old attempted to serve its mother; when three months old this animal became so troublesome, owing to its attempts to cover other foals and even calves, that castration was necessary. The same author describes a case of masturbation in a foal only two months old; the animal masturbated by arching the back to an extreme degree, and pushing the hind feet forward along the surface of the belly on either side of the penis.

Several allusions have been made in passing to the subject of sexual perversions. A detailed consideration of these manifestations is now necessary, owing to the fact that perversions exhibit peculiar relationships to the sexual life of the child, such relationships being of two distinct kinds. In the first place, perverse modes of sexual sensibility are very common during childhood; and since erroneous views on the subject are widely prevalent, the true significance of such perversions demands very careful study. In the second place, it is maintained that certain influences affecting the sexual life during childhood are competent to give rise to permanent sexual perversions. We will discuss these two questions in the order here stated.

Adult sexual perverts frequently declare that their first experience of perverse sexual sensibility dates from the eighth year, or even earlier. Thus, by homosexuals we are told that the homosexual inclination was felt in very early childhood, in one case directed towards a school-fellow, in another towards some near relative, or towards a resident tutor—- or in the case of female homosexuals, towards a girl-companion or a governess. Moreover, homosexuals often assure us that the homosexual inclination has been persistent, and that it has never been interrupted by any manifestation of heterosexual desire. The assumption that in homosexuals the sexual impulse becomes active earlier in life than is normal, was one of several considerations by which von Krafft-Ebing was led to regard homosexuality as a degenerative phenomenon, consequent upon neuropathic or psychopathic hereditary taint; and this author held the same view regarding other sexual perversions—sadism, for instance. In opposition to this opinion, attention may be drawn to the fact, which was fully considered in the last chapter, that very commonly indeed the activity of the normal sexual life can also be traced back into the early days of childhood. This fact has hitherto to a large extent been overlooked simply for the reason that recent investigations dealing with the sexual impulse have in most cases dealt exclusively with morbid manifestations; whilst the psychologists by profession, whose province it was to study the normal sexual life, have with few exceptions (Max Dessoir, Binet, Jodl, and Ribot) completely ignored this field of inquiry. For this reason many phenomena, e.g., early activity of the sexual impulse, and hyperæsthesia of that impulse, have been assumed to be characteristic of the perverse modes of sexual sensibility, whereas the like phenomena may readily be observed in association with a qualitatively normal mode of sexual sensibility.

The theory of the congenital nature of homosexuality was based for the most part on the common assumption that the condition is primary and premature in its occurrence, and that it is exclusive of the opposite mode of sexual sensibility. But for several reasons the inference is not justified. For, first of all, for many cases it is incorrect to assume that the homosexual inclinations are thus exclusive in their character; as I have previously explained, the adult homosexual's belief that from early childhood he has never experienced any other than homosexual inclinations, depends in many instances on an illusion of memory. Owing to the fact that in consequence of the fuller development of homosexuality he is no longer interested in the heterosexual, he is apt to forget any early heterosexual inclinations. Secondly, the primary appearance of homosexual inclinations does not prove that these inclinations are congenital; for in homosexuals, as in heterosexuals, the specialised mode of sexual sensibility is preceded by a period in which the sexual impulse is undifferentiated; and, in homosexuals and heterosexuals alike, chance plays a great part in determining which mode of sexual sensibility first manifests itself. The congenital nature of heterosexuality is not disproved by the fact that one who in adult life possesses a normal mode of sexual sensibility, may as a schoolboy have first experienced sexual desire towards a school-fellow; just as little, then, does a similar early history in one who in adult life is homosexual in his inclinations, prove that his homosexuality is congenital. In the animal world also, before the occurrence of sexual maturity, the love-games occasionally display a similar confusion of rôles, so that the sexually immature female animal may attempt to cover the youthful male. The congenital nature of homosexuality is displayed, not by the primary appearance of this mode of sensibility, but by the fact that when the puberal development takes place, the homosexual sentiments persist, and are not replaced by heterosexuality.

The congenital nature of homosexuality has been assumed more particularly in those cases which are described respectively as effemination and viraginity. The former name is given by von

Krafft-Ebing to cases in which in homosexual men the entire system of feelings and inclinations is influenced by the abnormal mode of sexual sensibility. Such a male homosexual has a strong dislike for smoking and drinking, and for all masculine sports; on the other hand, he delights in self-adornment, in art and belles-lettres and even in literary affectations. The corresponding condition in women was by von Krafft-Ebing termed viraginity. Such female homosexuals do not merely experience sexual attraction towards members of their own sex, but they also exhibit other peculiarities usually characteristic of the male, such as dislike of ordinary feminine occupations, a neglect of the arts of the toilet, and a rough and masculine mode of behaviour. They exhibit inclinations for science rather than for art. They sometimes attempt to drink and smoke in a masculine manner. Von Krafft-Ebing and many other writers have assumed that the characteristics of effemination and of viraginity are displayed in early childhood. We are told that a boy with these tendencies prefers the society of little girls to that of boys, that he likes to play with dolls, and to help his mother in her housework. He takes naturally to cooking, sewing, and darning; and becomes clever in the selection of feminine dress, so that he can help his sisters in the choice of their clothes. Contrariwise, the girl who is destined in later life to display the characteristics of viraginity will be found frequenting the playground of the boys. Such a girl will have nothing to do with dolls, but exhibits a passion for the rocking horse and for playing at soldiers and robbers. It is indisputable that these descriptions apply to many cases. But it is necessary here to repeat my previous warning against over-ready generalisation; for we find that there is quite a number of boys and girls who exhibit during childhood such contrary sexual qualities and inclinations, and yet subsequently undergo a perfectly normal, or at any rate a non-homosexual, development of the sexual life. During the period of the puberal development, the normal heterosexual characteristics come to predominate. The non-differentiated character of the sexual life during childhood forbids us, from the mere existence at this period of life of such contrary sexual tendencies, to infer that these tendencies will necessarily persist, and that the subsequent sexual development will also be of an inverted character. We must point out, in addition, that from childhood onwards many women and many men fail to exhibit the psychical tendencies appropriate to average members of their respective sexes, without this justifying the conclusion that we have to do with homosexuality. There are heterosexual men who are fond of needlework; and there are heterosexual women in whom housework and the care of children, and even in many cases the details of their own toilet, arouse no interest whatever. Because we observe, in any individual, certain contrary sexual tendencies of this character, to draw the inference that in such a case we necessarily have to do with homosexuality, would be a most disastrous error.

Apart from these considerations, we have, when there is a history of such tendencies in childhood, to take into account the possibility of illusions of memory just as much as we have in the cases in which adult homosexuals assure us that in childhood they never experienced any other than homosexual inclinations—a matter discussed in the first chapter. A homosexual man, recalling his memories of childhood, lays especial stress on all that appears to be connected with homosexuality; he is apt to remember those instances only in which his conduct exhibited girlish characteristics, and to forget all instances of an opposite kind. Finally, we have to take into consideration the various interpretations which are tenable of occurrences during childhood. An adult homosexual who as a child once did some needlework for a joke, sees in this later a characteristic of effemination. A girl who, for lack of companions of her own sex, was accustomed to join in her brother's sports, comes to believe, when subsequently she has developed into a homosexual woman, that her conduct in childhood resulted from congenital perversion, whereas in reality this conduct was the purely accidental result of her childish environment. On the other hand, the withdrawal during childhood from the companionship of members of the same sex is explicable in a converse fashion. Homosexual adults often tell us that even in boyhood they shunned the company of other boys, and sought girl companions, to join in the games of these latter—and they endeavour to explain this conduct on their part as determined by contrary sexual inclinations in early childhood. Yet, in many cases, boys avoid those of their own sex, and seek the companionship of girls, not for the reason just alleged, but solely because these boys thus early experience erotic stimulation when associating with girls. In any case, we must carefully avoid over-estimating the importance of what may appear to be contrary sexual phenomena during childhood, and we must not be too ready to accept the occurrence of such phenomena as a proof that sexual perversion had manifested itself already during childhood. The general possibility of this occurrence is, of course, not disputed; but the far too common exaggerations of the matter cannot be too decisively rejected.

The case I have now to describe is that of a woman whose characteristics during childhood were thoroughly boyish, and who at this time experienced homosexual inclinations; during the period of the puberal development, however, the homosexual tendencies disappeared, never to return.

Case 10.—Mrs. X., twenty-six years of age, happily married for five years past, enjoys excellent health, with the exception of pains during menstruation, has normal intercourse with her husband, experiencing sexual impulse of full intensity, and a normal voluptuous sensation. The family history is healthy on the whole; some of the mother's relatives are described as "nervous"; but in so large a family, otherwise healthy, this is of trifling significance. Most of her blood-relations are, so far as inheritable morbid conditions are concerned, thoroughly healthy. As a girl, X. (whose statements, in so far as I was able to inquire, were in all important respects substantiated by her mother) was at first accustomed to seek the companionship of boys only. She was continually playing with her brothers and their friends, and was always the leader in their wildest games including war-games, and playing at Indians. During childhood she was almost always regarded as "the baby," although she had a sister two years younger than herself, this sister being altogether girlish in her ways. Very seldom did X. play with anyone but the boys; when she did on rare occasions seek other companionship, it was always that of the sister of one of her boy friends. The two girls had obviously great sympathy each for the other, manifested when they were as yet only nine years of age, and increasing as the years went on. The closer her association became with this girl, the more did X. withdraw from the companionship of the boys, to devote herself to her girl friend. The association became more and more intimate; and when they were both thirteen years old their endearments passed from kisses and embraces to manipulation of the genital organs. In those latter, X. always played a passive part, not herself touching her own genital organs nor those of her friend. Occasionally X. would feel drawn towards some other girl, but such errant inclinations never lasted long. At about the time when her fondness for the other girl began, that is to say, during her tenth year, X., who was then accustomed to compassionate herself for not having been born a boy, began to assume a more definitely boyish behaviour. Under the pretence of "dressing up," she used to wear her brother's clothes; occasionally she smoked, although in her home, and in the circle to which her family belonged, smoking was disapproved of even in grown women. At the age of fourteen, X. began to menstruate. The friendship between the two girls continued until the seventeenth year of life. Then X. gradually "came out," her homosexual tendencies disappeared, and at the same time her feminine nature became apparent. The desire to dress up as a man and the desire to smoke passed away, and have never returned, although X. now moves in circles in which many women smoke. And, most important fact of all, the homosexual relations were now completely broken off. The two girls remained on friendly terms; but alike in X. and in her friend the homosexual inclinations disappeared, and the improper sexual practices were entirely discontinued. X. began to flirt, now with one man, now with another, until when nineteen years old she fell in love with her present husband, and married him after a two years' engagement.

This case shows that neither the existence of homosexual inclinations during childhood, nor the simultaneous exhibition of other contrary sexual mental qualities, necessarily foreshadows the development of permanent homosexuality. On the other hand, we must not from the subsequent appearance of heterosexuality draw the conclusion that this was first acquired intra vitam, for it very often happens that congenital heterosexuality first manifests itself during the period of the puberal development. In an analogous case, in which the homosexual and other contrary sexual tendencies and inclinations of childhood have persisted during the adult sexual life, it would be equally erroneous in the absence of further evidence to conclude that the homosexuality was congenital. I recognise the existence of congenital homosexuality, but I consider that the reality of this condition is established by other grounds than those just mentioned. This question has been fully discussed by me elsewhere, and cannot here be further considered.

Many investigators regard homosexuality as an acquired manifestation. In cases in which the existence of homosexuality can be traced back into childhood, they explain this on the ground that at a time when the individual concerned was in a state of sexual excitement, some other person of the same sex must have made a marked impression upon his imagination. In this way, they suggest, is effected an association whose influence endures throughout life. I will here say no more than this, that this association theory does not suffice to account for the facts. The deficiencies of the association theory will to some extent become apparent from the account I am about to give of the other sexual perversions.

For the dispute to what extent sexual perversions are congenital and to what extent they are acquired, prevails not only concerning homosexuality, but also concerning sadism, masochism, sexual fetichism, &c. In the case also of these latter perversions, some maintain that in those instances in which the perversion began in childhood, some early association was the originating cause; whilst others, from the very fact that the perversion appeared very early in life and was apparently primary, infer that it must be of a congenital character. For instance, a man experiences sexual excitement whenever he sees a cook or other woman kill a fowl; and when revived in memory, the corresponding ideas exercise a similar exciting influence. On inquiry, we learn that when he was eight years old he by chance saw a fowl killed, and then immediately felt strong sexual excitement. Similarly, many masochists and sadists assure us that their first experience of their peculiarly tinged sexual excitement occurred during childhood; e.g., in the case of the masochist, when being punished with a whipping, and so on.

Beyond question, the impressions of childhood may result in the formation of enduring associations. From experiences during childhood may originate terrors and feelings of disgust which are never subsequently overcome. A child who for any reason has several times felt a strong loathing towards some particular article of food, will retain throughout life a dislike to this same substance. Felix Platter relates his own experience as follows. When a child, he once saw his sister slicing rings of "boiled gorge" (see note, below.), and sticking these rings on her finger. The sight was so unpleasant to him that he had to go away. The disagreeable memory has been so persistent, that ever since he has been unable to bear the sight, not merely of such "rings of flesh," but rings of gold, silver, or any other material. A child who has once been frightened by a dog, may ever after be terrified of all dogs. An individual may also, by a kind of moral contagion, be affected by the experiences of others. A child who has seen another child frightened by a cat, may for this reason acquire an antipathy to cats lasting for the whole of life. It is upon the undoubted fact of such experiences as these, that those build their case who maintain that sexual perversions originate in chance impressions during childhood or early youth. But weighty reasons can be alleged against any such generalisation.

Note on the expression "Boiled Gorge."—This is a literal translation of the German gesottne Gurgeln, an apparently forgotten article of diet. Finding no account of it in any German dictionary, I applied to Dr. Moll, who writes as follows:—"Gurgel denotes a particular part of the neck, in human beings the front part, comprising the hyoid bone, the larynx and trachea, the pharynx and the upper part of the oesophagus, the thyroid body, and the adjoining muscles. As far as I am aware, this part of the animal body is not now used for food. Presumably it was so used in Felix Platter's time, but I cannot say if the 'rings' of which he speaks were cut from the trachea, the oesophagus, or perhaps the great blood-vessels."—Translator's Note.

To return to the instance of the man who is sexually excited by the sight of fowls being killed, it is true that on superficial consideration the case may appear to support the theory that we have here to do with an acquired perversion. We cannot assume that in this child the complicated image of the killing of a fowl was inborn, and the first inference will therefore be that his perversion is purely an acquired one. But on closer examination we perceive that the matter is less simple than appeared at first sight. First of all we have to inquire why it is that in this particular instance the sight of the killing of a fowl induced such a perversion, when in hundreds of other cases no such result follows the same stimulus. The assumption that in the particular case there chanced to occur sexual excitement simultaneously with the sight of the fowl-killing, is altogether inadequate as an explanation. For, first, this assumption of the simultaneous occurrence of sexual excitement is in most cases a pure supposition, quite unsupported by proof. Secondly, even when the two processes, the sight of the killing, and the sexual excitement, do occur simultaneously, it is still open to question whether the latter may not have been determined by the former; that is to say, it may be that the perverse mode of sexual sensibility previously existed, at least as a predisposition, and that the connexion between the phenomena is the reverse of what is supposed. Thirdly, moreover, the chance view of some occurrence in association with sexual excitement does not suffice to explain the enduring association of sexual excitement with such an occurrence throughout the whole of life. Think of persons who have masturbated during childhood. When they were masturbating, their eyes have rested on various indifferent objects: underlinen, articles of furniture, pictures, books, &c.; but this does not induce the association throughout life of sexual excitement with the sight of any of these articles.

Apart from these considerations, the fact that some external process, such as the killing of a fowl, has important relationships with the content of a subsequent perversion, does not prove that this perversion is an acquired one. We may rather suppose that in the case of one endowed with a congenital predisposition to the excitement of the sexual impulse by the sight of cruelty, the particular cruel act which will prove the determinant in a particular case, must depend upon the chance circumstances of the individual's life. On this view, if, in the case under consideration, the fowl-killing had not happened, at the appropriate time, to awaken the sexual impulse, it must be assumed that some other but similar process would have been competent to effect this. In any case, the association theory alone will not suffice to account for these cases; and the possibility cannot be excluded that in cases of sadism there is a specific abnormal disposition of the sexual impulse, and that the experiences during childhood influence the matter only in so far as they may determine the special manner in which the sadistic tendency will subsequently manifest itself. It is, in fact, very remarkable how often some particular act of cruelty will, in a certain individual, exercise throughout life a sexually exciting influence: in one person the desire to strike may be associated with sexual excitement; in another it may be the desire to stab or to cut; in one individual sexual excitement results from the sight of a fowl being killed; in another, when the victim is a fish, and so on. Although we encounter some in whom the particular cruel act associated with sexual excitement changes many times during life; yet, on the other hand, we find that there are many persons in whom sexual excitement is aroused by some special sadistic practice, and by that alone; and on careful inquiry we ascertain that even in childhood such an act was associated with voluptuous excitement.

I will take this opportunity of explaining very briefly that there is still another possible way of explaining these enduring associations as being based upon impressions received during childhood, without the supposition that these impressions of childhood are the exclusive determinants; this is the assumption that there exists a congenital weakness of the rudiment of the normal sexual impulse, and that it is owing to this primary defect that the paths of nervous conduction involved in the activity of the normal sexual impulse so readily become impassable.

No further discussion of such disputed problems of the sexual life can now be attempted. What has been said should suffice, on the one hand, to prove that the experiences of childhood have important relationships to the occurrence of sexual perversions; and, on the other, to put the reader on his guard against numerous exaggerations. I will merely add that whilst the examples I have given concern only homosexuality and sadism, similar considerations will be found to apply, mutatis mutandis, to other sexual perversions.

Notes of a few cases will now be given in which more or less perverse tendencies can be traced back into the days of childhood, at least in so far as the memories of those concerned can be regarded as trustworthy.

Case 11.—X., thirty-one years of age, is a foot-fetichist. He believes that his preference for feet dates from the age of six years, when he began to regard with extraordinary interest the feet of a servant girl in his father's house when she was engaged in washing the floor. From the age of six to the age of eleven years, X.'s memories are somewhat confused. Thenceforward, however, in the matter of his fondness for feet, his memories are distinct enough. When he was twelve years old he saw in his parents' house a young girl standing bare-footed before the kitchen fire; he seized the opportunity of crouching down on the ground quite close to the girl's feet, giving as his excuse that he wanted to bask in the heat of the fire. While doing this, he yearned to touch or to kiss the girl's feet. Between the ages of thirteen and sixteen he was crazy about the naked feet of girls and women. He took every opportunity of seeing the servants' feet when they were scrubbing the floors, and this sight sufficed to induce in him erection of the penis. This foot fetichism has persisted, directed sometimes towards the feet of women, sometimes towards the feet of men. Since he grew up, X. has from time to time had normal heterosexual intercourse.

Case 12.—Y., twenty-five years of age, homosexual, with a special preference for soldiers. In early childhood he noticed in himself a great fondness for handsome men. When walking in the streets of the town as a small boy, it was the soldiers, in especial, from among the men he met, who made a strong impression upon him. He remembers that when he was seven years of age, he allowed a soldier to take him on his knees, and that it gave him great pleasure to stroke the man's cheeks. The roughness of the cheeks gave him an extremely agreeable sensation, and he sought every opportunity of renewing this sensation. He found cavalry soldiers especially stimulating. From the age of eleven dates his peculiar delight in the well-rounded nates of a cavalry soldier. As he himself puts it, with the lapse of time, this has become to him a genuine fetich. Subsequently, young men-servants also aroused his interest, but never to the same degree as cavalry soldiers. The homosexual tendency has persisted into adult life.

Case 13.—Z., twenty-seven years of age, has several times been prosecuted, on account of his attempts to spy upon women in public lavatories. It is his custom, when in such a place he can observe the genital organs of a woman in the act of defæcation, to masturbate. He states that this tendency was well marked in him at the age of thirteen years. He believes, indeed, that at this time he was inspired mainly by curiosity—by a desire to see what the genital organs of a female were like. But he recalls that when a child, at about the age of eight or nine years, he experienced sexual stimulation when a girl cousin of six sat on his face; and he thinks that when only five or six years old he crawled under the petticoats of a servant girl, in order to lay his face against her nates. Even as early as this he experienced great pleasure in the act.

Case 14.—X., is now twenty years of age. He always experiences sexual excitement when he thinks of the act of whipping. It is unnecessary for him to play any active part in this himself; and it is a matter of indifference to him whether a man beats a woman, a woman beats a man, or an adult of either sex beats a child. In all cases alike the sight induces sexual excitement; and the imaginative reproduction of such a scene is his customary stimulus during masturbation—this being a fairly frequent occurrence. He traces back to childhood the stimulus exercised on him by a whipping seen or imagined. When from seven to nine years of age, he began to find such experiences sexually stimulating; by the age of ten, he was quite clear as to the existence of this peculiarity in himself. At this early age he struck himself with a stick, under the influence of an obscure impulse to arouse voluptuous sensations by means of the blows; he did this fairly frequently.

As regards his sexual sensibilities in general, he is by no means indifferent to members of the opposite sex. He gladly seeks social intercourse with females, and likes to kiss them; but he does not experience any definite sexual impulse towards them, such as might culminate in sexual intercourse. Three times he has had actual intercourse, but on each occasion he has been able to effect erection and ejaculation only by means of all kinds of artificial stimulation. It is a noteworthy fact that when he was fifteen or sixteen years of age he became intimate with the members of a homosexual circle, and only by considerable effort was he able to free himself from these associations.

In autobiographical literature we from time to time come across accounts of such perverse modes of sexual sensibility. Ulrich von Lichtenstein, in whom masochistic inclinations were unmistakably present, relates that when he was barely twelve years of age he became the devoted slave of a grown woman; and he describes his sentiments, at this early age and subsequently, towards this woman, who was well born, good and beautiful, chaste in mind and body, and in every respect virtuous. Well known, too, is the case of Rousseau, of which I shall have to speak again later; this writer traces his masochistic perversion back to the seventh year of his life. I may allude also to Rétif de la Bretonne, who was born in

1734, and certainly experienced sexual sentiments in very early childhood. In his Monsieur Nicolas, which must be regarded as an autobiographical work, Rétif relates the beginnings, in the years 1743-44, of his fetichistic fondness (which endured throughout his life) for women's feet and women's shoes. In purely fictional works, analogous cases are also described. Thus, in his Pour une Nuit d'Amour, Zola depicts a sadistic-masochistic relationship between two children:—

"From earliest childhood Thérèse von Morsanne used Colombel as the scapegoat and the sport of her caprices. He was about six months older than she. Thérèse was a dreadful child. Not that she was wild and uncontrolled, like the ordinary unruly child; on the contrary, she was extraordinarily serious, with the outward aspect of a well-brought-up young lady. But she had most remarkable whims and caprices, When she was alone, she would from time to time utter inarticulate cries or angry howls.

"From the age of six she began to torment little Colombel. He was small and weakly. She would lead him to the back of the park, to a place where the chestnut-trees formed an arbour; here she would spring on his back and make him carry her about, riding sometimes round and round for hours. She compressed his neck, and thrust her heels into his sides, so that he could hardly breathe. He was the horse, she was the lady on horseback. When he was tired out, and ready to drop from exhaustion, she would bite him till the blood flowed, and would cling to her seat so tightly that her nails sank into his flesh. And the ride would thus start once more. The cruel queen of six years old, borne on the back of the little boy who served her as beast of burden, hunted thus on horseback with her hair streaming in the wind. Afterwards, when they were with their parents, she would pinch him secretly, and by repeated threats would prevent him from crying or complaining. Thus in secret they led a life of their own, very different from that which was apparent to the eyes of others. When they were alone, she treated him as a toy, to be broken to fragments at her pleasure, simply to see what might be inside. Was she not the Marquise? Were not people on their knees before her? And when she was tired of tyrannising over Colombel in private, she would take a peculiar pleasure, when a number of others were present, in tripping him up, or in running a pin into his arm or leg, whilst at the same time she forbade him with a fierce glance of her black eyes to show even by the movement of an eyelid that she was to blame.

"Colombel bore his martyrdom with a dull resentment. Trembling, he kept his eyes on the ground, to escape the temptation to strangle his young mistress. And yet he did not dislike being beaten; it gave him a bitter delight. Sometimes, even, he actually sought for a blow, awaiting the pain with a peculiar thrill, and feeling a certain satisfaction in the smart when she pricked him with a pin."

I have now recounted a number of cases in which the perversions observed in adults can be traced back to early childhood. I have shown that it remains doubtful, when the specific perversion first makes its appearance, whether it results from a congenital predisposition which is merely aroused to activity by an outward stimulus, or whether the outward stimulus is also the true determinant. A further point has now to be considered, and it is one which, as far as I know, has hitherto been completely ignored in the literature of the subject. The majority of sexual perverts trace back the origin of their perversion to a time at which the detumescence impulse had not yet been awakened. Thus, the homosexual tells us of a peculiar impulse he felt in childhood to kiss his tutor; we learn from the hair-fetichist that when still a child he loved to play with girls' hair; and so on. And we are told that these impulses, voluptuously tinged, occurred at a time when erection and ejaculation had not yet taken place, and that there was not as yet any of that peripheral voluptuous sensation which can be clearly differentiated from the purely psychical voluptuous sensation. The question then arises, was this voluptuous sensation excited during childhood of a truly sexual nature at this early age? Was the boy's impulsive desire to kiss his tutor a sexual impulse? From the fact that later in life such an impulse is unmistakably sexual, the conclusion is often drawn that the earlier inclinations, and the pleasurable sensations associated with the corresponding mental processes, were also sexual. The inference is an obvious one, and is doubtless justified in many instances. But the following point must be taken into consideration. It is a fact that the psychosexual processes of the child are less sharply differentiated from other psychical processes than is the case in the adult; and it is therefore possible that the specific sexual perversions, and the specific sexual sensibility, develop out of a corresponding sensibility in the child which is not yet of a sexual character. The observation of Stanley Hall that children display a peculiar interest, not only in their own feet, but also in the feet of other persons, would appear to confirm this view. He writes: "Quite small children often display a marked fondness for stroking the feet of others, especially when these feet are well formed; and many adults testify to the persistence of such an impulse, whose gratification gives them a peculiar pleasure." It may readily be supposed, in many cases of foot-fetichism, that this unmistakably sexual phenomenon has originally developed out of such a non-sexual fondness for feet.

Unquestionably, many of the processes of childhood are not to be regarded as sexual, although they are closely related to the sexual life. This statement applies to many of the friendships between boys or between girls, such as are formed during the period in which the sexual impulse is still undifferentiated, or after its differentiation has occurred—and such friendships must not be identified with sexual feelings. At this period of life, we occasionally observe a desire in boys to form romantic friendships with others of their own sex; and the same is true also of girls. In many cases of this kind, there is no question of the presence of any sexual element, and we have no right, therefore, to regard as manifestations of the sexual impulse such instances of enthusiastic friendship during the period of undifferentiated sexual impulse. Each case must be separately analysed, in order to determine its nature. On the other hand, the sexual character of an inclination may sometimes be recognised in the early years of childhood, even in cases in which the boy's own genital organs are in no way involved. It may happen that a boy of eight will display a marked interest in the genital organs of youths or of men, and will seize every opportunity of peeping at them; and in such a case we are as a rule justified in assuming the existence of a homosexual tendency, even when there is no reflection of sexual disturbance to the boys own genital organs. But we must guard against the mistake of seeing a sexual element in every friendship between boys.

As with human beings, so also with the lower animals, it is not always possible to differentiate friendship from the sexual impulse. Robert Müller has collected a number of interesting observations bearing on this matter. He states that the so-called animal friendships, friendships between animals of different species, are in many cases determined by sexual feelings. He mentions the case of a dog ten months old, which made sexual attacks on hens, and thereby killed them; in another instance, a thorough-bred dog, two years old, exhibited a similar perversion, and had a lasting sexual relationship with a hen. He also quotes a case of which a man named P. Momsen was the witness, in which a gander attempted to pair with a bitch. These examples show that in the cases of animal friendship so often reported in the newspapers, the existence of an element of perverse sexuality is at least possible. But it does not, of course, follow that every strange animal friendship is of a sexual nature.

This is true, also, of other perversions—of sadism, for instance. The tendency to cruelty appears in early childhood, and it is only subsequently that this tendency becomes definitely associated with the sexual life. But even though this association (of cruelty with the sexual life) is demonstrable in so many instances, we are not for this reason justified in regarding every brutal act, all deliberate cruelty, as manifestations of sadism; and this reservation applies no less to adults than to children. Thus, delight in the sufferings of others, though it may be regarded as analogous with sadism, has no necessary connexion with the sexual impulse. Just as little can we assume that the deliberate ill-treatment of animals, whether on the part of children or on that of adults, is necessarily the outcome of sadism.

Felix Platter relates in his autobiography that when as a boy verging on maturity he had already chosen his future profession as a medical man, he came to the conclusion that he ought to accustom himself to the sight of disagreeable things; with this end in view, to habituate himself to see without emotion the heart and other viscera, he frequented the slaughter-house. Subsequently he experimented on a little bird, to ascertain if it had blood-vessels, and if it could be "bled"; he opened a vein with a penknife, and the little bird died. He did the same thing with various insects—stag-beetles, cock-chafers, and the like. Actions of this kind performed by children have, of course, no connexion with the sexual life. When a child tears off the feet of an insect, or mutilates any other animal, the motive is often simply that with which the same child will pull a watch to pieces. The same act may result from various motives; and for this reason we must guard against the misconception which might lead us, from every cruel act performed by a child, to diagnose the existence of sadism, or the certainty of a subsequent sadistic development.

In a case of rose-fetichism, which I have published elsewhere, the subject was a philologist, thirty years of age, who had never masturbated during his school days, and until he was nineteen or twenty had remained sexually neutral, experiencing sexual inclination neither towards females nor towards members of his own sex. But he had from an early age exhibited a very great interest in flowers, and while still a child used to kiss them. He is unable, however, to recall the existence in this connexion of any sexual excitement. When about twenty-one years old he was introduced to a young lady who at the time was wearing a large rose fastened into the front of her jacket. Henceforward, in his sexual sensibility, the rose assumed extraordinary importance. Whenever he was able, he bought roses, kissed them, and took them to bed with him. The act of kissing a rose induced an erection of the penis. In his seminal dreams, the image of the rose always played a leading part.

This case is extremely instructive. A great love for flowers, leading to the act of kissing, occurs in many children without any subsequent association, when these children have grown up, of sexual sentiments with flowers. Such persons will lay little stress on their memories of such occurrences in childhood—indeed, in adult life these incidents are for the most part forgotten. But to X., who when grown-up became affected with rose-fetichism as a sequel of a specific experience, it seems that his sexual fetichism is causally dependent upon his childish love of flowers—and probably he is right in so thinking. But we must not for this reason assume that his childish preference had any sexual character. It is more likely that the abnormally great fondness for flowers, beginning in childhood, was a favouring factor of the subsequent development of the rose-fetichism. What applies here to a pathological instance, may also be assumed to be true of the normal sexual life. That is to say, the experiences of childhood, which have not as yet any relationship with sexual life, are nevertheless of great significance in relation to the subsequent upbuilding of the sexual life, and above all in relation to the development of the psychosexual sentiments.

For the sake of completeness I must allude here to two additional processes which are also related to the sexual life of the child, viz., exhibitionism and skatophilia. As regards exhibitionism, Lasègue describes as exhibitionists those persons who display their genital organs to others from a certain distance, without attempting any other improper manipulations, and above all without making any endeavour to effect sexual intercourse. Kovalevsky contends that the tendency to exhibitionism is observed in the male sex especially during childhood at the approach of puberty, and in old age. He records the following case: "The headmistress of a boarding-school one day brought to see me a boy fourteen years of age, very well behaved and intelligent, who experienced from time to time an irresistible impulse, when he met one of the little girls of the school, to expose his penis. As a rule he was able to withstand this terrible impulse, but occasionally he yielded to it. He then experienced a sense of confusion in his head and his vision, and his whole body seemed to become tense, whilst at the same time he experienced a voluptuous sensation in the penis and in the body generally. This state lasted for one or two minutes, and was succeeded by a moderate sense of weakness and a very distressing sense of shame. The acts of exhibition were never accompanied with seminal emission, although he sometimes had such emissions during the night." I have myself hardly ever observed this form of exhibitionism in children. Somewhat commoner, however, is the mutual and perfectly voluntary exhibition of their genital organs by children, generally boys and girls together; in these cases, as previously explained, the acts are determined rather by curiosity than by the sexual impulse. It is necessary to insist upon this fact, as distinguishing exhibitionism in children from exhibitionism in adults. A like question arises regarding the skatological inclinations and interests of children, which are assumed by Havelock Ellis to be intimately connected with the sexual life. It is an undoubted fact that many children before puberty are greatly interested in the excretions from the bladder and the intestine. Stanley Hall, to whom Havelock Ellis refers, is of opinion that "micturitional obscenities, which our returns show to be so common before adolescence, culminate at ten or twelve, and seem to retreat into the background as sex-phenomena appear." He distinguishes between two classes of cases: "fouling persons or things, secretly from adults, but openly with each other," and, less often, "ceremonial acts, connected with the act or the product, that almost suggest the skatological rites of savages." I can myself, as a result of numerous inquiries, confirm the existence of skatophilia in children. But I have not yet been able to satisfy myself that these processes always, or even usually, have any connexion with the sexual life. Such a connexion unquestionably exists in some cases, but no less certainly it is not an invariable one. Skatological acts—those, that is to say, in which the more

disgusting excreta play a part—arise in some instances out of a masochistic mode of sensibility. In cases in which adult masochists have such inclinations, it is often impossible to trace their existence back into childhood. It rather appears, in most of the instances of skatological inclinations which have come under my own observation, that these inclinations have been superimposed upon other masochistic tendencies, and these latter may sometimes be traced back to the days of childhood. But in a few cases I have found skatological perversions to have originated very early in life. A man with a university education, with an inclination to the practice of cunnilinctus, assured me that this inclination began in childhood. Another man, whose interest in the female nates and anus was unquestionably not the result of any excesses, stated positively that he was able to refer the origin of this inclination to a definite experience of his childhood. When only seven years of age, he experienced the impulse to look at the nates of a servant-maid; and he believes that this inclination, which in his case was certainly generalised at a very early age, arose from a still earlier experience, viz., the chance sight of his mother's nates, when she urinated in his presence. His whole account of the matter suggests the existence of a fetishism directed to the nates, impelling him to the most disgusting acts, which he has several times performed. A similar case, but on a homosexual basis, will be found recorded as Case 20 in my work on Sexual Inversion.

No detailed account of other pathological manifestations of the sexual life will now be attempted, since this work professes to deal only with subjects of a wide and general significance. We cannot consider those cases, for instance, in which there is developmental defect of the reproductive organs; those, for example, in which there is no discoverable development of the reproductive glands. But some reference may be made to hermaphroditism. In the human species true hermaphroditism is a very rare occurrence, whereas apparent hermaphroditism, the so-called pseudo-hermaphroditism, is comparatively frequent. The sexual life of pseudo-hermaphrodites has in some instances been very carefully studied, more especially with reference to the relationship of pseudo-hermaphroditism to the direction of the sexual impulse. It appears that in a number of cases of pseudo-hermaphroditism, not only did the secondary sexual characters exhibit an inverted or contrary sexual development, but the sexual impulse was also

inverted—was directed, that is to say, towards individuals of the same sex as that to which the pseudo-hermaphrodite really belonged. Beyond question, cases have been observed in which pseudo-hermaphrodites with testicles have had sexual inclination towards males; and pseudo-hermaphrodites with ovaries, sexual inclination towards females. In many of these cases, such contrary sexual tendencies could be traced back into childhood. We have, of course, to reckon with the fact that in the case of pseudo-hermaphrodites the diagnosis of the sex is usually based upon the formation of the external genital organs, and without any expert examination of the reproductive glands; thus they are often brought up as members of a sex to which they do not really belong, and in consequence of this their education is sexually inverted. In such cases it may reasonably be suggested that the homosexuality is the result, not so much of a congenital inversion of the sexual impulse, as of the contrary sexual education.

For a detailed treatment of the subject of hermaphroditism, reference should be made to the special literature of the subject, and above all to the exhaustive and laborious work of Neugebauer.

CHAPTER VI

ETIOLOGY AND DIAGNOSIS

The last chapter dealt with pathological phenomena in the sexual life of the child. From the considerations urged in this and in earlier chapters, it will have become apparent that sexual manifestations in childhood are not necessarily to be regarded as pathological. This conclusion does not conflict with the assumption that certain factors influence the sexual life of the child. The numerous individual differences suffice to indicate the existence of such factors. Many of these are of a pathological character, but others have no connexion with the domain of pathology. Among the factors thus influencing the sexual life of the child, we can distinguish those affecting the germinal rudiments from those which exercise their influence later. Those of the former group first demand our attention.

In certain families, the early awakening of sexuality is observed with remarkable frequency. These are often neuropathic or psychopathic families, and moreover the early awakening of the sexual life is frequently associated with neuropathic or psychopathic symptoms. But this is by no means always the case, and often enough such persons belong to healthy families and are themselves healthy. We are therefore not entitled to regard the occurrence of sexual manifestations in childhood as a proof of degeneration or of a morbid inheritance. But equally erroneous is the opposite view, that the early awakening of sexuality is an indication of exceptional endowments. It is true that in many persons of genius premature sexual passion has been observed, and such manifestations are by no means always confined to the contrectation impulse. We learn, too, in our consulting rooms, that not infrequently the most diligent schoolboys exhibit at a comparatively early age the phenomena alike of contrectation and of detumescence. But the fallacy of drawing general conclusions from this fact is shown by the additional fact that in idiots and imbeciles premature awakening of the sexual life is also of common occurrence. In cases such as were formerly described as moral insanity, but which in Germany to-day are classed with imbecility, sexual assaults on others are very common at an early age. This is true also of other forms of idiocy and imbecility. In asylums for such patients, feeble-minded children not infrequently make sexual attempts on nurses and on other inmates. In this connexion, we have to consider both components of the sexual impulse, the phenomena of contrectation as well as those of detumescence. In the case of low-grade idiots, we often see the phenomena of pure detumescence, without the accompaniment of any sexual inclination directed towards another person; this is simply physical masturbation, performed under the promptings of an organic impulse. But not only in imbeciles and idiots, and in persons of genius, but also in those with perfectly normal mental endowments, the sexual impulse, and more especially the phenomena of contrectation, may appear at a very early age. Persons with artistic tendencies develop in this way with comparative frequency. We must, for these reasons, guard against the misconception that the early awakening of sexuality is per se pathological. The fact that the study of the sexual life has been undertaken chiefly by medical men, and above all by neurologists and alienists, has inevitably introduced a certain bias into the results of the investigation. Opportunities for the study of the sexual life of normal persons have been comparatively rare; for those in whom the early awakening of sexuality has been recorded have for the most part sought medical advice and treatment for some other reason, and the physician has taken the opportunity to make inquiries into the patient's sexual history. The boundary-line between what is pathological and what is normal can be determined only by an extended study of the sexual life in normal persons. By very numerous inquiries I have done my best to effect this; and a careful examination of the accumulated material leads to the above-mentioned conclusion, that an early awakening of the sexual life is commoner in those with an abnormal nervous system than it is in healthy persons: but it also appears that an abnormal sensitiveness of a non-pathological character, such as is exhibited by persons with the artistic temperament, and likewise a disposition excitable to a degree which cannot yet be called morbid, predispose the subjects to an early awakening of sexuality.

To attain to clear views on this question, it is necessary to bear certain distinctions in mind: first, as regards the different periods of childhood; and, secondly, as regards the two components of the sexual impulse (detumescence and contrectation). My own investigations have led me to draw the following conclusions. During the first period of childhood, that is to say, up to the end of the seventh year of life, the occurrence of manifestations of the sexual impulse must arouse suspicions of the existence of a congenital morbid predisposition. But as regards the phenomena of detumescence, which are confined to the peripheral genital organs, we must make an exception to this rule if they do not appear spontaneously, but result either from local inflammatory or other morbid changes, or from deliberate seduction of the child to the performance of sexual manipulations; at any rate, in such cases, the probability of the existence of congenital morbid predisposition is greatly diminished. I am also forced to regard as suspicious the occurrence of phenomena of contrectation during the first period of childhood, although not to the same extent as are the peripheral manifestation of the sexual impulse—and I hold this view notwithstanding the numerous cases recorded by Sanford Bell. Passing to the second period of childhood, the phenomena of contrectation may appear at the very beginning of this period, that is, during the eighth year of life, without justifying the inference that any morbid predisposition exists. Regarding the phenomena of detumescence, we must not hold them to be necessarily morbid when they make their appearance during the last years of the second period of childhood; but when this occurs earlier, during the tenth or eleventh year of life for instance, some suspicion may reasonably be aroused. In this general survey of the material, it did not appear that any important difference existed between the two sexes in the matters under consideration; but I believe that in girls the phenomena of contrectation often make their appearance somewhat earlier than in boys, whereas, on the other hand, the occurrence of the phenomena of detumescence at an early age is more likely to indicate the existence of congenital morbid predisposition in girls than it is in boys.

In the delimitation of the pathological from the healthy, I have endeavoured to lay down broad general lines. It must not be supposed that precisely at the close of the first period of childhood, that is to say, at the end of the seventh year of life, the sexual life, and our opinions as to the significance of its manifestations, undergo sudden alterations. Our estimates as to the significance of phenomena occurring during the early months of the eighth year of life, will not differ materially from our estimates as to the significance of the same phenomena when they occur during the last months of the seventh year. My conclusions have no more than a general application, based as they are on the recorded experiences and on my own personal observations of numerous persons, healthy and diseased.

Let us consider further what are the factors favouring an early awakening of the sexual life. I have previously mentioned the fact that in certain families a remarkably early sexual development is quite common. This is true also of certain races. But the data bearing on this question are not quite so trustworthy as might be wished. The fact that among certain nations marriage sometimes takes place at a remarkably early age, is no certain proof of the early awakening of sexuality in persons of this nationality; for the marriage may be a purely ceremonial affair, and may be effected long before the individual is ripe for sexual intercourse or for procreation; and the first act of intercourse may not take place until several years after the ceremony of marriage. Among ourselves, marriage, especially in the case of men, does not as a rule take place until long after the age of puberty, and it therefore seems to us very remarkable when, in another race, men marry ten years earlier; but this must not be taken as a proof that sexual development occurs at an earlier age. We can gain some knowledge of the subject from the statistical inquiries which have been made regarding the appearance of that manifestation of puberty which is most readily available for such inquiries, namely, the first occurrence of menstruation. Ribbing has made a study of this question, and gives the following figures regarding the commencement of menstruation in women of different nationalities in various places: Swedish Lapland, 18 years; Christiania, 16 years, 9 months, 25 days; Berlin, 15 years, 7 months, 6 days; Paris 15 years, 7 months, 18 days, and 14 years, 5 months, and 17 days; Madeira, 14 years, 3 months; Sierra Leone and Egypt, 10 years. From these data we should naturally he led to infer that there would be great variations in the age at which other manifestations of the sexual life first make their appearance, and experience justifies this inference.

Some writers attribute to climate a great influence in this respect; whilst others regard this view as erroneous, and believe that the differences observed depend rather on racial peculiarities. By advocates of the former view it is assumed that a hot climate leads to the early appearance of menstruation, whilst a cold climate retards the development of this function. Those who dispute the influence of climate bring forward instances of a contrary kind. Thus, among the Samoyede Eskimos, menstruation begins at the age of twelve or thirteen, notwithstanding the fact that they dwell within the Arctic circle; whereas, among the Danes and the Swedes, menstruation begins at about the age of sixteen or seventeen years. Again, we are told that among the Creoles of the Antilles, as in France, menstruation rarely begins before the fourteenth year, whilst in the same islands, girls of African race begin to menstruate, as in Africa, at ten or eleven years of age. These objections to the climatic theory are certainly serious ones. But when we are considering the possible influence of climate upon menstruation, we have to remember that it is possible that climate may exert its influence cumulatively in successive generations, and may not produce its full effect upon the age at which menstruation begins, until after the lapse of several generations. We certainly lack evidence to show that in isolated individuals a change of climate affects the first appearance of menstruation. But it is not impossible that climate may exert such an influence in the course of several generations. Such a view would appear to receive support from our observations on animals, for the sexual life of the latter is notably influenced by the seasons, and change of season resembles in many respects change of climate. In most animals, and more especially in those living in a state of nature, the sexual impulse becomes active at stated intervals only, and these intervals are related to the duration of pregnancy in such a way that the birth of the young occurs always at a season in which the nutritive conditions are favourable. It is widely assumed that even in the human species there remain vestiges of such a periodicity in the sexual impulse. I have discussed this matter very fully elsewhere, and will here do no more than draw attention to the fact that the poetry of spring, which sings partly of love alone, and partly of the relations between love and the annual awakening of nature, bears upon the influence of this season of the year upon the sexual impulse. It seems that the spring also exerts an influence upon the love-sentiments of the child. It is possible that suggestion here plays a certain part, inasmuch as from childhood onwards poetry and many observations teach that there is a connexion between love and the season of spring. Sanford Bell considers that the importance of spring in this connexion depends on the fact that at this season children begin to meet one another in the open, subject to less restraint, and perhaps more frequently. But he does not exclude the possible existence of an inherited vestige of periodicity in the sexual impulse.

It is widely assumed that among the higher social classes the awakening of the sexual life occurs earlier than among the lower. But it can hardly be said that trustworthy statistics exist to illustrate this point; and the most we can admit is that it may be true of the commencement of menstruation —though even here the data available hardly suffice to afford proof of the thesis. It is said that in girls of the upper classes menstruation begins on the average at an earlier age than in girls of the lower classes; and also that menstruation begins earlier in towns than in the country. Rousseau asserted this long ago, taking his facts from Buffon, who attributed the fact to the sparer and poorer fare of the country folk. Rousseau, while admitting that menstruation began later in the country districts, considered that diet had nothing to do with the matter, since even where (as in Valais) the peasants enjoyed a liberal fare, puberty, in both sexes, occurred later than in the majority of towns, in which an excessively rich diet was often customary. He believed that the difference between town and country in this respect depended rather upon the more enduring repose of the imagination in the country, this latter itself arising from the greater fixity of customs in the rural districts. Speaking generally, however, the question whether in the country the sexual life awakens later than it does in the towns, cannot be said to have been decisively answered.

Closely connected with the question of the alleged later awakening of the sexual life in the country is the belief that in the country children are also more moral and remain longer uncorrupted.

I myself do not believe that children are more moral in the country, or that they here remain longer uncorrupted than in towns, whether large or small. Nor is it proved that in former times the country possessed any advantage in these respects, as compared with our own days and with the modern town. The entire fable of rural innocence appears to rest, not upon an actual comparison between town and country, but rather upon the more lively interest felt in town life, and especially in the life of the great towns: in towns, immorality has been more carefully studied and more often described; and on account of the greater concentration of town life, it is also more readily apparent. But any one who studies erotic literature and descriptions of manners and customs, at any rate, anyone who studies these without prejudice, will find ample ground for the opinion that even in earlier times morality stood in the country on no higher level than in the towns. The opinion that country life was more moral has existed from very early times, and it is interesting to observe the way in which in erotic literature we at times encounter a satirical use of this fact, describing the painful disillusionment of a man who has hoped to find perfect innocence in his loved one from the country, and has been bitterly disappointed.

I do not propose to give numerous examples of rural immorality in earlier times; two will suffice, both dating from the eighteenth century, and both bearing on the seduction of children. Laukhard, born in the year 1758, at Wendelsheim, in the Lower Palatinate, tells us how, when six years of age, he was introduced by a manservant into the secrets of the sexual life, so that he was speedily in a position "to take part, with consummate ability and to the admiration of all, in the most shameless lewd sports and conversations of the menials of the household." And Laukhard adds in a note that, in the Palatinate, obscenity was so universal, and among the common people the general conversation was so utterly shameless, that a Prussian grenadier would have blushed on hearing the foul talk of the Jacks and Gills of the Palatinate. He also relates that he soon found an opportunity of practising with one of the servant-girls what the manservant who had been his instructor had extolled to him as the non plus ultra of the higher knowledge. If we compare with this the descriptions given by Rétif de la Bretonne, who was born in the year 1734 in the village of Sacy in Lower Burgundy, and was the son of a well-to-do peasant, and if we study a number of similar accounts of country life, we shall hardly be inclined to take a very roseate view regarding rural morals in former days. We learn from Rétif, that while still quite a little boy, only four years of age, he had the most diverse sexual experiences with a grown-up girl, Marie Piôt, after she had induced an erection of his penis by tickling his genital organs. These and numerous similar accounts, which we find in the works of writers of previous centuries, are not likely to sustain the conviction that rural morals were formerly distinguished by exceptional purity.

But if this claim must be disputed as regards rural life in former times, it is still more certain that we must deny that to-day a higher moral level obtains in the country than in the towns, and this is true above all as regards children. It is certain that sexual activity in children does not begin later in the country. My views as to present conditions in the country are derived mainly from information directly communicated to myself. From a number of grown-up persons, now residing in the metropolis, but born and bred in the country, I have received details of their own early sexual experiences. I have in addition had opportunities for direct personal inquiries in rural districts and in the smaller country towns. Lastly, I have received reports voluntarily furnished to me by persons still residing in the country. Combining all these sources of information, I am justified in asserting that in the country sexual practices among children are of exceedingly common occurrence.

Just as the recent increasing development of large towns has been regarded as responsible for immorality and for premature sexual activities in children, so also has modern civilisation in general been blamed for the same results. There has always existed a tendency to depreciate the morals of contemporary periods, and to exalt in comparison the morals of an earlier day. In books of earlier generations, in those, for instance, which appeared between the middle of the eighteenth century and the middle of the nineteenth century, we find, just as we find in the writings of our own day, lamentations upon existing corruption, especially as regards the morals of children, and panegyrics upon the morality of an earlier time. But when we examine the documents of the past, we find adequate proof of the fact that morals stood at no higher level in former times than to-day, and, more particularly, we learn that the sexual morals of children were no better then than now. If this were otherwise, how could we explain the fact that, in the year 1527, for instance, the Town Council of Ulm issued an order to the brothel-keepers of that town that they were no longer to admit to the brothels boys of from twelve to fourteen years of age, but rather were to drive them away with birch-rods. This fact, with many others, is recorded by Hans Boesch; and collectively they suffice to prove, not merely that the children of former times were no whit more moral than those of our own day, but also that the awakening of sexual activity occurred just as early then as now.

But although I contest the alleged general influence of the life of large towns and of modern civilisation upon the morality and the sexual activities of children, I admit at once that peculiar conditions of place and time may exert a great influence in these respects. Frequently, no detailed analysis of these conditions is possible; but sometimes such an analysis can be effected. Only by the assumption that these special influences exist can we understand how it is that such marked differences exist at different times in the same place. I know certain schools in Berlin in which masturbation, and even mutual masturbation, are widely diffused; and I know others regarding which in this respect no unfavourable reports can be made. I know, indeed, of schools about which I have received from former pupils, persons whose trustworthiness I have absolutely no reason to doubt, reports which prove that a remarkably high level of sexual morality must have existed in these schools. On the other hand, ex-pupils of other schools, attended by boys of very various classes of the population, have informed me that at these schools there was hardly a boy who did not masturbate. It is not always possible to ascertain the causes of such differences. One child, perhaps, may corrupt an entire class. But I believe also that the influence of the schoolmasters, and especially that of the headmaster, may be of enormous importance in this respect. Similar differences exist in the country. It is even believed by some that there are differences between the Catholic and Protestant inhabitants of the rural districts. How extensive may be the differences even within a comparatively small area, is shown by an example, which I will quote, from C. Wagner. One of the districts studied by him was the Province of Jagst in Würtemberg, and he reports that there is a striking difference between the Alt-Würtemberg and the Franconian districts. The report states that in the former district the greater number of parents appear to recognise it as their sacred duty to bring up their children properly and to watch over their development. Moral depravity could not be said to be general among the children of this region. Very different was it in the Franconian districts, in which not only were the children cared for much less perfectly, but in which also "the children saw and heard much too early things which impair or destroy the innocence and purity of the heart." We are told that shamelessness in the satisfaction of natural needs was general; some cases of self-abuse were reported; and obscene and lascivious conversation was common. The causes assigned for this in the report are: overcrowding in the dwellings, there being in some cases but a single bed for children of school age of different sexes; also that children had been present when cattle were performing the sexual act. Often in the country we are told that children have been corrupted by grown persons, through sleeping in the same bed with the latter.

What has just been said bears upon the influences which at the opening of this chapter I classed with the second group of the influences affecting the sexual life of the child, namely, those that come into play only after birth. But whatever degree of importance we may attribute to these, it cannot be doubted that congenital predisposition plays a very important part in inducing an early awakening of the sexual life. What we see in this case is similar to what happens in respect of other qualities than the sexual. Some persons are congenitally predisposed to a one-sided development; and in some persons there occurs a phenomenally early development of certain particular talents. It will suffice to remind the reader of children who while still quite young can perform extraordinary arithmetical operations, and of those who at six or seven years of age can play beautifully on the piano or some other instrument. In these latter cases the most important feature is the congenital predisposition, but this predisposition has, of course, to be aroused to activity; and the same is true in the case of the sexual impulse. This explains why it is that the most careful education often fails to prevent the premature commencement of the amatory life; and it explains also, on the other hand, why it is that even in the most unfavourable circumstances, sexual phenomena do not always make their appearance during childhood. I know of persons who have passed the years of childhood in a brothel, amid surroundings obviously calculated to turn their attention to sexuality, but in whom nevertheless during childhood no development of the sexual life appeared to have occurred. The popular saying, "What is bred in the bone will not out of the flesh," may be to some degree an overstatement, but nevertheless corresponds to the actual facts. But we must not go to the other extreme, and refuse to recognise the importance of the influences surrounding the developing child. We must bear in mind that congenital predispositions vary in strength; and a little reflection will convince us that the awakening of the sexual life will be hindered by a favourable environment, but facilitated and accelerated by an unfavourable one. In cases of seduction, the congenital predisposition often plays no more than a secondary part. Sexual acts in childhood resulting from seduction often exhibit a merely imitative character, and do not appear to proceed from an organically conditioned impulse; in such cases the sexual malpractices are often discontinued when the seducing influence is withdrawn; but if this influence is exercised persistently and systematically, it may have a permanent effect even in cases in which the congenital predisposition is slight.

This is all I have to say about the relationship between the congenital predisposition and the external influences of life. Turning now to consider these influences by themselves, we have to distinguish between those that are somatic or physical and those that are psychical in nature. Influences of these two classes may co-operate simultaneously, or may pass one into the other; and, speaking generally, it is by no means always easy to maintain a sharp distinction between them.

Seduction may in some instances arise largely by way of physical stimulation, as, for example, when another person deliberately handles the genital organs of a child. Nurses sometimes stroke or tickle a child's genitals in order to put an end to a screaming fit. But in some cases—and these are more numerous than is commonly supposed—nursemaids do this under the impulse of their own lustful feelings. Such actions are not necessarily the outcome of a perverse sexual impulse, although they may be due to such an impulse in the form of pædophilia, as I shall have to explain in detail when I come to describe that perversion. Frequently the offenders are not in the least aware of the danger of what they are doing, and do it merely in sport. In many instances the seduction is effected by other children, and often at a very early age. Recently a case was reported to me in which a boy only five years of age led older children astray. In schools, a closet used by both boys and girls is by many considered extremely dangerous. In the country, the fact that children have a long way to go to school often gives opportunity for improper conduct; and this is especially likely to occur if there are copses near the road in which the children can conceal themselves from observation. When children in the country traverse long distances on the way to preparatory confirmation classes, misconduct is exceptionally likely, for such children are now at an age at which the activity of the sexual life is becoming more manifest. Whether the seduction be the work of other children or of adults, the child thus led astray is likely subsequently to induce artificially as often as possible the agreeable sensations with which it has now been made acquainted, more especially in view of the fact that in children the imitative impulse is far more strongly developed than it is in adults, in whom imitative inclinations are counteracted by numerous inhibitions. What is true of seduction is true also of the various affections of the genital organs which induce an impulse to scratch, such as eczema, prurigo, urticaria,

&c. Affections of regions adjoining the genital organs may also lead to similar troubles—for instance, threadworms in the rectum or the vagina.

Clothing, also, especially in boys the breeches, may give rise during childhood to unwholesome stimulation. Hufeland, in his Makrobiotik, long ago advised against the wearing of breeches by little boys. The Schaumburg-Lippe body-physician, Faust, in a work published in the year 1791, strongly recommended that boys should not wear breeches. Frequently the climbing of the pole in the gymnasium is regarded as being the etiological factor in the induction of premature masturbation. Experience shows that occasionally the first voluptuous sensations do actually arise during the act of climbing the pole. A similar report is made also in regard to the climbing of trees and of gymnastic exercises on the parallel and horizontal bars. It is obvious that pressure on the genital organs will very readily arise in these ways. But cases are reported in which the child experiences sexual excitement from exercising on the horizontal bar, not when he is straddling the bar, but when he is hanging to it by the hands. It must in these cases remain doubtful whether the sexual excitement results from the pressure of the breeches, or is a direct result of the hanging posture. Where pressure is exerted on the genital organs, it is not always the strength of the stimulus which is most significant. A nursemaid may do much more harm by gently tickling a child's genital organs than by pressing them forcibly. Nor have we to think only of the quality of the stimulus, but also of its newness; for an unfamiliar stimulus may cause sexual excitement simply because it is unfamiliar. Various stimuli have to be considered, in addition to those previously enumerated. I may refer here to flagellation. It is well known that in many children the first experience of sexual excitement results from a whipping; indeed, a perverse mode of sexual sensibility lasting throughout the whole of life may thus originate. I shall return to this matter in the chapter on Sexual Education. I will merely refer here to certain other stimuli which have in many cases aroused sexual excitement for the first time. Penta reports the case of a girl twelve years of age who first experienced sexual excitement during a railway journey. Certain men have informed me that they became sexually excited for the first time while driving over a rough stone pavement. It is obvious in these cases that the rapidly repeated succussion stimulates the peripheral genital organs, and that in this way sexual sensibility is awakened. Havelock Ellis reports cases in which boys first experienced sexual pleasure when wrestling. Thus, a physician wrote regarding a boy of twelve or thirteen, that he experienced an extraordinarily pleasant sensation whilst wrestling with another boy, and that thenceforward he sought every opportunity to wrestle, often three or four times daily, and continued to do this until he was nearly nineteen years of ago. Whilst in this instance we are told that contact of the penis with the opponent's hips was effected, and that probably the sexual excitement was induced in this manner, I must point out that a masochistic-sadistic form of excitement may also result from wrestling, and that it is to this that we must refer the sexual desires and voluptuous sensations that are aroused in many males by the act of wrestling.

Chemical stimuli must be regarded as a sub-variety of physical stimuli. It is sometimes asserted that a diet too rich in meat or otherwise too stimulating is dangerous in this regard. But an examination of the available material will show that this opinion lacks foundation. There is no proof that the sexual impulse can be prematurely awakened by a meat diet, or by any other particular diet. I cannot regard such an assertion as proved even as regards alcohol. Although I hold very strongly that no alcohol should be given to children, this is not because there is any proof that in children to whom alcohol is given the awakening of the sexual impulse occurs earlier than in others. But once the awakening of the sexual life has taken place, it is true that alcohol may have an exciting influence, and this in two different ways. On the one hand, if so much alcohol is taken as to interfere with the natural psychical inhibitions, sexual practices may occur that would not otherwise have occurred. On the other hand, also large quantities of alcohol may often induce an after-effect, after the intoxicating effects have completely passed away, manifesting itself, it may be, in the form of sexual excitement, but also, and chiefly, in the form of common sensations in the genital organs. To complete the account of this matter it is necessary to add that there are many persons who consume large quantities of alcohol, who yet are extremely moderate in sexual relationships. But alcohol should not be administered to children, for reasons altogether independent of its influence upon the sexual life.

Psychical stimuli are perhaps even more important than physical stimuli. Here also seduction has to be considered, especially during the second period of childhood, in which danger may arise from playmates or school-fellows. This applies equally to children of either sex. Danger may also arise from adults, not only through systematic seduction on the part of grown persons who deliberately debase the mind of youth, but also in other ways. The conversations of adults often lead to sexual acts on the part of children, who understand far more of what is said in their presence than grownups commonly believe. While the child is to all appearance immersed in a book, while a girl is playing with her doll, or a boy with his tin soldiers, the parents or some other adults carry on a conversation in the child's presence under the influence of an utterly false belief that the latter's occupation engrosses his or her entire attention. Yet many children, in such cases, are listening to what is being said with all their ears. Especially foolish, however, are those parents who believe that by the employment of innuendo they are able to conceal from any children who may be present the true inwardness of their conversation. In these matters children are as a rule far sharper than their elders are accustomed to believe. It is hardly necessary for me to point out that opportunities for direct observation are especially dangerous to children. I allude more particularly to the case of children living in the same house with prostitutes; but the danger is hardly less when the children have an opportunity of observing their own parents engaged in sexual acts, or even in the mere preparation for such acts. Forel quotes the report of an experienced physician to the effect that the children of peasants who have watched the copulation of animals often attempt to perform such acts with one another, when bathing, or when any other opportunity offers.

In the preceding portions of this chapter I have attempted to distinguish individual influences from general influences, to distinguish congenital influences affecting the germinal rudiments from environmental influences acting after birth, and to distinguish psychical stimuli from physical stimuli. But it is obvious that the maintenance of a sharp distinction in these respects is very difficult, and indeed often quite impossible. A few additional considerations will elucidate this statement. Let us consider, for instance, seduction: here the separation of the psychical from the physical element cannot possibly be effected, because, as a rule, in these cases the two elements co-operate simultaneously. Let us consider the cases in which, owing to a congenital racial peculiarity, the sexual life awakens earlier than is usual among ourselves. In such cases, the manners and customs of the race in which this early development of sexuality is usual will be found to be especially adapted to attract the child's attention to sexual matters earlier than is here customary. It suffices to remind the reader of the celebrations of puberty and of the early marriages common among such races. Here it is hardly possible to separate the congenital characters from the effects of environment. But although, for the reasons given, the discrimination between the individual factors may be exceedingly difficult, still an attempt at discrimination must be made, more especially in view of the fact that a purposive sexual education can be attempted only when due consideration has been paid to the various etiological factors.

It would naturally be of the utmost importance to be able to foresee the cases in which it is likely that the sexual processes of childhood would undergo an exceptionally early development. But as a rule we are unable to do this; and we must therefore be satisfied with the attempt to determine in individual cases whether manifestations of the sexual life occur during childhood, and if so, which manifestations. But even here we encounter difficulties, which in many instances are insuperable, but in others arise from the incompetence of adults. This is all the more deplorable because the effectiveness of sexual education is minimised through the lack of insight. Just as in the practice of medicine an accurate diagnosis is an indispensable prerequisite to correct therapeutics, so also here. Since in the earliest years the child has no conscious understanding of sexual processes, whilst children in whom a sexual consciousness has begun to dawn conceal most carefully from their elders all manifestations of their sexual life, diagnosis is possible only through knowledge of mankind in conjunction with tact.

Let us first consider the phenomena of contrectation. We shall notice sometimes that a little boy, perhaps seven years of age or even younger, will withdraw from the society of other boys, and will seek the company of some particular individual, for example that of a girl friend of his sister, of about his own age. Similar phenomena occur in girls. A little girl in her tenth year will frequently be noticed to find something to speak to her mother about whenever a particular male friend of the family visits the house. Even a shrewd and observant mother will often fail to take note of the reason why on these occasions her little daughter invariably comes into the room. The child will have every possible kind of excuse ready to enable her to seek the company of this particular person. At times this goes further. We then notice that the child endeavours to come into physical contact with the object of affection, showing him great tenderness, and showering on him caresses.

Such a desire for intimate physical caresses must always arouse the suspicion that sexual feelings have now been awakened. We must not, of course, assume that every childish caress is sexually determined; but we should always bear in mind this possibility in cases in which the child's desire to caress someone is well marked. If such feelings manifest themselves towards the end of the first period of childhood or at the beginning of the second, observation will be comparatively easy, for the younger the child is the less competent is it to conceal its feelings. The consciousness that there is anything wrong in the gratification of such sentiments awakens as a rule very gradually indeed.

Similarly, it will be far easier in the case of children to observe peripheral processes in the genital organs than it is to make such observations in adults. Thus, even in the case of infants in arms, but more often in the case of boys who are somewhat older, the mother or the nurse may be surprised to observe erections when the boy is undressed for his bath or some other reason, or when he has kicked off the bedclothes at night. In other cases the child may be seen handling his genital organs, either openly or beneath his clothing. Often, in the absence of manual stimulation, the child adopts some other means of stimulating his genital organs. Thus, in girls the legs will be crossed, and the thighs rubbed lightly each against the other. In other cases, both in boys and in girls, the child will lean against a piece of furniture in what appears to be a perfectly innocent manner; but in reality pressure is being exercised on the genital organs, it may be by the corner of a table, it may be by the back of a chair; and then the stimulus is strengthened by various movements. In some such way children will effect masturbatory stimulation and obtain sexual gratification, in the presence, not only of their mother, but in that of quite a number of other persons. Guttceit reports the case of a woman who squatted down so that her bare heel came into contact with the genitals, and she then masturbated by rubbing the two parts together. I myself have known the case of a young girl who sat with her legs beneath her, and masturbated with the boot she was wearing. In many instances we are enabled, by watching the child's movements, to ascertain with such certainty what it is doing, that no confirmatory evidence is needed. We notice, especially, that when the orgasm is approaching, the movements change in character and rhythm. The eyes become bright, and the face assumes an excited and voluptuous expression. This may be observed even in infants in arms. Townsend reports the case of an infant, eight months old, "who would cross her right thigh over the left, close her eyes and clench her fists; after a minute or two there would be complete relaxation, with sweating and redness of face; this would occur about once a week or oftener; the child was quite healthy, with no abnormal condition of the genital organs."

In the absence of these definite indications, it is necessary to be cautious in coming to a diagnosis. Failing such caution, mistakes which may entail serious consequences are likely to arise. Two cases are known to me in which, after suspicion had rightly or wrongly been aroused, the child's most harmless movements were regarded as masturbatory in character. If a child becomes aware that its mother or some other person in authority is making such a mistake, the effect will naturally be very unfavourable. We have also to reckon with the fact that children who are somewhat older, from eight or nine years upwards, hardly ever masturbate when others are present, but only when they believe themselves to be unobserved—in bed, in the closet, or when out walking. In such cases it is hardly possible to diagnose masturbation with certainty; more especially in view of the fact that the signs that may betray an older boy—stains on the shirt or other articles of underclothing—are usually lacking during the first two periods of childhood. It must be added that such stains on linen resulting from ejaculation do not at first contain spermatozoa, and for this reason their diagnostic value is greatly lessened. Still, the possible appearance of these stains is a matter to which attention should always be paid, and this in girls as well as in boys. In many instances, also, our diagnosis may be supported by the discovery of articles used for onanistic purposes. In the case of boys we shall seldom, comparatively speaking, be able to do this; although, even in boys, operation is sometimes needed for the removal of articles used for onanistic purposes, which have found their way into the urethra or the bladder. In girls, such operations are more frequently required. Hairpins, pencils, and various other articles used for onanistic purposes, are from time to time removed from the vagina or the female bladder. Other signs that are supposed to indicate the habitual practice of masturbation are of little diagnostic value. It is traditionally held that masturbation in girls leads to elongation of the clitoris, but there appears to be no warrant in fact for this opinion. As I have previously pointed out, laceration of the hymen does not in general result from masturbation. Other signs, such as local irritation or swelling, are hardly ever seen in boys, and in girls are seen only in cases in which they masturbate to excess. In girls, moderate reddening of the external genital organs has no significance whatever; and I take this opportunity of giving a special warning against inferring from the existence of such reddening that masturbation is practised, and also against attaching any importance to this symptom in a case in which a sexual assault is supposed to have been committed on a little girl.

Certain other signs which have been believed to support a diagnosis of masturbation, do not even justify suspicion. Among these reputed signs may be mentioned: black lines under the eyes, pallor of the cheeks, inflammation of the eyes, &c. Generally speaking, it must be said that in sexually immature children nothing but direct observation will justify a definite diagnosis of masturbation, except in cases in which the child itself makes confession to someone in its confidence. For the diagnosis of auto-erotism, however, it is not necessary to establish the occurrence in the child of the voluptuous acme; it suffices for this diagnosis if there occur signs of those general voluptuous sensations which were described earlier. In many cases in which the practice of masturbation is diagnosed, and in cases in which children themselves confess to masturbating thirty times a day or more, we can hardly suppose that the voluptuous acme or orgasm is attained.

It is sometimes maintained that the early appearance of the physical manifestations of puberty is an indication that psychosexual processes are also occurring prematurely. Thus, Kisch expresses the opinion that in many cases premature sexual development manifests itself in children by the enlargement of the breasts, and by the growth of the axillary and pubic hair, in the absence of the commencement of menstruation, Kussmaul also observed cases in which, in comparatively early girlhood, all the physical signs of puberty were present although menstruation had not yet begun. According to my own experience, we must be careful to avoid taking an exaggerated view of such a connexion. Passionate psychosexual processes may occur in young children in the absence of any physical signs of premature sexual development. An impulse to masturbate may also arise quite independently of the commencement of the adult development of the external genital organs. Psychically determined erections may likewise occur, although the physical development is by no means far advanced. We shall therefore do wisely to avoid taking a narrow view of such a connexion, inasmuch as it may be that the physical signs of puberty on the one hand, and the phenomena of detumescence and contrectation on the other, may occur in conjunction at a very early age, whilst, in other cases, phenomena of the one class or of the other may occur in isolation. This statement is true, not merely of the secondary sexual characters, whose development by no means always affords a measure for the degree of development of the sexual impulse, but it is true also of the reproductive organs themselves. Halban reports the case of a boy six years of age, whose penis was as large as that of a full-grown man, but in whom, apart from the erection, all the characters were infantile. Still more often do we note the independence in many young men of the individual symptoms of sexual development from the growth of the beard, for this latter is often still lacking at an age when the sexual life in general has attained an extensive development. Still less importance must be attached to other occasional signs. According to Marc d'Espine "puberty occurs early in girls with dark hair, grey eyes, a delicate white skin, and of powerful build; late, on the other hand, in girls with chestnut hair, greenish eyes, a coarse, darkly-pigmented skin, and of delicate, weakly build;" but the evidence to justify any such generalisation is lacking. It is possible that the opinion quoted is supported to some extent by certain associated racial peculiarities, but we must be on our guard against accepting inferences of too sweeping a character. Still less, of course, are such peculiarities a trustworthy aid for the diagnosis of the occurrence of sexual acts at an early age.

The safest way of obtaining accurate information as to the practice of masturbation and other sexual acts is by means of confessions made to some person in the child's confidence. Cases are known to me in which children have very readily confided in some elder person. If this does not often occur, the fault commonly lies with the child's elder associates, who do not understand how to establish a truly confidential relationship with the children under their care. If a child finds that no one will speak to it about sexual matters, it must ultimately become secretive about its own sexual life. The child sees very clearly that every word it utters about such things is repressed as improper, and soon learns that the whole field of sexuality is regarded as something unclean, about which not a word must be uttered. The ordinary behaviour of adults inevitably produces this impression in the child's mind, and it will readily be understood what an effect this has in preventing us from gaining information about the sexual life of the child. In many mothers, the abhorrence of the sexual is carried to such an extreme that while in other respects they keep their children scrupulously clean, they feel so strongly that the genital organs must not be touched, that they neglect to secure the ordinary cleanliness of this region of the body.

The best confidant for a young child will usually be the mother, not only because she sees more of the child than the father and because her relationship is a more intimate one than his, but in addition because a woman's insight into certain things generally excels a man's. As a matter of fact, for the reasons stated, masturbation in young children is in most cases discovered by the mother. It will be obvious that I speak here only of those mothers who have real affection for and sympathy with their children, and who share their children's interests; I do not refer to those mothers who think they have adequately fulfilled their maternal duties by paying a nurse or a governess, whilst themselves immersed in the pleasures of society—or perhaps engaged in the preparation and delivery of lectures on the best way of bringing up children, on the Woman's Movement, Woman's Suffrage, and similar topics—or, it may be, attending these same lectures—those who, in any case, prefer some other occupation to the care of their own children.

Above all, let not those who have the care of children be deceived, either by diligence, or by conduct exemplary in other ways, or indeed by earnest study of the Bible, by pious protestations, or by regular attendance at church. I know a boy of twelve, reputed to be extremely religious, and ostensibly on religious grounds going to church every Sunday; but whose real motive in the church-going was the hope to meet the girl of whom he was enamoured. Extensive experience of the conduct of adults should teach us the necessity for extreme caution in these respects. I recall the case of a gentleman whose reputation was that of a paragon of all the virtues. When others of an evening went out to enjoy a glass or two of beer, or in search of even lighter pleasures, he was supposed always to turn homewards, ostensibly in order to work. Only after some years was the fact disclosed that he was an habitual loose-liver, enjoying indiscriminate sexual intercourse with unmarried girls and with his neighbours' wives, although to his friends and comrades he had appeared to be a man of exceptionally strict life, and this above all in sexual relationships. The same may be true also of quite little children. Hebbel relates that in his first year at school be sat next to a boy who appeared to be engaged in the most earnest study of the catechism, whilst under the rose he was pouring into young Hebbel's ear all kinds of obscenities, and was asking him if he was still stupid enough to believe that children were brought by a stork or were found in a basket in the cabbage-patch. Many parents, too, know so little about their children in these respects, that they are utterly astonished when some day their eyes are opened to the facts of the case by their family physician. I knew a boy of fourteen who went regularly to church, and who in other respects was a fine fellow, and a diligent pupil at school He was brought to see me because he was affected with spasmodic movements. On examination, I found him to be suffering from a severe attack of gonorrhoea, which he had contracted in intercourse with his aunt's servant-maid. When I told his mother the truth, she was at first extremely angry at what she was convinced must be a mistake on my part; but further inquiry disclosed the fact that for a year or more the boy had been intimate with prostitutes and other girls.

I have been writing of processes occurring in the reproductive organs, such as erections, seminal and other discharges, and masturbation; and of the means for the recognition of these processes. But it is necessary to recognise that we must not assume without further inquiry that all processes occurring in the genital organs are of a sexual nature, although in individual instances the distinction between the sexual and the non-sexual may be extremely difficult, or even impossible. Thus, of erections occurring before the reproductive glands ripen, not all are of a sexual nature. We know, too, that even in the adult, non-sexual erections may occur. The clearest instances of this are met with in the form of priapism, the principal characteristic of this condition being the occurrence of permanent erection which has nothing at all to do with the sexual impulse. The same is true for the most part of matutinal erections, the precise cause of which is not yet determined. They are commonly referred to distension of the bladder, which is supposed by reflex action to lead to distension of the corpora cavernosa of the penis. It is certain, at any rate, that these matutinal erections are not caused by sexual thoughts, nor as a rule do they induce sexual feelings. We must distinguish between these processes; just as recently we have learned to distinguish herpes progenitalis, the characteristic of which is its localisation to the genital organs, from herpes sexualis, which is directly dependent upon sexual processes. If we regard this distinction between sexual and non-sexual erections as applicable also to erections in childhood, we are justified in assuming that many erections, in infants-in-arms, for instance, are non-sexual in nature, even though in appearance there is nothing to distinguish them from sexual erections. In infants, erections may arise from external stimuli or from distension of the bladder, which must be distinguished from the erections which have a definitely sexual causation. We must, of course, admit the possibility that such primarily non-sexual erections may secondarily give rise to sexual processes; inasmuch as by the stimuli resulting from the erection, the child's attention may be directed to the genital organs. Just as we must guard against regarding every erection in the child as a sexual process, so also must we be cautious in our estimate of the significance of manual stimulations. Children often stimulate various parts of the body. Some children will rub the lobule of the ear, others will suck their fingers, or will stimulate their mouths in other ways. Some children have the offensive habit of picking their nose; and it is evident that many cases in which children stimulate the genital organs manually are on the same footing with nose-picking and numerous similar habits. In such cases we have not to do with a specific genital sensation to which the child responds; but with a stimulus which may be pathological, but is not necessarily sexual. In many cases, indeed, the stimulus is not even pathological. We have to take the following point into consideration. As soon as the child begins to become conscious of the existence of its organs, it fingers them. It does this with its nose and its ears, just as it does with its feet; and it is obvious that the genital organs will receive the same treatment. A gentleman who had grown up in the country related to me that as a child he had often been present when cows were being milked, and that in the evenings, after he had gone to bed, he performed the milking movement on his penis, and was greatly astonished at the fact that no milk flowed forth. He assured me that the like experience had occurred to quite a number of boys who had been his playmates in the country. It is certain that such manipulations of the genital organs, entirely non-sexual in origin, may lead to the practice of masturbation. But we must not immediately conclude that every manipulation of the genital organs in a child is sexually determined.

It is true that many investigators regard numerous movements on the part of children as sexual processes, even when the genital organs are in no way involved. Freud above all, discovers sexuality in the life of the child in cases in which, I am convinced, sexual elements play no part whatever. Sucking movements in children are regarded by Freud as sexual phenomena. He considers that the lips and the fingers are erogenic zones. With just as much reason, every movement might be regarded as sexual—as, for instance, the clenching by a child of its little fists. As long ago as 1879, Lindner, of Budapest, published an able essay about the movements made by children sucking their fingers, lips, &c., and suggested that there was some connexion between these sucking movements and sexual processes. He stated that many children, when sucking the lips, the fingers, the back of the hand or some other part, or when sucking a rubber teat, simultaneously rubbed some other region of the body—in some cases the lobule of the ear, the nipple, or the genital organs; this was sometimes done with one hand only, sometimes, if both hands were free, with both. This statement is perfectly correct. It may happen that the child stops rubbing the genital organs as soon as the sucking is interfered with; or, conversely, the sucking may cease as soon as we withdraw the child's hands from its genital organs. But, even in these cases, the friction of the genital organs does not necessarily possess a specifically sexual character, since friction of the lobule of the ear or of some other part of the body is an equivalent act. It is certain that there is here no intimate connexion between the act of sucking and the sexual life. Thus, there is no proof whatever for the view of Lindner, which has recently been carried to a still greater extreme by Freud, that this "voluptuous sucking" (Wonnesaugen) is a truly sexual process. We may, indeed, assume, as does Rohleder, that such sucking movements occur with especial frequency in children with a congenital morbid predisposition, and that to this extent therefore it is connected with masturbation. But in my opinion it is essential to regard the two movements as clearly independent in character.

Certain other childish habits, such as nail-biting, have also been described as sexual manifestations. What I have said of sucking movements applies to this also. It is true that nail-biting and masturbation may both occur in the same child, and French writers have maintained that there is a causal nexus between the two processes. If we regard nail-biting as a "tic" occurring chiefly in neuropaths, and if we assume that the neuropathic congenital predisposition is the basis of the premature awakening of sexuality, it may be supposed that to that extent there exists a relationship between the two phenomena, inasmuch as we may refer both manifestations to a common cause, viz., the neuropathic predisposition. But there is no justification whatever for regarding, as some do, one manifestation as the direct consequence of the other.

Speaking generally, we shall do wisely to exercise caution in defining the limits of the sexual life of the child. If a boy runs after a girl, and if the two flirt one with the other, it will often be merely from a desire to imitate their elders. In many instances, even, in which the genital organs play a part in such imitation, we must distinguish what is done from the sexual life proper of the child. If children play at "father and mother," if the "midwife" comes, and "childbirth" takes place, the play may certainly depend upon an early awakening of the sexual life; but this is not necessarily the case. There may be no more than innocent imitation of grownups, as the following case shows. A number of little boys and girls, almost all under eight years of age, played at being prostitutes, souteneurs, and men-about-town. The little girls each demanded a penny when they had allowed the little boys to touch their genital organs. It was an extremely characteristic fact that the leader of this band was a feeble-minded boy, whose parents I had advised to send him to an asylum, because, after various dangerous actions, he had attempted one night to kill his little sister eighteen months old by inserting beans in her nose. Such acts as that first described may, of course, depend upon a premature awakening of the sexual impulse; and when a number of children engage in amusements of this kind we not infrequently find that in the leader and seducer the sexual impulse is already awakened, whilst the others act merely in obedience, at first, at least, to an imitative impulse. Certainly, I have known a few instances in which children with premature sexual development very rapidly came to a mutual understanding, and in whom their intimate association was dependent upon prematurely awakened sexual impulses.

Just as sexual acts in which the genital organs play a part occasionally arise, not from premature awakening of the sexual impulse, but from imitation merely, so also, as previously explained, may this happen in the case of more harmless processes. Braggadocio here plays a great part, and also the desire to act like grown-ups. Thus, the boy who runs after girls, and makes appointments with them, sometimes does this merely to show off before his companions, and to produce in them the impression that he is a "manly" fellow. We must take care to separate these cases, also, from those that are genuinely sexual.

If it is difficult to separate the sexual from the merely imitative, no less difficult may it be to distinguish psychosexual processes from others. If a child lavishes caresses on mother, governess, or sister, it may be difficult to discover definite characteristics enabling us to distinguish whether the motive is or is not sexual. But, generally speaking, when a child exhibits an intimate and caressive affection for its mother we shall not incline to think of processes of the sexual life. We cannot dispute the truth of the statement made by various authors, that in these caressive inclinations sexual elements are intermingled. But this talk of the intermingling of sexual sentiments arises in reality only from the fact that neither on theoretical nor on practical grounds are we in a position to draw a clear line of demarcation between the sexual and the non-sexual; and we must avoid stretching this idea of the intermixture of sexual elements beyond the fact that a scientifically based practical distinction is not always possible.

We have to admit that above all in the mind of the child the various feelings comprised under the idea of "sympathy" (friendship, affection for parents, love of children, sexual love) cannot always be marked off each from the other after the manner of provinces on a map. Even jealousy, which is often regarded as characteristic of the erotic sentiments, does not necessarily possess a sexual basis. The boy, in his love for his mother, is jealous of his father, jealous of one of his brothers or sisters, jealous even of a dog to which his mother pays attention. How little jealousy may depend upon a sexual motive, may be learned by the observation of animal life; a dog becomes jealous if its master takes notice of another dog, or even pays attention to his own children. In children, more especially, the extension of jealousy is far greater than it is in adults. Whereas in adults this sentiment is chiefly, if not exclusively, associated with the erotic feelings, in children this is by no means the case. In the child, jealousy may clearly be associated with every possible variety of sympathetic feeling. For this reason, it is impossible for us to draw a distinction between sexual and other psychical processes, simply on the ground of the associated manifestation of jealousy.

On what grounds, then, can we decide that certain processes are of a sexual nature? In many instances, only the subsequent development will show that one process was sexual, another non-sexual. If one day a boy, embracing, as often before, his girl friend, has an erection, and then perhaps endeavours to draw her towards him so that her body presses against his genital organs, or even has an ejaculation with a voluptuous sensation, we may assume the influence of a contrectation impulse, which has existed for some time, but only now has for the first time been localised in the peripheral genital organs. On the other hand, if in the same boy when he hugs his mother no peripheral sexual manifestations occur, either now or subsequently, we must assume that in the earlier embraces of his mother there was no sexual element. But no such simple solution of the difficulty is really possible. It may happen that in the case of feelings originally sexual their further development is inhibited. A boy might experience sexual sentiments towards his mother; but it is very probable that in such a case convention, education, and perhaps also the very frequent association with his mother, would repress the growth of these sentiments. This criticism is a sound one, and in my opinion the materials are lacking to enable us to overcome its force. For why should certain processes occurring in childhood—for example, a boy's impulse to caress his mother—be regarded as non-sexual; and yet the same processes subsequently be regarded as sexual, merely because they ultimately become associated with the phenomena of detumescence? Take the case of a boy seven years of age; he loves and cuddles his mother; he is drawn also to a girl friend of the same age as himself, and kisses her with equal pleasure. The boy grows older, and after some years begins to have definite erections when he embraces and kisses his friend; but nothing of the kind occurs when he embraces and kisses his mother. Now, have we any right to assert, simply owing to the subsequent appearance of these peripheral manifestations in the one case and not in the other, that originally, when between the boy's inclination towards his girl friend and his inclination towards his mother no clear distinction could be drawn, the former was sexual, the latter non-sexual in nature?

The dilemma is unanswerable, unless we admit that, in the child, sympathetic feelings, which we shall subsequently be able to classify without difficulty, are, when they first appear, not always susceptible of any such differentiation; and that for this reason we are just as little able to distinguish a boy's love for his mother from has non-sexual friendship for a little girl, as we are able to distinguish either from a sexual love for another girl. To a very acute observer, certain slight indications may in many cases give some idea of how the matter really stands; but we are here largely concerned with subjective interpretations, rather than with distinctions that are objectively demonstrable. The difficulty of drawing distinctions is all the greater in view of the fact that in the case of non-sexual feelings sexuality constantly plays a certain part. Our sentiments are complex, and compounded of many and various elements; sexual contrasts play their part in family relationships; and it is not by pure chance that harmony exists by preference between father and daughter, and between mother and son. This sexual contrast tends to manifest itself in all displays of family affection. Thus, many men will tell us that in early boyhood they loved to kiss their mother and sisters, rather than their father and brothers. In my experience, the analogous sexual contrast does not show its effects so clearly in the case of women as in the case of men. I cannot be certain if the differences I have observed in this respect depend merely upon chance. It is certainly a fact that men, in their confidences to me, have remarkably often reported childish memories of the working of this sexual contrast. And conversely, many homosexuals have assured me that in boyhood they kissed their father with much greater pleasure than their mother.

Our diagnosis will, naturally, be greatly facilitated in those cases in which the phenomena of contrectation are plainly reflected to the reproductive organs. I, at any rate, believe that in practice such an association suffices completely to establish the diagnosis. We can, indeed, recognise this also in the dream life, at least as soon as the first nocturnal emissions have occurred. In the first edition of my work on Contrary Sexuality (Berlin, 1891), I drew attention to the fact that those affected with perverse sexuality commonly have perverse dreams; and Näcke has further discussed the significance of sexual dreams for the diagnosis of sexual perversions. In children also we shall find in their sexual dreams, especially when these dreams have begun to be accompanied with seminal emissions, a certain assistance in the delimitation of their sexual sentiments from other manifestations of sympathetic sentiment. But this aid in diagnosis is not available till comparatively late in childhood, i.e. not until ejaculation has already begun. Even before this epoch dreams may have a sexual character, and may be conditioned by sexual processes. But practically, before the occurrence of ejaculation and orgasm in dreams, an exact diagnosis is opposed by so many difficulties, that little of value can in this way be gained.

In this chapter we have examined the considerations that must guide us in our study and diagnosis of the sexual life of the child. It is, naturally, an important question, whether signs exist pointing to an abnormal development of the sexual life, and more especially to the growth of a sexual perversion. This matter has been discussed with considerable detail, and I need not, in conclusion, add anything to the emphatic warning previously given, against making apparently perverse manifestations in childhood the basis of a definite diagnosis or prognosis.

CHAPTER VII

IMPORTANCE OF THE SEXUAL LIFE OF THE CHILD

The problem of the significance of sexual phenomena in the

child is naturally one of great importance. We have here, in fact, two problems to consider: first, whether the appearance of sexual phenomena in childhood indicates a morbid or in other ways abnormal state; and, secondly, what are the consequences of the occurrence of sexual phenomena in the child. An example will help to illustrate the need for drawing this distinction. Certain malformations of the external ear are indications of the existence of a morbid degenerative condition; but from the malformation itself there is nothing to fear. Similarly with the sexual life of the child, it may happen that a manifestation indicates the existence of morbidity, although the manifestation does not by itself entail upon the child any serious consequences. On the other hand, sexual phenomena in the child deserve in some cases the most attentive study, owing to the dangers likely to result from their occurrence.

With regard to the first question, whether sexual manifestations in the child indicate per se the existence of a morbid state, it is not necessary to say much here, since the subject has been fully discussed in the section on Etiology. In any case, we must avoid exaggerating the importance of sexual feelings in the child. Ribbing contends that we must regard it as abnormal when a boy of thirteen or fourteen is obsessed (hanté) by erotic ideas. This is true enough if there is real obsession by such ideas, but it is not true if there is no more than an occasional uprising of sexual feelings. I explained that an over-development of the sexual life in the child was an indication of the existence of a congenital morbid predisposition.

Passing to the second question, as to the consequences of the occurrence of sexual phenomena in the child, these consequences may be very various in nature. They arise more especially in the hygienic, social, ethical, educational, forensic, and intellectual domains.

First of all, then, let us consider the dangers to health.

The earlier the sexual impulse awakens, the earlier also arises the danger of sexual practices, and more particularly of masturbation. Common sensations in the genital organs, the feelings associated therewith, the impulse to allay the unsatisfied libido—all these may lead the boy to handle and rub his penis. The girl is affected by similar stimuli. In these cases, the first act of masturbation does not depend upon the desire to enjoy a voluptuous sensation, but results from the impulse to allay vague feelings of uneasiness. Only subsequently, when the child has learned by experience that mechanical stimulation of the genital organs induces voluptuous sensations, or when he has been taught this fact by a seducer, does the desire to produce voluptuous sensations become the mainspring driving to masturbation. The danger, of course, increases, in proportion as the child comes fully to understand that in this way it can produce agreeable sensations, all the more because the child is either unaware of the injurious consequences of the practice, or, if it has been informed of these consequences, the knowledge cannot weigh in the balance against the easily induced enjoyment. But, let me say here at the outset, the dangers of masturbation have been greatly exaggerated. Chiefly since the publication, at the end of the eighteenth century, of Tissot's book on masturbation, but to some extent also even earlier, it has been usual to refer to masturbation the occurrence of innumerable diseases, including mental disorders and locomotor ataxia. I do not propose to reproduce the account given by Tissott, and after him by Hufeland, and also by the innumerable quacks

and swindlers who trade in the "cure" of "secret diseases"—these latter, preying upon the fears of humanity, declare that every possible affliction in both sexes may result from masturbation, and recommend innumerable miraculous remedies for these often imaginary ills. Disorders and displacements of the uterus, ulcers and cancer, gastralgia and gastric spasms, jaundice, pains in the nose, are supposed in women to result from masturbation, as well as fluor albus, nymphomania, &c. There is hardly a single organ of the body of which disease and destruction have not by many been referred to masturbation. In reality all this is false. It is more than doubtful whether, as far as adults are concerned, occasional masturbation is necessarily more harmful than normal sexual intercourse. According to my own observations, the principal question is whether, in masturbation, the bodily and mental stimuli employed to obtain sexual gratification involve an especial shock to

the nervous system—a greater shock than results from normal sexual intercourse. More powerful shock may, indeed, arise from the fact that the masturbatory act is apt to be repeated with excessive frequency; and we have to admit that the chief danger of masturbation lies in the fact that there is so grave a risk of sexual excess. Owing, too, to the frequency of repetition, a need will very readily arise for an increase in the stimulation, and this may apply alike to the bodily stimuli and to the mental; and the stronger the stimuli have to be, the more powerful also will be the general effect on the nervous system. Thus the danger of shock to the nervous system from masturbation will be seen to depend, first, upon the frequency with which the act is repeated, and, secondly, upon the increasing intensity of the stimulation. To this extent, therefore, masturbation may be more dangerous than normal sexual intercourse; for this latter also, unless it is to exert an unfavourable influence on the health, must not involve mental and bodily stimulation of too powerful a kind. The good effects of sexual intercourse depend upon its adequacy to the feelings, upon the absence of any exhausting imaginative activity, and upon the absence also of artificial bodily stimulation. But artificial stimuli and exhausting imaginative activity are often associated with coitus also, in cases in which the stimulus evoked by the personality of the sexual partner is inadequate. Again, the powerful efforts which must as a rule be made by persons who desire to repeat the act of intercourse several times within a brief period, will have a similar effect upon the system to the powerful imaginative activity in cases of masturbation. The resemblances, on the one hand, and the differences, on the other, between masturbation and normal sexual intercourse, will be apparent to those who carefully consider the facts just stated; and it will also become apparent in what circumstances masturbation must be regarded as injurious. This is all I have to say concerning masturbation in adults.

The idea that masturbation is, generally speaking, dangerous, is by many restricted to the practice during childhood and youth, the belief in its danger at this stage of life being based upon the view that the organs are at this time insufficiently developed. But even this contention cannot be regarded as fully established. I will, in the first place, consider those cases only in which masturbation is practised after the formation of semen has begun, but when the processes by which bodily maturity is attained are not yet fully completed. To the theoretical assumption that masturbation is especially hurtful in cases in which the organs are not yet adequately developed, we may oppose the consideration that the completer development of organs is favoured by exercise. We cannot further discuss such theoretical speculations, which lack the firm foundation of experience. On the whole, I agree with the estimate of the consequences of masturbation expressed by

Aschaffenburg, a man to whom we are indebted for the refutation of many extravagant views. Experience teaches that almost all men, healthy and unhealthy, moral and immoral, have masturbated for some years, once or several times a week, towards the end of the second and during the beginning of the third period of childhood. In view of this experience, what right have we to maintain seriously that masturbation is, generally speaking, dangerous to health. It is, of course, possible to contend that these persons would have developed better if they had not masturbated. But there is equal ground for asserting the opposite. We possess no evidence whatever to show that those young persons who never masturbate are in after life stronger and healthier than the others. I know some persons who have never masturbated. In the case of some of these, it was because the impulse to masturbate was lacking; others, notwithstanding the existence of a strong impulse, refrained from masturbation under the influence of religious or ethical motives. In both of these groups, I have seen persons exhibiting the very morbid symptoms which Tissot and his followers referred to masturbation; and I was quite unable to convince myself that abstinence from masturbation secured any notable advantage. Whilst I do not assert that the morbid phenomena which I observed in these individuals arose in consequence of their refraining from masturbation, I consider that there is no justification for the converse assumption in the case of those who did masturbate. I believe that many of those patients who never masturbated were the subjects of congenital morbid predisposition, and that, as a direct consequence of this fact in many of them, the sexual impulse was of minimum intensity or developed exceptionally late; I consider, therefore, that the morbid manifestations in the domain of the nervous system were dependent, not upon the fact that they did not masturbate, but principally upon the congenital morbid predisposition.

Whilst I thus reject the view that masturbation in children is generally dangerous, this must not be regarded as implying that I consider the practice altogether indifferent as far as its influence upon health is concerned. In the child, as in the adult, there is danger in the fact that the act is so easy that it is likely to be repeated very frequently, and thus to become habitual. In addition, the masturbator is apt to require strong physical and mental stimuli, and this increase of the stimulus may become dangerous. A special danger of persistent masturbation is to be found in the possibility that impotence may result. The masturbator, being accustomed to stimulate his genital organs by manipulations, and by various methods increasing in intensity of stimulus, will often find subsequently that the normal stimuli, acting in part in the form of the sensory processes in the genital organs, and in part in the form of the normal psychical influences proceeding from without, are no longer competent to induce the normal sexual reactions (erection and ejaculation). This affects chiefly members of the male sex, but in some instances the same is true also of women. It is true that in women the sexual act is rather of a passive character, erection not being in them essential as it is in the male; but in the case of women also, long-continued masturbation, whether practised in childhood or subsequently, may bring about so intimate a dependence of sexual desire, ejaculation, and gratification, upon the artificial stimuli, that the occurrence of these phenomena in normal coitus may be hindered or completely inhibited.

Some writers contend that sexual perversions, homosexuality, for example, may be induced by masturbation, but I myself doubt this. For such a development to be possible, it is necessary that very special influences should be in operation, more particularly a congenital predisposition, or the cultivation of the perversion by perverse imaginative processes—this latter, indeed, occurring very readily in masturbators. But masturbation to excess is far more likely to induce general neurasthenia than to give rise to sexual perversions. When I speak of excessive masturbation, however, it must be admitted that the term is a relative one. What is harmful excess in one person is not necessarily excess in another. This is true of children as well as of adults. I have seen children who, owing to premature awakening of the sexual life, have begun to masturbate at a very early age, without any serious effect upon health. Having seen such children again in adult life, after the lapse of more than fifteen years, I consider that I have had opportunities for forming a sound judgment upon this point. We have to take into account the fact that when a youthful masturbator subsequently exhibits nervous manifestations, these often result from the anxiety he has experienced on being informed of the serious consequences of masturbation. Not masturbation itself, but fear of the effects of the practice, is here responsible for the resulting injury to health. Experience teaches that a certain sort of popular literature has an especially unfavourable influence in this respect.

Moreover, in many cases, self-reproach on moral grounds, it may be in childhood, but more often later in life, must in such persons be regarded as the cause of the appearance of nervous and mental symptoms. The dread of having committed a deadly sin, or an extremely immoral act, explains a part of the results which are commonly referred directly to masturbation. The dangers of masturbation must not be underestimated, but exaggeration must equally be avoided. I do not believe that in children masturbation is, generally speaking, more dangerous than it is in adults; but I consider that masturbation resulting from a spontaneous impulse is less harmful, than when artificial bodily and mental stimuli are freely employed. And though the dangers are slightest when masturbation is not continued for a long period, still, in this connexion, a period of a few years cannot be regarded as so very long; at any rate, practical experience shows us that we must avoid over-estimating the importance of masturbation even if continued for several years.

A particular description must now be given of masturbation as practised in boys before the formation of semen has begun—that is, before the fourteenth or fifteenth year of life. Féré regards orgasm without ejaculation as very dangerous, and compares its effects with the phenomena of fatigue. The nervous discharge occurring in the orgasm may certainly explain the depressed state of many masturbators, also their tired appearance, dilated pupils, and languid movements. We note also mental disturbances as well as physical, especially diminished powers of attention and memory, and somnolence up to the point of narcolepsy. According to Féré, the physical and the mental symptoms alike can be detected by precise investigations. In children suspected of masturbation, dynamometric observations disclosed a notable diminution, to the extent even of one-half, when the children were not kept under constant observation and when other signs of masturbation existed; and in these cases experimental observation also showed a diminution of the power of attention. The test applied was to erase some particular letter of the alphabet from one page of a book. When such a test is employed, the practice of masturbation is said to have an unfavourable effect, and to cause mistakes. I do not think that these so-called precise investigations are of much value, for suggestion on the part of the experimenter, who is sometimes prejudiced, may play a great part in producing the results. Even when transient phenomena of fatigue appear, and are demonstrable by experiment, it does not follow that any permanent injury has been done, and just as little do otherwise transient manifestations of fatigue necessarily indicate anything pathological, or foreshadow the onset of any progressive morbid state.

The clinical material offered in support of the idea that masturbation is especially dangerous in children too young to have an ejaculation should, moreover, be carefully and critically examined. I myself formerly accepted the view of most authoritative writers as to the grave danger of masturbation in these circumstances. But we can no longer do this unconditionally. The gradual change in my own views arose as follows. From the commencement of my medical practice I was frequently consulted about masturbation in children. Many of these cases date from ten, fifteen, and even twenty years back. I have recently instituted inquiries as to the present condition of my former patients. In so far as information was obtainable, I have been astonished to learn how well boys, who from the age of eight, nine, or ten had masturbated for several years, had developed as youths and as full-grown men. I have had similar experiences in the case of girls. Among my patients, I have had girls who masturbated at the age of five or six years; and ten to twenty years later, when some of them have married, I have gathered information regarding their subsequent development, either from the patients themselves or from their associates. Here also it was very remarkable to learn how rarely unfavourable consequences have occurred from the practice of masturbation in early childhood, notwithstanding the dangers commonly supposed to attend thereon. Especially rare have ill consequences been in those cases in which masturbation was not pushed to the point of inducing orgasm, but in which the children have masturbated simply in order to procure agreeable local stimulation. But in some instances also, in which orgasm without ejaculation had been observed, no bad results have occurred. Such results are, however, much more likely to follow in cases in which there has been prolonged sexual excitement preparatory to the orgasm, whilst this latter has been artificially deferred as long as possible. Where this has been habitual, I have, in some of the patients, seen serious consequences, and especially neurasthenic symptoms, result from masturbation. But the persons thus affected were in many cases the subjects of such severe hereditary taint, that it was impossible to decide to what extent their troubles were due to congenital predisposition, and to what extent they were referable to masturbation or to other noxious influences. It is, moreover, probable that when the nervous system is less resistent in consequence of congenital predisposition, the bad effects of masturbation will more readily appear than in those whose inheritance is a sound one.

As a result of these experiences, I feel justified in coming to the following conclusions regarding masturbation during childhood. It has not been proved that masturbation during childhood, with or without ejaculation, is generally dangerous. The possibility of danger resulting from the practice is, however, increased by long-continued and frequently repeated masturbation; also by the artificial postponement of the voluptuous acme, and by congenital predisposition to nervous disorders. My notes of the cases which I have seen during many years of medical practice show that, even in children, masturbation does not necessarily do any harm.

Case 15.—The girl X., four years of age, was brought to see me because it had been noticed that she frequently tried to handle her genital organs, and also that she stimulated the same organs by means of rubbing movements of the crossed thighs. Her mother had further from time to time noticed rocking movements, associated with a fixed stare, which had aroused suspicions of the occurrence of the sexual orgasm. Various methods were tried to put a stop to these practices, but without result. Hypnotic treatment was not tried, because the child was still too young and her attention wandered too much. Mechanical methods of control were also fruitless. The trouble continued for five years, during all of which time the child was under my own observation. She went to school, where she proved a diligent scholar, and was one of the most successful pupils; her physical condition was also excellent. Thenceforward, for several years, I received no precise information about the patient, although from time to time I saw some of her associates. But after about eight years, I had an opportunity of learning her later history. The child which had begun to masturbate when four years old was now a young lady of eighteen. When fourteen years old she had for some months suffered from chlorosis, but had never been troubled by any other serious illness. I could not learn with certainty whether the habit of masturbation had been discontinued; but there had been no definite evidence of the practice of masturbation, or of any other artificial sexual stimulation, after the age of nine. At the present time X. is perfectly healthy.

Case 16.—The boy Y. was brought to me when eight years old. It had been noticed that at night, whether sleeping or waking, he very often handled his genital organs. Erection of the penis had also been observed from time to time. His mother and his governess believed that he masturbated every night. When this had been going on for several years, the patient was brought to me for suggestive treatment. Mechanical means were simultaneously employed, his hands being fastened at night in such a way that he could not bring them into contact with his genital organs. But he speedily loosed himself from his bonds. The trouble abated in severity, but continued none the less for several years. I saw the patient again when he was twenty-four years of age. No abnormality whatever could be observed. He had normal sexual potency, and was entirely free from neurasthenic symptoms.

I have hitherto, in this chapter, spoken only of the dangers of auto-erotism. It is hardly necessary to mention the fact that the nervous system of the child may be injuriously affected by other sexual acts, as, for instance, by premature sexual intercourse. The occurrence of such acts is naturally favoured by a premature awakening of the sexual life.

We have also to consider the results of passionate love in children, apart from actual sexual intercourse. In children with congenital neuropathic predisposition, these results may be serious; and, as Bell points out, symptoms of severe nervous shock may ensue, more especially owing to separation from the beloved object, or in consequence of rejected affection. The same writer even records several attempted suicides consequent upon the death of the loved one; two of these occurred in boys of eight and nine years of age respectively; two occurred in girls, aged nine and eleven years. Eulenburg, who has made a special study of suicide and attempted suicide during school-life, in his enumeration of the causes of such acts, mentions several that are germane to our subject. Among these are the following: becoming acquainted with the existence of a liaison on the part of the loved one with another;

unfortunate love; love for a married woman; neglect of school work owing to a love-affair and consequent fear of expulsion; and, finally, love-anxiety. It must, however, be freely admitted that Eulenburg's cases relate to schoolboys who were fairly old. Thus, one of these cases was that of a Catholic boy in one of the higher forms, who had formed a liaison with a girl of sixteen in a neighbouring girls' school, and whose Director had intervened, very judiciously, as it appears, on learning of the affair. The other cases in which Eulenburg mentions the age of those concerned were also those of boys no longer very young; in some of these, double murder or double suicide resulted. In the other comprehensive works on suicide, and even in those dealing especially with suicide in children, I have been able to find comparatively little material bearing on this particular question. Brierre de Boismont, indeed, tells us that children occasionally commit suicide on account of jealousy; here, however, he does not refer to sexual jealousy, but to jealousy of a more general character aroused by preference shown to another child. Although such serious consequences occur chiefly or exclusively in children who cannot be regarded as perfectly normal, it is nevertheless possible for erotic influences to act as the final determinant. But such serious results are certainly comparatively rare.

Just as in former times masturbation was believed to be the cause of all kinds of illness, so to-day, according to Freud and his followers, the general sexual experiences of children are responsible for various subsequent illnesses. Four neuroses (neurasthenia, anxiety-neurosis, hysteria, and compulsion-neuroses) are referred by Freud to all sorts of disturbances of the sexual life, past or present. Hysteria and compulsion-neuroses are regarded as a reaction to the sexual experiences of childhood; neurasthenia and anxiety-neurosis are referred to later sexual experiences. Freud originally assumed that during the childhood of hysterical patients sexual seduction by adults or by older children played the chief part; but at a later date he has advocated the view that the imaginative activities of the days of puberty, which intervene between the sexual experiences of childhood and the appearance of the hysterical symptoms, are responsible for the occurrence of the latter. Quite recently, Abraham has insisted that a sexual experience may be of some importance in relation even to the onset of dementia præcox. But I do not consider that Freud's assumption is justified, nor do I think that he adequately excludes the effects of hetero-and auto-suggestion. It is out of the question that in every case of the above-mentioned neuroses, sexual experiences should be the cause; and it is equally erroneous to suppose that every sexual experience in childhood has the effects which he assumes. It is true that Freud and his followers report cases which they regard as proving their thesis. But I am by no means satisfied with these clinical histories. They rather produce the impression that much in the alleged histories has been introduced by the suggestive questioning of the examiner, or that sufficient care has not been taken to guard against illusions of memory. The impression produced in my mind is that the theory of Freud and his followers suffices to account for the clinical histories, not that the clinical histories suffice to prove the truth of the theory. Freud endeavours to establish his theory by the aid of psycho-analysis. But this involves so many arbitrary interpretations, that it is impossible to speak of proof in any strict sense of the term. Dreams are interpreted symbolically at will, and other definite objects are arbitrarily assumed to be symbolic representatives of the genital organs. I detect the principal source of fallacy in this arbitrary interpretation of alleged symbols.

However this may be, there is no justification for the assumption that hysteria or other neuroses are always, or even in the great majority of instances, to be regarded as dependent upon masturbatory or other sexual acts during childhood. We must on no account forget that an illness often has a dozen causes or more; and although one or another of these may have had a preponderating influence in the causation, we have no right arbitrarily to select one of them as the efficient cause. I do not deny that occasionally the sexual life during childhood plays a part in inducing a subsequent neurosis; but this applies only to a comparatively small proportion of cases, and we must guard against exaggeration in the matter.

This is all I have to say concerning the relationships of the sexual life of the child to the occurrence of nervous diseases. The sexual life has, of course, important bearings on health in other ways. The venereal diseases, in most cases, result from sexual intercourse; and it will readily be understood that since early sexual intercourse is rendered more likely by a premature awakening of the sexual life, an increased danger of venereal infection will thus arise. Although infection in children occurs comparatively seldom in consequence of spontaneously practised sexual intercourse, and more frequently as the result of the mishandling of children by perverted or criminal adults, still cases are from time to time observed in which infection with venereal disease arises in children from spontaneously sought sexual intercourse. In Jullien's work we find a striking chapter on gonorrhoea in children, illustrated with appropriate cases. He writes. "In other cases, little boys, sexually premature, make early attempts at sexual intercourse. In Paris we see hardly grown youths appearing at the specialist's clinic, quite proud that they need to be treated for gonorrhoea. The very fact that they present themselves so coolly at the places for the special treatment of venereal diseases, suffices to show that they fully understand the cause of their illness." In Jullien's opinion, venereal disease is especially serious in children, because many of them conceal their condition as long as possible in the hope of avoiding punishment. Barthélemy reported a case in which the parents came to consult him because the boy was passing water every few minutes, and because at school he was repeatedly asking to leave the room in order to go to the urinal. Examination showed that he was suffering from cystitis, and that this was a sequel of gonorrhoea. As regards children of the other sex, I have myself seen cases of gonorrhoea in which sexually immature girls have been infected in sexual intercourse of which they themselves had been the instigators. In most cases, infection in children results from intercourse with grown persons, but it sometimes happens that children infect one another. Little need be said here about the dangers of gonorrhoeal infection. Although in children the course of the disease exhibits many peculiarities, the general results are much the same as in adults, viz., pain, orchitis and epididymitis with atrophy, cystitis, &c.; and in girls, more especially peritonitis. Other venereal infections may of course also occur in children, such as soft chancre and syphilis. No detailed account will be given of these diseases. Although we need further information as to the results of venereal infection in children, in well-informed medical circles the numerous and severe ill consequences of such infections are well understood.

I have in this chapter spoken more especially of the dangers threatening the child's health from the side of its sexual life. These are, of course, not the only dangers; the moral and social dangers are even greater. First of all, in this connexion, we have to consider the practice of masturbation; but in our estimate of its effect upon morals, we must be careful to avoid sanctimoniousness. The question why masturbation is regarded as immoral has never yet been answered, declamation being here commonly mistaken for argument. And yet reasons may be found for the belief that masturbation may sometimes be a positively moral act; as, for instance, when one who is dominated by a very powerful sexual impulse, avoids injury to another by means of masturbation. Consider a case, for example, in which one who masturbates would otherwise transmit venereal infection to another, or would injure another by illegitimate sexual intercourse. In cases of perverse sexual practices in which the offender's liability to punishment was under discussion in the law court, I have more than once called attention to this point. Take the case of a man whose sexual impulse is directed towards children, and who finds great difficulty in restraining himself from sexual malpractices against children. His action is assuredly a far more moral one if he satisfies his impulse by the practice of masturbation, rather than by a sexual assault upon a child! If, notwithstanding these considerations, masturbation is generally regarded as an immoral act, the reason for this opinion must obviously be sought in deeper and more general grounds. In the first place, we have to take into account the fact that according to the moral code of many persons, and certainly according to the official theological code, the only kind of sexual intercourse that is morally permissible is that which is known as "legitimate," i.e. connubial intercourse; extra-connubial intercourse is stigmatised as immoral. Masturbation, like extra-connubial sexual intercourse, is sexual indulgence outside the limits of that which is alone permissible by the canons of theological morality. Owing to the definite teaching of the Church in this matter, the views of the common people are inevitably influenced thereby, although the practical relationships of life are thus completely ignored; above all, the fact is ignored that marriage does not as a rule become possible until long after the awakening of the sexual impulse. The purpose of the proscription by theological morality of illegitimate intercourse and of masturbation is to effect the prevention of all varieties of sexual indulgence except under the form of marriage, and, if possible, under the form of marriage blessed by the Church. The importance attributed to receiving the approval of theological morality is seen from the fact that in all strata of the population, however much alike in private conversation and in political assemblies they may protest against the dominion of the Church, nevertheless almost invariably the ecclesiastical ceremony is superadded to the civil marriage. In our moral estimate of masturbation, we have to take another point into consideration. We have seen that long-continued and excessive masturbation is dangerous to health; now every voluntary action, and every action that is commonly believed to be voluntary, the effects of which are injurious to body or to mind, is considered to be immoral, unless it

is performed in pursuit of some lofty aim—as, for instance, in the case of the doctor who exposes himself to some deadly infection for the sake of his patient's welfare. But these reasons do not suffice to account for the fact that masturbation is commonly regarded as a more immoral act than illegitimate sexual intercourse. Here, however, as so often happens, the popular instinct contains a kernel of truth, which in this case relates not so much to the individual ethical judgment as to the general interest. The popular instinct, or we may rather say the soul of the people, commonly regards that as immoral which, if approved, would entail serious general consequences. In this ethical judgment we have, as it were, the manifestation of an instinct of self-preservation on the part of the soul of the people. We must not forget that the practice of masturbation is extraordinarily easy, and that if it were recognised as a morally permissible act, its frequency would be notably increased. The reason last given, namely, the injury to health that may result from masturbation, explains one way in which the practice is opposed to the general interest. But another reason is still more important. The practice of masturbation naturally limits the frequency of sexual intercourse, not only in its illegitimate, but also in its legitimate form. The easier an act is, the more readily, if it is deleterious, will popular sentiment build a protective wall around it. In individual instances, such popular valuations are devoid of logical foundation, and for this very reason it is often impossible to reject them on logical grounds. But they are largely based upon considerations of the general interest, and for this reason it is often just as well that they are impervious to logic. Hence, although in concrete cases of masturbation physicians and schoolmasters will not always take a severe view, and, in certain instances, as explained above, it may even be considered that masturbation is a morally permissible act, this will not affect the general disapproval, in consequence of which a very large number of persons refrain from masturbation. Moreover, the absence of such disapproval would lead to extremely serious consequences. Merely in order to prevent interference with normal sexual intercourse between man and woman, it is necessary that in the popular judgment masturbation, as the greatest enemy of sexual intercourse, should be condemned. In addition to these motives, there are others closely connected with them, which in some cases operate unconsciously. Since masturbation is practised in solitude, if masturbation were regarded as morally permissible to men, the value of woman would diminish, since her wooing and winning would be no longer necessary to man, Analogous considerations naturally apply to masturbation in women. The need that each sex should regard the other as indispensable is a powerful motive in bringing about the popular condemnation of masturbation; and it must further be remembered that the amatory life, and more especially its psychical accompaniments, in truth only attain their fullest development through the mutual intercourse of the sexes.

The general condemnation of masturbation is, in my view, most readily explained on the considerations just outlined. However this may be, we have certainly to reckon with the fact that masturbation is regarded as an immoral act. But inasmuch as the early awakening of the sexual life, or at least the early appearance of the phenomena of detumescence, leads almost inevitably to the practice of masturbation, it will readily be understood that the child is apt to be forced into a line of conduct which conflicts with the generally accepted ethical code.

The social dangers of masturbation are very closely connected with the ethical dangers, and we frequently find them appearing concurrently. In isolated instances, as Lombroso and Ferrero have shown, premature awakening of sexuality may lead to prostitution. In the chapter on Biology and Psychology, a special section is devoted to sexual prematurity, and the authors contend that in Italy this factor plays a greater part than it does elsewhere. It is further characteristic that in erotic literature women who are famous or notorious for their love-adventures are commonly described as having been the subjects of premature sexual development. From the beautiful Helen, who at the ago of seven, according to one story, and at the age of twelve, according to another, was deflowered by Theseus, down to modern times, we find that premature sexual development is frequently adduced as a characteristic of such women. Although it is true that in many cases of the seduction of children there is no question of sexual prematurity, still, for a part of the cases, premature sexual development is responsible. For it can hardly be disputed that the crime of the child-seducer is greatly facilitated, if the child meets the seducer halfway. In cases in which sexual offences were committed on little girls, Tardieu made a special class of those in which the offence was frequently repeated upon the same individual. Of the 60 cases of this kind, 29 were in little girls under eleven years of age, and 26 were in girls from eleven to fifteen years. He states that in these chronic victims, he was first of all struck by the premature development of the genital organs and the remarkable prematurity of general sexual development, both of these conflicting with the age and the development of the girls in other respects, Tardieu certainly paid especial attention to the physical peculiarities of the genital organs, and he was inclined to refer the premature development to the early experience of sexual intercourse. But it is possible that the real connexion was the reverse of this—and, indeed, many other observations support

such a view—in that owing to their sexual prematurity the children experienced a powerful sexual impulse at an unusually early age, and that for this reason they became the victims of sexual attempts much earlier than others. Kisch also believes that in many cases of premature puberty, premature sexual intercourse is observed, and parturition may even occur at a very early age. He writes: "A girl in whom menstruation began at the age of one year, gave birth to a child when she was ten years old (Montgomery). A girl who began to menstruate when at the age of nine years, became pregnant very shortly afterwards (d'Outreport). The well-known case recorded by Haller, in which at birth the pubic hair was already grown, and in which menstruation began at the age of two years, was also one of very early pregnancy, the girl giving birth to a child when nine years old. Another girl in whom at birth the pubes were already covered with hair began to menstruate when four years old, copulated regularly from the age of eight, and at nine years became pregnant, and was delivered of a vesicular mole with an embryo (Molitor). A girl began to menstruate at the age of two, had

a growth of hair on the pubes and developed mammæ at the age of three, and became pregnant at the age of eight (Carus). With these cases must be classed that observed by Martin in America of a woman who was a grandmother at the age of twenty-six. Lantier, in his travels in Greece, speaks of a mother of twenty-five with a daughter of thirteen."

Whatever the real sequence of events—whether in a little girl the occurrence of sexual intercourse is favoured by the spontaneous premature awakening of the sexual impulse, or, conversely, it is the premature intercourse which awakens the impulse and keeps it active thereafter—the consequences of premature awakening of the sexual impulse are always extremely serious, and often result in the permanent social extinction of the girl concerned. Although in many cases she may be fortunate enough to escape the fate of the prostitute, none the less in modern civilised countries the loss of virginity is a serious disgrace, by which her future will be affected altogether apart from the moral shocks resulting from sexual intercourse in early childhood, and from the possibility of impregnation. The case is much the same as regards children of the male sex. The fact that a boy is sexually precocious, will greatly facilitate his being led astray by grown females to whom his extreme youth acts as a stimulus. Moreover, his sexual precocity may deliver the boy to the embraces of homosexual men, an outcome which is rendered the more likely by the commonly undifferentiated character of the childish sexual impulse. There are certain homosexual adult males whose impulse is especially directed towards boys still possessing the milk-white face of the child, and his encounter with such a pervert may make all the difference to a sexually premature boy. Although I have been engaged for years in the collection of facts bearing on this question of homosexuality, I have recently been astonished to learn, in an ever-increasing number of cases, how adult homosexuals, men of thirty years and upwards, form homosexual relationships with schoolboys, and regard their right to do this as practically self-evident. It is obvious that this is likely to do grave moral injury to the boy—altogether apart from the fact that the production of homosexuality is thereby greatly facilitated, however much interested homosexuals may contest this assertion. It is clear, too, that boys upon whom such relationships are imposed will sometimes tend to grow up as male prostitutes, just in the same way as little girls prematurely seduced in consequence of an early awakening of sexuality often adopt a life of prostitution.

Children in whom sexuality has awakened are especially dangerous to their associates, since they readily seduce others to sexual malpractices. Thus, it sometimes happens, though happily not often, that children attempt sexual intercourse with one another. A question in forensic medicine formerly much discussed, is the age at which children are first able to effect sexual intercourse. I have no doubt whatever that by the end of the second period of childhood, in a comparatively large number of boys, spontaneous erections occur adequate to allow the introduction of the penis into the vagina to be effected; but no doubt it might be difficult for such a boy to effect complete penetration into the vagina of a girl in whom the hymen was still intact. Pouillet even asserts that all boys have the faculty of erection in quite early childhood; and he places on record the following experiment, whose repetition had better be avoided. If in an infant lying in its cradle the edge of the foreskin be tickled with a feather, we shall at once see the penis swell up and become erect, and the infant will grasp at it with the hand. There is no doubt that boys in whom the sexual impulse is prematurely awakened may be a danger to little girls through attempting intercourse with them. More frequently, however, the danger lies, not in attempts at coitus, but in other improper manipulations and contacts, which may take almost every conceivable form. Mutual masturbation is fairly common among children, or one child may manipulate the genitals of another; such practices occur more often between two boys than between two girls or between boy and girl. But experience shows that other and more advanced sexual acts may occur, though fortunately less often; for instance, pæderastic acts between boys, introduction of the penis of one individual into the mouth of another, &c. Ferriani has collected a number of cases of this kind, occurring in youthful criminals. In boys he distinguishes two groups, those from the tenth to the fourteenth, and those from the fourteenth to the eighteenth year of life. He made inquiries regarding the sexual life in 69 boys belonging to the former group, and in 48 belonging to the latter. Of the 69 belonging to the former group, 48 were found to masturbate, in 25 improper sexual acts with the mouth were admitted, in 12 active pæderasty, and in 17 passive pæderasty. It is evident that these data must not be generalised, for Ferriani's studies related to boys who had been morally neglected from the earliest days of childhood, and who had been sent to prison as thieves, beggars, and vagabonds. A great danger attendant on sexual acts in which one child is led astray by another is, of course, the moral harm which threatens the other associates of such children. Girls and boys are equally exposed to such seduction, and the seducer also may be of either sex. In cases of an altogether exceptional character, danger threatens in this respect from a child's own brothers or sisters. Among cases which have come under my notice, I may mention one in which a boy began to carry out all kinds of perverse sexual acts with his sister, who was about eight years younger than himself, and continued to do this when he had attained the age of twenty-nine years. Forel sees, rightly, as I believe, especial danger in the leading of others astray by young homosexuals, alike in boys' and in girls' boarding-schools. In some of these cases the seducer's act is merely a manifestation of the early undifferentiated state of the sexual impulse, but in others it is an early sign of a real homosexual development.

I append here certain cases from the literature of the subject showing the great dangers that proceed from such premature sexual development. One case reported by Forel was that of a girl nine years of age. "This girl would stimulate sexually all boys of her own age or somewhat younger whom she could induce to allow her to do so. She did this so secretly, that by mishandling the genital organs of her two little brothers, both younger than herself, she slowly brought one to his death, and in the other caused serious injury to the bladder and urethra. With an older boy, she was accustomed to have actual sexual intercourse in the woods. I could not, in this case, gain any definite information regarding hereditary taint. Such persons commonly become criminals in later life, or at least indulge in the most shameless masturbation or give themselves up to prostitution."

A case which at one time attracted great attention in France may here be given in the actual words of the report. "Leo, thirteen years old, demanded the favours of eleven little girls, offering in return, as the girls confessed, a small reward—a penny or a sweet. Many others must have been compelled by their parents to make no complaint, in order to avoid a mortifying publicity. Leo is the son of a good fellow, a shoemaker by trade, and also a lamplighter. The mother having run away, and the father being often out at work, the boy was left much alone. He would then entice into the house little girls of the neighbourhood, one after another, in order to commit immoral acts with them. One day he invited in a little girl of five. The girl's brother peeped through the window, and saw Leo standing naked in front of Mary, as if he posait pour le torse. Ultimately the matter was reported to the police superintendent of the district, and it transpired that not less than ten or eleven little girls of the quarter had been thus led astray. From time to time he invited into the house a number of good-for-nothings of the same stamp as himself, and here this youthful Casanova organised pleasure-parties of a kind usually unknown to those of his age. The lad was bound over to come up for trial if called upon. Such cases as this are commoner than is generally believed; and perhaps commoner in the country than in the town."

The way in which such practices spread by moral contagion is shown by a report of Ferriani, who made inquiries of nine boys, at ages varying between eight and twelve years, how they had learned to masturbate. I. had been taught by a certain K., II. by I., III. by IV., IV. by I., V. by II., VI. by III., VII. by IV., VIII. by VI., IX. by II. Not long ago, I myself came across such an epidemic, in which there occurred, not only masturbation, but, in addition, all sorts of mutual sexual contacts between boys and girls; a boy of five was the primary seducer, having undertaken the sexual enlightenment of a girl of seven, and beginning this process with the remark that she need no longer believe that babies were brought by a stork. These two went on to improper contact, and subsequently quite a number of children were gradually corrupted by the two.

To the jurist, also, the question of the sexual life of the child is one of great importance. I do not myself share the view of Ferriani and others, that the sexual life of the child, when it awakes prematurely, is a common cause of crime—although this may be true of certain special cases, presently to be described. But the sexual life of the child is of importance from another point of view. In cases in which children are the objects of sexual offences, such as have recently so often come before the courts, the question of the capacity of the children to give evidence frequently plays a great part. The lawyer, who is often ignorant of the extent to which sexual imaginations and sexual acts may prevail among children, is apt to assume that the child is of necessity sexually inexperienced, and for this reason to put a trust in childish evidence which is in many instances not justified by the facts of the case, because the supposed inexperience may not really exist. If judges and magistrates knew how much and how often children's brains are occupied with sexual imaginations, without speaking of the sexual acts which many children have engaged in while still quite young, they would be more guarded than they are at present in their acceptance of children's evidence in sexual matters. Not infrequently, when such a child describes the sexual offence which is supposed to have been committed, it is assumed without further inquiry that the child's account must be accurate, the grounds for this assumption being stated as follows: "How could such an accusation be invented? The poor child has had no previous experience of such matters; what is now described must have actually happened, for it is impossible that an inexperienced child could construct it all out of its own imagination." But to anyone who has seriously studied the sexual life of the child, this logic is utterly fallacious. Still, the argument is none the less a very dangerous one; and as an expert witness I have assisted at several trials as to which I remain convinced to this day that the judge has assumed the offender to be guilty simply because he (the judge) was ignorant of the nature of the sexual life of the child, above all as regards psychosexual imaginations. Some years ago there was tried in Berlin a case in which a wealthy banker was accused of misconduct with a little girl. In the end the accused received a severe sentence. In that trial I was called as an expert witness, and I believe that as regards the principal charge the banker was wrongfully condemned. The principal witness was a girl twelve years of age, and it was her accusation which formed the main ground of the conviction, and this notwithstanding the fact that the child had subsequently withdrawn her charges. In common with other expert witnesses, I pointed out, in rebuttal of the girl's evidence, that the person on whom the alleged offence had been committed was not, as the police magistrate and the judge had both assumed, an inexperienced child, but one in whom sexuality had prematurely awakened, and in whom strongly sensual tendencies were manifest; we showed that in her imaginative activities the sexual life played a leading part, and that the child herself had at an earlier date performed some of the actions with which sho charged the accused. But the child had made so favourable an impression on the police magistrate and the judge that they firmly believed her first statement, and held that her subsequent withdrawal of her accusation was due to outside influence. It would be well, in some cases of the kind, to insist upon a complete examination of the girl who makes the accusation, this examination to include her bodily state, to ascertain if there are indications of a prematurely awakened sexual life—for example, any irritation of the genital organs by masturbation. We shall also do well, in such cases, to endeavour to ascertain whether the child is already fully informed concerning the nature of sex. We must always bear in mind that things which may give an indication regarding this are usually kept very secret, and that none of the child's associates may be able to give us any information. Even though among the witnesses we have parents, masters, or governesses all uniting to assure us that the child's mind is still perfectly innocent, and that not a suspicion regarding matters of sex has yet been aroused, the judge should not allow himself to be deceived. Sexual imaginations often dominate the consciousness of the child, at the very time when a display of shamefacedness in relation to such things deceives the onlookers. In such trials, it is sometimes put forward as a defence, that some third person, some police official, the examining judge, or even an enemy of the accused, has reiterated the false accusation to the child, and has, as it were, suggested it. Such an assumption is, for many cases, altogether superfluous, even if we do not believe a word of the child's accusation, for it completely underestimates the power of the childish imagination. The French physician, Bourdin, in his work on Lying Children, gives the case of a little girl who by her good behaviour and affectionate disposition had won the love of her foster-parents. One day they were reading aloud the report of a scandalous trial, while the child was in the room playing with her dolls, and to all appearance paying no attention to the reading. A few days later the foster-parents saw the little girl putting her dolls together in an indecent posture. In answer to earnest inquiries, the child said she was only doing what someone had once done to her; she then went on to make detailed and serious accusations against certain other persons. A clever and experienced physician was asked to investigate the matter before any application was made to the law courts. As a result of a physical examination of the girl, he declared that what she described could not possibly have taken place; and ultimately she admitted that the whole accusation was false. As a reason for her lies, she said, "qu'elle avait voulu faire comme les dames que l'on avait mises dans le journal." Such imaginative activity may occur in healthy children, but it is in the case of those with a morbid inheritance that we have especially to reckon with these possibilities. As with the grown woman, so with the child, the degenerative form of hysteria makes those subject to it untrustworthy witnesses. This applies above all to accusations of sexual offences. Feeble-mindedness is also dangerous in this connexion, for its existence is apt to be overlooked by the judge, although an expert examination of the witness—who, in most of these cases, is of the female sex—would facilitate the diagnosis. Among the feeble-minded, we find, not only sexually premature individuals, but also persons with a tendency to pathological deceit, this latter sometimes manifesting itself in childhood, and of course lessening or completely abolishing the subject's credibility as a witness to the occurrence of alleged sexual offences.

These considerations must not lead us to the opposite extreme, of altogether discrediting the assertions of child-witnesses; but they should convince us of the need for the recognition of a source of fallacy often completely overlooked by parents, namely, the indulgence by children in sexual imaginative activity, and the frequent existence of unsuspected sexual enlightenment. To this extent only do such questions form part of my subject. Following Hans Gross, I have already drawn attention to the fact that girls of a certain age are untrustworthy witnesses regarding their own experiences. But to guard against too comprehensive a generalisation in this respect, I must point out that during the second period of childhood a girl may be a highly competent observer, and this precisely for matters in which her interest has been aroused by the development of her sexual life. I may quote from Hans Gross certain remarks bearing on this. "We have to recognise that in the observation and understanding of certain matters, there is no one cleverer than a growing girl. Her school-life, and her personal experiences and occupations, do not adequately occupy her energies. Sexual influences are beginning to become active, and half-unconsciously the girl studies her environment in search of experiences bearing, however remotely, on this sphere. The little interests and amours of the nearer and further environment will be by no one discovered so speedily as by a bright and lively half-grown girl. Every variation in the mutual interest of the pair she has under observation will be noted by such a girl with the keenest sympathy. Long before the two have come to an understanding, she will be aware of their sentiments for one another. She notes when they are drawing nearer together, and she knows at once when they have given open expression to their love. Whether they become engaged or whether they draw apart from one another, the little one knows all about it before any of their intimates. Moreover, such a girl will take note of all the doings of certain of her acquaintances. An interesting beauty, or a young man living near at hand, will have no more watchful observer of all their doings than a young girl of twelve years. She, too, will take note more accurately than anyone else of all the changes of mood of those who are under her observation."

But the sexual life of children is of importance, not only in relation to the question of their credibility as witnesses, but also in respect of our decision as to matters of fact. Sexual attempts on children under fourteen years of age are legally punishable offences, and it is a matter of indifference whether the offender or the child was the instigator. In determining the degree of culpability it is, however, of important whether the child against whom the offence has been committed was innocent and uncorrupted, or was one with previous sexual experiences. In addition to this, we have also to take into account the question whether the child incited to the offence, under the influence of the spontaneous activity of its own sexual impulse. All these considerations will make it clear that from many points of view the sexual life of the child is a matter of forensic importance.

We must not forget that the child itself may be threatened with legal dangers as a result of the activity of its own sexual impulse. The German legal code decrees different degrees of penal responsibility at different ages. Children not yet twelve years of age are not liable to criminal prosecution. A child over twelve, but under eighteen years of age, must be exonerated if when the offence was committed the child did not possess the knowledge enabling him or her to understand its culpability. By the third paragraph of section 176 of the German criminal code, any one who has improper sexual relations with a person under fourteen years of age, or who induces such a person to practise or suffer such relations, is liable to severe punishment.

If, therefore, two children of eleven engage in mutual misconduct, they incur no liability to legal punishment. But two boys of thirteen are liable to prosecution for the practice of mutual masturbation. Each of them has performed an improper act with a child under fourteen years of age, and the liability to punishment in each case depends upon the answer to the question whether the offender possessed sufficient knowledge to enable him to understand his culpability. This knowledge is not identical with the knowledge that the offence was legally punishable; that is to say, either boy would be liable to punishment, even though he had no idea whatever that improper sexual relations with children under fourteen constituted an offence against the law. All that is necessary is that he should possess a sufficient degree of intelligence to understand his culpability, which is quite another thing from his possessing knowledge of his legal liability to punishment. Generally speaking, however, the public prosecutor is disinclined to initiate proceedings in such cases, for the most part because it is held that the necessary understanding of culpability is commonly lacking. But such prosecutions have more than once occurred. In the year 1899, in a little town in the Mark of Brandenburg, proceedings were taken against eighteen school-children, boys and girls, and five pupil-teachers. These twenty-three persons, who appeared in the dock, had all reached an age at which they became liable to criminal prosecution; in the case of a number of other boys and girls who were concerned in the affair, no prosecution could take place. Ultimately, all the accused were discharged, as it was held that when the offence was committed they did not possess the requisite understanding of its culpable character. But by order of the court several of the accused were transferred to a reformatory. Since a prosecution may take place in such cases, a conviction is also possible. It is evident that as soon as a child is twelve years old, it may incur legal liabilities in consequence of the activity of the sexual impulse.

We must not overlook the fact that the intellectual side of development may be influenced by an early awakening of the sexual life, the child inclining, in this case, to occupy its mind with sexual thoughts, to the neglect of educational opportunities. I have seen cases which were regarded as instances of aprosexia, the lack of the power of concentration being attributed to adenoid vegetations, but in which the defect might, with at least as much reason, have been referred to the play of sexual ideas. To the teacher, his pupil's inattentiveness is often an insoluble riddle, merely because he ignores in the child the play of erotic imagination, and, in fact, ignores the child's inner life in general.

And yet, in such cases, the child's failure to attend to the work of the class sometimes depends upon nothing more than occupation with thoughts about a beloved person. In other instances, the inattention is due, not to sexual ideas, but to sexual acts. As a patient of my own put the matter: in boyhood, while in the Latin class he was supposed to be learning his amo, amas, amat, he and his school-fellows were studying the subject practically beneath the table. Naturally, the stronger the child's sexual impulse, the more will the attention wander; and although in most cases, in children, the impulse is comparatively weak, in isolated instances it may from the first be abnormally powerful, entailing dangers to the intellectual development as serious as those other dangers previously enumerated. According to Sanford Bell, unfavourable consequences to intellectual development cannot, as a general rule, be attributed to the early amatory inclinations of childhood. All that is likely to be noticed is that on days when the child loved by another is away from school, the latter child will be less attentive than usual. But the circumstances are somewhat different when the object of affection is not a school-fellow. Bell speaks only of cases in which the child-lovers are members of the same class, and he refers to heterosexual inclinations only. In such cases, the results of early amatory inclinations may even be good. Hebbel relates of himself, how zealously as a little boy he attended school, simply in order to meet in the class the girl he loved. The presence of the loved one may, in fact, powerfully stimulate ambition and the desire to work. A little girl who has fallen in love with her schoolmistress or governess, will strive to please the latter by hard work and attention; and, similarly, a boy who loves a boy or a girl classmate, very often attempts to make an impression on the feelings of the loved one by his performances at school. Whilst we recognise the dangers attendant on the development of sexuality in the child, we must not overlook the fact that this development may have its good side.

For, just in the same way, a child's altruistic feelings may be stimulated by love. We see cases in which a child tries to help the beloved schoolmate in every possible difficulty or trouble. Such a love may also spur the lover on to excellence in other fields than the mere work of the class. The boy, while still quite young, seeks to make an impression on the girl by courage and steadfastness, just as he will seek to do this somewhat later, when he has attained early manhood.

A spirited description is given by Grünstein of boys engaged in a sham fight. At first the contending parties are timorous, appearing afraid of one another:—

"But when the girls draw near, to view
The slaughter of a stricken plain,
In mimic battle, at this cue,
The boys now join with might and main.

Under the spell of girlish eyes
Each strives his courage to display;
For wounds or death he may despise,
Who helps his side to win the day.

And as the factions join in strife,
They shout amid the battle's din;
Fighting as if for very life,
Each one will do his best to win.

Each hopes the victory to gain;
Each would the bravest warrior prove.
Hurrah! they cry, and each is fain
To win bright glances from his love."

As I have previously explained, the existence of sexual perversions may sometimes be traced back into early childhood, although, in individual cases, the experiences of childhood may throw little light on the subsequent sexual life. But we saw that cases certainly occur in which the abnormal tendencies of the sexual life are manifested in early childhood, and in which, also, other tendencies of childhood are determined by the abnormal sexual life. In such cases, the mental life of the child is also profoundly affected. Such a child feels unhappy on account of its abnormal sexual relationships. The boy would rather have been a girl, the girl a boy. In such a case, the choice of a future profession will also be affected by mental peculiarities closely associated with the sexual life. The homosexual ladies' tailor, the music-hall artiste who makes a speciality of feminine impersonations, the ladies' hairdresser, and others in like occupations, will often tell us that the choice of their trade or profession was made while they were still children. In this connexion, I may also refer to the sexual life of

Catholic priests. It is certain that some of these exhibit homosexual tendencies. It is often suggested that it is their repulsion from heterosexual intercourse which leads such men to take the Catholic vow of celibacy. But there is another possible factor which must not be overlooked. It is not unlikely that certain persons, not homosexual, but in whom sexual inclination towards women is primarily wanting, may incline to enter the priesthood. Yet another possibility is pointed out by a Catholic priest who has written on this subject. He is of opinion that homosexually inclined boys often exhibit even in childhood caressive tendencies; such boys early attract the attention of priests, who make use of them in the performance of various ecclesiastical ceremonies. For this reason, such boys come under the influence of the priesthood at an exceptionally early age; and thus it comes about that in an exceptionally large proportion of cases they themselves enter the priesthood.

There are other sexual perversions, in addition to those just mentioned, by which the inclinations and occupations of the child may be influenced. A hair-fetichist, whose case I had occasion to study carefully when, at the age of fifteen, he had to stand his trial on account of cutting off girls' plaits of hair, informed me that for one or two years before he first committed this offence, he had experienced a peculiar stimulus whenever he handled hair. In other cases of fetichism which I have had under observation, the abnormal fetichistic tendency went much further back. An underclothing fetichist began at the age of seven to be greatly interested in his sister's and in the maidservant's underclothing, touching such articles of clothing as often as he could, and pressing up against them in a caressing way. The choice of reading is sometimes determined by perverse sensibilities, the sexual nature of which may often not become apparent until a considerable period has elapsed. I know certain persons with masochistic and with sadistic tendencies, who in childhood preferred to read stories about robbers and slaves, the use of fetters and the descriptions of violence of all kinds playing a peculiar part in their imaginations. It must be regarded as definitely established that children sometimes deliberately incur corporal punishment in order to enjoy masochistic sexual sensations. The best-known instance is that of Jean Jacques Rousseau, who at the age of seven was chastised by Mademoiselle Lambercier, and thereupon experienced agreeable sensual feelings. He himself tells us how sincere was his affection for Mademoiselle Lambercier, and his extremely tractable disposition would have tended to prevent his deliberately seeking to commit an improper act. And yet in spite of this the chastisement was repeated, and again he experienced a secret stimulation. In a little erotic work of the eighteenth century, Le Joujou des Demoiselles, we find under the heading of "Le Fouet" ("A Whipping"), the following short poem, relating to a girl twelve years of age:—

"A l'âge de douze ans, pour certain grave cas,
Que je sais et ne dirai pas,
Lise du fouet fut menacée
A sa maman, justement courroucée,

Lise repondit fièrement,
Vous avez tout lieu de vous plaindre,
Mais pour le fouet tout doucement,
Je suis d'âge à l'aimer et non pas à le craindre.

At the age of twelve, for a good reason,
Which I know, but will not tell,
Lise was threatened with a whipping.
To her mother, justly incensed,

Lise answered proudly,
You have just cause of complaint,
But as regards a moderate whipping,
I am of an age to enjoy and not to fear it."

The awakening of sex has further effects upon the mental life of the child. Its curiosity is aroused, as soon as the phenomena of pubescence make their appearance, either in themselves or in other children. Long before this, as a rule, the navel has to the child been an object of curiosity. This part of the body seems strange and perplexing, and even in early childhood the genital organs may inspire similar sentiments. The child observes that in respect of such things some reserve is the rule, that a certain shyness is manifested in looking at and touching the genital organs, and for these very reasons the child's attention is apt to be directed to these organs. But curiosity becomes much keener when the signs of puberty manifest themselves. To many a child, the looking-glass serves as a means for the thorough observation of these remarkable signs of development. With amazement the child watches the growth of the axillary and the pubic hair; and in girls attention is aroused by the enlargement of the breasts. Curiosity then leads the child to seek information about these things from various books, and especially from an encyclopædia. It is a matter of general experience that the article on Masturbation is eagerly studied by many children, even before the end of the second period of childhood. A search is made for anatomical illustrations, in order to see the genital organs of both sexes. In many cases brothers and sisters arrange to satisfy one another's curiosity on this point. Elder brother and younger, elder sister and younger, or brother and sister will often seek to enlighten one another as to differences in bodily structure, especially as regards the external genital organs, by means of mutual inspection. Such childish curiosity may be, and often is, altogether independent of the awakening of the sexual life; the real motive is then the rationalist one, if the expression be permitted. But in other instances the curiosity is determined, or increased, by the awakening of the sexual life. Similar considerations apply to the observation of the sexual acts of animals, for which opportunities occur more especially in the country, but sometimes also in the town; in most cases, the motive for such observation in the first instance is pure curiosity, independent of sexual processes in the child. Parents who surprise their children thus engaged, usually regard such investigations as signs of gross immorality; but it is unnecessary to take so tragic a view. It is simply childish curiosity, on the part of those who see nothing wrong in what they are doing. That which is immoral in the adult is not necessarily immoral in the child, who is merely led by curiosity, and by his astonishment at the changes taking place in his body, to study these changes closely. It is not immoral for a child to wish to study in propriâ personâ matters about which information has been withheld. Adults are far too ready to interpret the actions of children in the light of their own feelings—a mistake which cannot be too strongly condemned.

The curiosity of the child about his own body is often intermingled with fear; above all in the perfectly innocent, completely unenlightened child, the first seminal emission, whether it occurs during sleep or in the waking hours, and in the girl, the first appearance of the menstrual flow, may readily cause serious alarm. It must not be supposed that such alarm is of rare occurrence. Even in large towns, which our moralists are apt to regard as altogether corrupt, we sometimes find that a boy of fifteen or sixteen may be greatly alarmed, on waking, to discover that he has had a seminal emission, for which he has been prepared neither by experience nor by instruction.

Additional wider influences of the sexual life of the child cannot here be fully discussed. But when we see that in great poets and other artists much of their creative work may be effected in childhood, and when, on the other hand, we observe the connexion of many artistic productions with the psychosexual sphere, we cannot fail to admit the possibility that the sexual life of the child is to some extent related to art. Thus, we sometimes see children endeavouring, however imperfectly, to express their feelings in verse; and in cases in which nothing of the kind occurs, the erotic feelings of childhood may still exercise influence later in life. As examples from world-literature, I may mention: Heine, who was still a boy when he was so greatly attracted by his Sefchen, the executioner's niece, whose personality made a definite impression on the poet's maturer work; Goethe, whose friendship with the sister of the little Derones, likewise had certain artistic results; Dante, who first met his Beatrice at the age of nine years, and ever thenceforward remained under her spell. If in such cases we inquire as to the impressions of childhood, we unquestionably find, in poets and artists, traces, sometimes of direct, but more frequently of indirect influences.

Mantegazza goes so far as to regard the premature development of psychosexual sentiments as a peculiarity of richly endowed and talented natures. An obscure, shamefaced feeling, by which the boy is drawn to the girl, is, he thinks, manifest in such natures, even before sex has made its profound impression upon the developing organism, and before the reproductive organs have assumed their adult forms. He compares such feelings with the rosy tint which appears on the horizon before the sunrise, and he considers that in men of a lower type or less highly gifted by nature, the new sentiments known by the name of love do not appear until after the adult development of the reproductive organs. I do not believe that this generalisation is well founded; although, as previously mentioned, I consider that the alarm which is often caused in elders by the appearance in the child of such early psychosexual manifestations is not warranted, as a rule, by the facts of the case.

The question as to the quality of the offspring resulting from the sexual intercourse of children, either of two children who are both sexually mature, or of a sexually mature child with a grown person, has not, in Europe, any great or immediate practical interest. With us, procreation is rarely possible on the part of those who are still children, for the boy is hardly competent for procreation before the completion of the second period of childhood, and in the case of girls such competence is rarely met with till towards the very end of the second period of childhood. But if we put the question in a somewhat more general form, and study the quality of the offspring of youthful persons in whom bodily development is not yet fully completed, the matter becomes one of greater practical interest. But for a decision even on this point, data are insufficient, notwithstanding the fact that, according to Pauline Tarnowsky, among the Russians a young girl frequently marries while still sexually immature, at the age of sixteen or seventeen, when, in that country, menstruation has often not yet begun. But there is a country from which data bearing on this problem can be obtained—

data of considerable, and, as some think, of decisive importance— viz. India. In India, child-marriages occur with extraordinary frequency, and, according to Hans Fehlinger, their number continues to increase. Originally almost confined to the Hindus, these marriages have spread to the Mohammedans, the Buddhists, and the Animists, notwithstanding the fact that religious reasons for such marriages exist only in the case of the Hindus. In the year 1881, for every 1000 persons under 10 years of age, 99 were married, of these 24 being boys, and 75 girls. In the year 1901, the number of married persons under 10 years of age was 158 per 1000, of whom 20 were children under 5 years old. This is an enormous percentage: and although Fehlinger himself draws attention to the fact that marriage in childhood is not always tantamount to the beginning of sexual intercourse, since in many cases years will intervene between marriage and the commencement of cohabitation, yet in many other instances no such interval exists. E. Rüdin also deals with the question of child-marriages in India, discussing it from the point of view of racial degeneration. He states that, with one exception, modern writers are agreed that the consequences of the Indian custom of child-marriage are altogether bad—that not a single point can be urged in favour of the practice. The solitary writer to urge anything in favour of the custom of child-marriage is Sir Denzil Ibbetsson, who asserts that in the Western Punjab, where child-marriages are exceptional, immorality and assaults upon women are commoner than in the Eastern Punjab, where child-marriages are the rule. Those who strongly disapprove of child-marriages, point more particularly to the fact that when a girl-child is married to an adult man, she often receives mechanical injuries in the act of intercourse; and they contend, in addition, that child-marriage is injurious to the offspring. For, by child-marriage, we obviate any possibility of sexual selection within the limits of a particular caste, inasmuch as persons are bound together in marriage whose defective constitution and inferior mental endowments may not become apparent until long after marriage, and yet the couple, tied to one another for life, will continue to procreate an inferior stock. But, in this connexion, it must not be forgotten that in India puberty is attained far earlier in life than it is in Western Europe.

Having dealt with the premature development of the sexual life, a few words must now be allotted to the consideration of an abnormally late awakening of sexuality. This latter phenomenon must, unquestionably, be regarded as a morbid manifestation. In the course of my experience, I have seen quite a number of people in whom the sexual impulse made its first appearance very late; in childhood, and also later, some of these were regarded by their associates as models of chastity. They had no intercourse with prostitutes, because even at the age of twenty they had not yet experienced any definite sexual impulse. They despised other young men who practised irregular sexual intercourse, and they themselves had no difficulty in refraining from such intercourse. But many such persons are the subjects of a remarkable self-deception; for a long time they really believe themselves to be exceptionally moral, and succeed in convincing themselves that their abstinence from sexual intercourse is dependent upon ethical motives, whereas often the real reason has merely been the lack of inclination and of capacity for sexual intercourse. In most cases the real nature of the case subsequently becomes clear to them, and they come to understand that their previous sexual abstinence was not determined by ethical motives. When we analyse such cases more accurately, we often find that we have to do with abnormal individualities; abnormal not merely in respect of the retarded development of the sexual life, but also as regards other phenomena. Not infrequently we have to do with neuropathic and psychopathic natures, and the reality of this is quite unaffected by the fact that the superficial observer is convinced that such persons are exceptionally moral. I possess a considerable number of autobiographical case-histories of this kind, and it is quite usual to find that they state that their associates have wrongly accredited them with peculiar virtue, whereas in reality their apparently irreproachable conduct depended simply upon abnormality of development, and the strict morality was an illusive appearance. Many of them also produce an altogether unmanly, effeminate, bashful, and timid impression. Although I have always honoured, and continue to hold in honour, those young men who avoid illegitimate sexual intercourse on genuinely moral grounds, the persons exhibiting the peculiarities just explained must be regarded as pathological subjects. If our moralists hold up to us as exemplary specimens such young men as these, we have to answer that in that case sexual abstinence, and also chastity and morality, may depend upon a pathological inheritance. Just as we are unable to regard eunuchs as exceptionally virtuous individuals, so also must we be cautious in our assignment of moral motives for the sexual abstinence of young men of this nature.

In the female sex, also, there are persons in whom the sexual life, and especially the sexual impulse, awakens very late. This may happen notwithstanding the fact that menstruation has begun at the normal age. Both the peripheral phenomena of detumescence, and also the phenomena of contrectation, may be thus retarded; and the former especially may permanently fail to appear. We see girls who appear remarkably virtuous, because, while other girls are rejoicing at having found an admirer, they pass coldly along, in the streets and elsewhere, their eyes directed forwards, and rigidly avoid exchanging glances with any male person. Although this delayed sexual development does not arouse in us the same unsympathetic feelings in the case of young women as it does in the case of young men, it is none the less necessary to recognise the phenomenon in the female sex as well, and this not on medical grounds merely, but also on educational, ethical, and social grounds. In fine, in such cases, we have to do with something very different from cases in which from a true sense of shame or on moral grounds a girl maintains her mental and bodily chastity; different, also, from the cases in which we have to do with women whose bodily development is normal, but who in other respects resemble rather the type of those in whom the reproductive glands have been removed.

I may take this opportunity of insisting upon the fact that the unduly retarded awakening of the sexual life, or the complete failure of the sexual impulse to appear, is not especially to be desired, and entails dangers and disadvantages just as does a premature development of sexuality. I may recall, in this connexion, certain earlier experiences. At one time it was assumed that there was a mental disorder known as pyromania; the pyromaniac was one with an irresistible impulse to light incendiary fires. To-day, we no longer admit the existence of any such disease, and the impulse to light incendiary fires, when such a morbid impulse manifests itself, is regarded as a symptom of imbecility, of cerebral degeneration, &c. But we may take this opportunity of reminding the reader that Henke, an earlier investigator, regarded pyromania as due chiefly to arrest or disturbance of the physical and psychical phenomena of puberty. Esquirol himself appears to have shared this opinion; and although modern psychiatry takes quite a different view of pyromania, we have none the less to insist that unduly retarded development may, just as much as premature development, give rise to undesirable consequences.

CHAPTER VIII

THE CHILD AS AN OBJECT OF SEXUAL PRACTICES

We have now to consider a matter which bears but indirectly on the sexual life of the child, and yet may be of the greatest importance in relation to that life; we have to consider cases in which the child is the object of sexual practices by others. I have previously referred to instances in which one child loves another. But the child may also be an object of sexual desire to adults; for in certain men and women, sexual inclination is directed towards children. By von Krafft-Ebing this state is termed pædophilia erotica.

Not all the cases in which sexual acts are performed on children belong to the province of pædophilia. It is well known that in certain countries—Germany is one of them—a superstition prevails among certain strata of the population to the effect that venereal diseases may be cured by means of sexual intercourse with children. Where this is the motive of the sexual act, the case does not belong to the class of pædophilia; and many other sexual acts in which children play a part must also be excepted from this class. It sometimes happens that debauchees, after having practised all kinds of venereal excesses, finally take to misusing children; nursemaids, again, and other servants, will carry out all sorts of sexual acts on the children entrusted to their care, sometimes merely in order to quiet the children, sometimes "for fun." Von Krafft-Ebing refers to a special group of young men who do not feel sufficient confidence in their sexual potency to attempt intercourse with grown women, also to masturbators affected with psychical impotence; such persons are apt to seek an equivalent for coitus in improper contacts with little girls.

One very large group of cases belongs to the sphere of psychiatry. In quite a number of congenital and acquired states of mental defect or disorder, sexual acts performed on children appear as symptoms of moral and intellectual degeneration. In this connexion may be mentioned, congenital imbecility, progressive paralysis (paralytic dementia), senile dementia, chronic alcoholism, cerebral syphilis, and post-epileptic dementia; with or without these conditions, epileptic disturbances of consciousness may lead to sexual offences against children.

None of these cases have anything to do with poedophilia erotica. And there are yet other cases which it is desirable to distinguish from this class, especially those cases in which a marked hyperæsthesia was the determining cause of the sexual act. In such a case, it is to the person thus affected almost a matter of indifference with whom the sexual act is performed. Anything warm and alive will do, and inasmuch as a child is often most readily available, a child often serves as victim, whilst in other cases an animal is utilised.

Fritz Leppmann, to whom we are indebted for a full and excellent study of cases of this kind, distinguishes the influences which are subjective to the offender from those which operate from without. Among the latter he refers especially to the Schlafbursch or night-lodger; it may be a young man in his prime, sleeping in the same room or even in the same bed with little girls; also to unemployment, which very readily gives occasion for sexual excesses; to the practice of allowing little girls to run about without proper supervision; to premature sexual development in children, which renders these latter especially liable to be the subjects of sexual misconduct; to child-prostitution, often at the instigation of the parents; to the lack of proper sexual reserve; to obscenity, dances, and popular festivals, whereby the sexual impulse may be stimulated; to unhappy marriage; and, above all, to the effects of alcohol. Occupation and position have also to be considered, for, in the case of many males, an authoritative position (that of schoolmaster, priest, doctor, employer, stepfather, tutor) gives extraordinary facilities for committing sexual offences against children.

Although children of all ages, and even infants in arms, may be the victims of sexual misconduct, in the majority of such cases we have to do with children who are no longer quite young; and this is true, more especially, of most cases of pædophilia erotica. This latter passion may be directed against children of the same sex as the offender, but more commonly it is directed towards children of the opposite sex. Not infrequently, however, the impulse in such persons lacks sharp differentiation, the pædophile showing inclination, now for immature boys, now again for immature girls. Occasionally, pædophilia is the only form in which sexual inclination exhibits itself in the persons concerned; but in other cases the pædophilic impulse alternates with normal sexual feelings, or with some other perverse sexual manifestation. A homosexual man, for instance, may one day be sexually attracted by children, the next by adult males. Less widely known, although, as I think, far commoner than is usually believed, are the cases in which women are sexually attracted by immature boys. Some of those cases of which mention has previously been made, in which nursemaids and other female servants seduce boys to the practice of masturbation, belong to this category; but this does not exhaust cases of such a nature. It is not necessary, when we see a woman caressing a boy, to assume at once and in every case that a sexual motive is at work; but unprejudiced observation will show that many of these cases are sexually determined. An interesting case of this nature has been published by Magnan. It was that of a lady twenty-nine years of age, with strongly marked hereditary taint, and suffering from very various mental abnormalities, with five nephews, the eldest of whom was thirteen years of age. At first, this eldest nephew was the object of her desires. "The sight of him caused in her intense sexual excitement; she experienced voluptuous sensations, which she was quite unable to repress, sighed, rolled her eyes, and became flushed; sometimes she had spasmus vaginæ, with local secretion." When this boy grew older, the next brother took his place in her desires; and in succession these were transferred to the other three. At the time when Magnan saw the patient, her sexual inclinations were directed towards the youngest nephew, a boy three years of age.

In many cases, the sexual inclination towards children is primary, existing from the first appearance of the sexual impulse; or it may appear simultaneously with other inclinations without there having been, as far as can be learned, marked previous sexual excesses. There can be no doubt whatever that in such cases we have to a large extent to do with morbid personalities. No small part in these cases is played by a purely psychological factor, namely, the innocence of the child. We know that also in the case of the normal sexual inclination of the male, innocence on the part of the female exerts a notable stimulus, in which connexion the question whether we have to do here with a result of conventional opinions or with an inborn mental disposition, must naturally be left open. But it is a fact that just as the knowledge of a woman's immoral past, or obscene remarks or gestures on her part, will in many men suffice to inhibit sexual desire; so, on the other hand, for many men, innocence in the woman heightens the stimulus. In many cases of desire for immature girls, the physical stimulus of the narrow vagina may also contribute to increase libido; but the part this plays is probably not considerable. Apart from the fact that in many cases in which men have sexual inclination towards such girls, immissio membri does not take place at all, this consideration would in no way explain those not very uncommon cases in which adult women experience sexual inclination for immature boys.

In connexion with this last point, it is of interest to recall the fact that in former days dwarfs, as well as fools, were kept at many courts. In view of the tender relationship which obtained between many ladies of position and such dwarfs, it has sometimes been inferred that the inclination was a sexual one, the small size and the undeveloped condition of the dwarf exercising a peculiar stimulus.

The depraver of children satisfies his desires in very various ways. It will readily be understood that the progressive paralytic (paralytic dement) will act in one way, and the true pædophile in another. I shall not, however, discuss these details here, but shall merely endeavour to give some general ideas on the subject. Often, and especially at first, the depraver of children merely seeks opportunities for seeing children; then he wants to touch the children with his hands, and often to handle their genital organs; and while attempting this, or while doing it, he has ejaculation. In other cases he presses the child more and more closely into contact with himself, and especially against his own genital organs. Finally, we may have more complete sexual acts; and, especially when the child is a girl, there may be attempts at intercourse, and even defloration; where the child is a boy, pseudo-coitus may take place. The depraver of children gains his opportunities by appeals to the child's peculiar weaknesses. He will, for instance, tempt the child by the offer of sweets, and in this way will obviously often gain his ends. Many such persons hang about in the neighbourhood of a school or a children's playground, simply with this end in view. Some years ago the police of a certain large town were informed that "child-lovers" haunted a particular place. It appears that here the children were in the habit of swinging on a chain suspended between two pillars, and that the watchers waited to catch a glimpse of the children's genital organs, or merely of their bare legs, when their petticoats flew up occasionally in the act of swinging. Many pædophiles become sexually excited at the mere sight of children sympathetic to them. In other cases, by no means rare, men experience sexual excitement whenever they see a little girl with short petticoats; these men will follow such little girls all over the place, without, as a rule, speaking to them or interfering with them in any way, being withheld from doing so either by the fear of punishment or by moral restraint. To many the mere sight of the child appears to afford sufficient sexual gratification; and to others the simple contact of their hands with the child suffices, and nothing more is attempted. But, in other cases, handling the child's genital organs plays the chief part, frequently because the offender can himself obtain sexual gratification only through inducing sexual excitement in the child and watching this excitement. Sometimes, however, the offender has no interest in the child's genital organs; far from being excited sexually by regarding or handling these organs, he may even find them repulsive; but in such cases the sight of general nakedness often induces sexual excitement. This is often associated with sadistic feelings, and this alike in men and in women. In other cases, a woman will make attempts at coitus with a little boy, having first induced erection of his penis by manipulating the organ, by tickling it, or in some other way. Finally, there are cases in which all kinds of other actions are performed. To the more complex perversions I shall return. Here I shall only point out that children may sometimes be utilised for the wildest orgies. A case was formerly published by Tardieu, in which servant-maids in conjunction with their lovers carried out with the children under their care all sorts of perverse acts: cunnilinctus, masturbation, the introduction of various objects into the vagina and the anus. Finally, it may be pointed out that in the lack of an object, the pædophile will naturally satisfy himself with the aid of imaginative ideas, masturbating the while, or he may be content with purely psychical onanism. We must not forget that the imagination usually suggests stimuli far stronger than those furnished by objective experience, and this applies in a most marked degree to pædophilia. Many pædophiles also satisfy themselves with the aid of erotic and obscene literature, containing descriptions of the acts in which they are interested, or with pictures of such acts. Among obscene pictures and photographs, not a few depict sexual acts performed with children; and there is no doubt that these are sometimes pictures taken from the life, children having actually been photographed in such obscene attitudes. The Latin countries appear to be the principal source of such pictures and photographs.

It will readily be understood that the performance upon children of sexual acts is a very serious matter for the children themselves, especially as affecting their sexual morality. It is true that in many instances pædophilia does not entail any consequences for the child, which completely fails to understand that it has been made use of for perverse purposes. The offender may know how to mask his actions, so that even a third person who is looking on may detect nothing more than tender caresses, and may remain altogether unaware of the existence of any sexual excitement. But in other cases the consequences for the children may be extremely grave. Not only is the child in this way prematurely introduced to sexual practices, but its moral corruption may result. The danger to the child is greater in view of the fact that the child depraver often fails to realise that he is trespassing against the child's rights. I remember a gentleman who had been punished with imprisonment on account of improper relations with a boy, and who continued to assure me that he had done nothing wrong in touching the boy's penis. In other cases, well-educated young men and women have no idea that unchaste conduct with children is an offence which may entail severe punishment, even in cases in which the child's genital organs are not touched.

It should not need demonstration that such sexual malpractices on children may have serious consequences for these latter. A girl may suffer most severely, alike morally and socially, even though defloration has not been effected. It is quite conceivable that in such a way a girl may be brought to prostitution. Certain investigators have studied the question at what age defloration had been effected in women leading a life of prostitution, and have ascertained that in many cases this had taken place in childhood. Martineau reports cases in which defloration had been effected at the age of nine or ten years. Experience teaches that boys also, especially when they have been seduced by sexual inverts, are very apt to adopt a life of prostitution. It must also be remembered that girls may occasionally become pregnant and give birth to a child even before they have themselves passed the years of childhood—another source of social danger. In addition, we have to reckon with dangers to physical health; among these we have the direct consequences of premature misuse of the genital organs, and, above all, the danger of venereal infection. In a great many cases, sexual offences against children are brought to light only when, on examining the child, gonorrhoeal or syphilitic infection is disclosed. Many authorities hold that the superstitious hope of curing venereal disease by sexual intercourse with an innocent child, is a comparatively frequent source of such infection in children. Freud, to whose views I have referred several times before, believes that sexual attempts on children may give rise in the latter to severe neuroses—an idea which forms an important part of the etiological system put forward by this author.

We must regard it as a peculiar danger of sexual relations on the part of a child with an adult, that sexual perversion may be induced. The chief danger does not arise from the fact that the child is occasionally utilised for a homosexual act, but from the circumstance that in the period of the undifferentiated sexual impulse, the child's sexual interest, and especially its contrectation impulse, is directed towards one of its own sex, and that thereby a permanent perversion may be induced. Edward Carpenter, indeed, considers that in such homosexual relationships the younger partner makes the advances. "The younger boy looks on the other as a hero, loves to be with him, thrills with pleasure at his words of praise or kindness." In his general views on this question, Carpenter takes a somewhat peculiar position. Unfortunately, he overlooks the fact that the elder is not to be exonerated because the younger made the first advances—at any rate, in cases in which the elder is in a position to understand the true nature of such relationships. Everyday experience shows that in many cases the elder person is of such an age that there can be no doubt upon this point. And apart from this, it is not usual to find that it is the younger person who makes the sexual advances. In most of the cases which have come under my own notice it was unquestionably the elder who began to lead the younger astray. The matter is not as harmless as Carpenter makes out. The same considerations apply to sexual intercourse with immature girls. Beyond doubt, there are many girls who meet sexual advances halfway, owing to the premature development of their own sexual impulse; and some such girls go more than halfway. A common practice of pædophiles is to begin by arousing sexual excitement in the child, either by manual stimulation, or else by showing the child erotic pictures, or by reading to it from an erotic book. We must also admit that in certain cases the child meets sexual advances halfway, not so much under the stimulus of its own sexual impulse, but for other reasons; for example, the child may be following the instructions of its parents, who regard their child as a marketable commodity, either because they have been well paid by the pædophile, or because they wish to use the child as an instrument in a blackmailing scheme. The point last mentioned is one of great importance—the fact that intercourse on the part of a grown person with a child under fourteen years of age is sometimes deliberately instigated by the child's parents or guardians, with the sole object of securing thereby a permanent income from blackmail. In other cases, the instigation may not come from the parents or guardians, or not directly from these, but from professional procuresses, who have undertaken to satisfy the desires of sexual perverts. I may refer in this connexion to the Pall Mall Gazette revelations of the London of nearly a generation ago.

False accusations on the part of children, especially on the part of little girls, who allege themselves to have been the subjects of sexual assaults, have been mentioned in an earlier part of this work, but the matter is one of such outstanding importance, that its further consideration will not come amiss. An experienced Berlin lawyer has recently emphasised this danger. He shows that it is a regular practice to utilise the existence of certain punishments as a means of getting undesired persons out of the way, by bringing false accusations against them. Immediately after the Franco-German War, these accusations dealt with offences against the laws providing for the safety of the Empire and of the individual States of the German Confederation. At a later date, persons seeking revenge made frequent use of accusations of lèse majesté. Still more recently, it is the section in the German legal code dealing with sexual offences against children, which is chiefly utilised for such purposes, "The good-natured householder who, because it is his birthday, presents a few sweets to children assembled in the courtyard of his house, is suspected of an offence against sexual morals;" when he finds it necessary to give warning to his untrustworthy hall-porter, this latter revenges himself by lodging a false accusation of this kind. It is a melancholy fact that an experienced barrister should find it necessary to make the following comprehensive declaration: "As a rule it is of no use for the accused person to call expert witnesses, who give the court long lectures upon the significance of children's evidence, and upon the import of evidence in general. In our own experience one accused of such offences rarely escapes conviction. He is hardly ever spared the terrible ordeal of examination and cross-examination. On all hands we hear the loud complaints of such persons, declaring that they have been wrongfully condemned." My own experience in the law courts leads me to accept these statements without reserve, and I regard as one of the gravest scandals of our present penal system the ease with which a girl who makes a pretty curtsy to the court, and who appears to be shamefaced when giving her evidence, is believed by the judge or magistrate. The dangers involved in this are obvious to many, especially to those who have much to do with children. An actor personally known to me, constantly received advances both from married women and from young girls, was pestered with letters from such persons, and to his great distress was several times followed in the streets by half-mature and immature girls. One day, in the street, he was walking with a friend, when two girls of about thirteen or fourteen years of age began to follow him. Turning round, he shouted to the girls that they had better run off home, or their father would give them a good spanking. To his astonished companion he explained that only by such drastic methods was he able, as he thought, to protect himself from false accusations.

It is very generally assumed that sexual offences against children are increasing in number. As regards the increase in Germany, the following figures are given by Mittelmaier. For sexual offences against children, the convictions in the year 1897 numbered 3085; and in the year 1904, 4378. But of hardly any offences specified in the code can we say with more certainty than we can of sexual offences against children, that the convictions bear no necessary relationship to the number of offences actually committed. My own experience in the law courts leads me to see in the figures nothing more than an increase in the number of convictions for such offences—convictions which may have involved the innocent as well as the guilty. However this may be, historical studies prove that sexual offences against children are no new thing. Long ago, Martial, in the sixth and eighth epigrams of his ninth book, complained of the procurement of children, referring to boys rather than to girls. Otto Stoll reports cases from uncivilised countries; and to his account of the defloration of children he appends the following words: "From all such details, we draw the ethnologically remarkable inference, that those human beings who have attained the highest level of civilisation, relapse frequently in the matter of the sexual life to the rudest instincts of savagery; and that in this respect neither does one civilised country much excel another, nor is 'civilised man' in a position to cast many reproaches in the teeth of the savage." Finally, I may refer to the experience of a Parisian Police Commissary, who in the middle of the nineteenth century described prostitution in Paris, and devoted a special chapter to the subject of child-prostitution. Beyond question, the committing of sexual offences against children is no peculiar privilege of the civilised world or of modern times; although it remains possible that there has of late been some increase in the number of such offences.

It is obviously right that children should receive special protection from the law. The higher limit of the age of protection varies from ten to eighteen years. Ten years is the age-limit in certain States of the American Union; seventeen is the age-limit in Finland. According to Mittelmaier, two considerations should guide us in regard to the protection of children: bodily immaturity, and moral weakness. The existence of the former leads the normal and healthy man to regard sexual approaches to children as unnatural and detestable. But, apart from the question of immaturity, we have to recognise that in children the moral sphere also deserves consideration; that notwithstanding the possible recent development of physical maturity, the child as such requires protection, in order to prevent the occurrence of such moral corruption as will render it incapable, when grown-up, of obeying the moral law. No thoughtful person can refuse to admit the child's right to protection.

But here a peculiar point needs attention, concerning, namely, the treatment in the law courts of such offences against children. I consider that by legal intervention in these cases the child's morals are sometimes more gravely endangered than by the original offence. If a man has momentarily laid his hand on the knee of a girl of ten, the child can hardly be said to have been injured, and will certainly have received much less injury than would result, if the case be brought into court, from cross-questioning of the child, not merely by its own relatives, but also by the police, the magistrate and his colleagues (in the court of first instance), by the public prosecutor and the counsel for the defence (in the higher court), and perhaps in addition by expert witnesses. When such a child is asked, whether the offender did not put his hand higher than the knee, whether he did or did not actually touch the genital organs, grave dangers may arise from such questioning. There is a further danger, in that some times, in such a case, the child is present in court throughout the entire proceedings. Some years ago, in Hamburg, I was called as an expert witness in a case of this kind. In this instance, the presiding judge, and also the public prosecutor and the defending counsel, exhibited the greatest possible delicacy, when one child was under examination, in sending the others, as far as possible, out of court. But I have also been present at trials in which no such precautions were taken, but in which every child was allowed to hear all the uncleanness in the evidence of the other children, and perhaps also in that of adults. Knowledge of the world, and, above all, tact, will best save the judge from treating children wrongly in this matter. The way in which a trial is conducted, which is often an extremely mechanical one, will not always enable the judge to avail himself of the means requisite for the protection of children from contamination in the course of such a prosecution. When we take a comprehensive view of the harm that may be done to children by sexual offences committed against them and by the consequent legal proceedings, we shall find, in my opinion, that from the legal proceedings arises a notable proportion of the injury.

The examination of the mental condition of the child-depraver is a matter of the utmost importance. In cases in which we find that the offender is suffering from some pronounced mental disorder, such as progressive paralysis (paralytic dementia), senile dementia, or an epileptic disturbance of consciousness, there can be no doubt as to the existence of irresponsibility; but it must never be forgotten that in the early course of such diseases, these sexual perversions often make their appearance at a time when no other definite signs of the brain disease have as yet appeared, and that for this reason the conviction of innocent persons—old men, for instance—on account of sexual offences against children, often occurs. Kirn, who in the Freiburg prison had under observation six old men at ages from sixty-eight to eighty-one, all convicted for sexual offences against little girls, states that in all of these there were intellectual defects, and in several of them pronounced symptoms of senile dementia. The psychiatric expert must examine all such cases with the utmost care. We may also express a wish that judges were not inclined to regard themselves as experts in this field, of which, as a rule, they have no expert knowledge whatever.

Cases in which there is no definite mental disorder belong to a different category. Fritz Leppmann, to whom we are indebted for the most comprehensive studies in this field of inquiry, comes to the conclusion that there is no such thing as a truly congenital sexual inclination towards children. Such inclinations often appear, indeed, in congenitally tainted or weak-minded individuals; but he considers that we have no right to speak of the perverse impulse as being itself congenital. Even if we admit this, and refuse to recognise the existence of a congenital perverse impulse towards children, still we have to admit that certain opportunities and conditions may not only lead to the committing of sexual offences against children, but may also induce pædophile tendencies. And the fact cannot be contested that this danger arises more especially in those who are much associated with children; especially, that is to say, in schoolmasters and tutors, on the one hand, and in schoolmistresses and governesses, on the other, Now, in every case that comes under our notice, two points must be taken into consideration. In the first place, if a remarkably large number of teachers come before the law courts charged with sexual offences against children, we have to remember that a certain proportion of these cases must arise from the false accusations to which those persons precisely are exposed who are much associated with children. The second point, on account of which limits are imposed on the extent of the last-mentioned etiological factor, is that certain persons adopt the profession of schoolmaster or mistress, or tutor or governess, either because they are aware of the fact that their sexual impulse is directed towards children, or else, and this is commoner, because, while they are but obscurely conscious of it, they are influenced thereby in the choice of a profession, without having any definite intention to make use of the children under their care in the gratification of their sexual desires It is an indefinite impulse towards children which is here operative, and sometimes determines the choice of occupation. I have seen cases in which there seemed to be a sort of mania for giving education and instruction, but in which on closer examination it appeared that the interest in the children was a sexual one. Two cases which have been reported to me show that in the case of women also opportunity very easily awakens the sexual impulse; in these cases the giving of baths to the children under their care, first definitely gave rise in two governesses to such perverse inclinations, and in one of them subsequently led to serious sexual malpractices with the children.

As regards the psychiatric treatment of true pædophilia, as a rule in such cases there is no possibility of pleading extenuating circumstances, as provided for by Section 51 of the Imperial Criminal Code. By this section, the offence escapes punishment if the offender was at the time in a state of unconsciousness, or was suffering from a morbid disturbance of mental activity, by which free voluntary choice was rendered impossible. In general, such persons must be held to be legally responsible. It may indeed, in individual cases, be possible to plead extenuating circumstances, or, when it is legally permissible, to plead the existence of partial responsibility—this latter more especially in cases in which symptoms of mental degeneration exist. But by itself a qualitatively abnormal sexual impulse gives the offender just as little right to plead irresponsibility, as a qualitatively abnormal sexual impulse gives the right to invade the sphere of interests of another. The fact that pædophile tendencies occur in those who are in other respects admirable persons does not countervail the need that children should be protected. It would be an error to assume that only morally defective persons are thus affected. I may mention in passing that Dostoiewski is said to have exhibited such pædophile tendencies—at any rate for a time. From the circle of my own acquaintanceship, I have learned that such a tendency may exist in those who are in other respects morally and intellectually sound.

In the sexual inclination of adults towards children, we find a source of serious danger; but the risks are greatly enhanced by the fact that the pædophile tendency is often complicated by other sexual perversions. Exhibitionism in the male is exhibited not only towards adult females, but also towards children, commonly towards girls, but in exceptional instances towards boys. It appears that in these cases the stimulus of innocence plays the chief part.

In many cases, the exhibitionist is satisfied with exposing his genital organs; and only in comparatively rare cases, which by many are not included in the category of exhibitionism, do we find that the exhibitionist also masturbates, sometimes in the presence of the child, sometimes after going elsewhere, The fetichistic tendencies of adults are also in many instances directed towards children. Well-known cases are those of the hair fetichists who not infrequently cut plaits of hair from the heads of schoolgirls; but other hair fetichists are satisfied with cutting from the head smaller fragments of hair.

Sexual inclinations towards children are especially apt to be associated with sadistic acts. In a comparatively large proportion of cases, children are the victims of lust-murder, if this term be used in its strictly limited signification, and not to include all possible sexual acts complicated with murder, but simply to signify cases in which the very act of murder provides a sexual stimulus, or when the corpse is utilised for a lustful act; that is to say, we must exclude from lust-murder proper, all the cases in which, for other reasons than a sadistic impulse, the sexual act is complicated with murder, as when the female witness of a previous sexual crime must be got out of the way. Children, too, are often the victims of other sexual acts, such as rape, which in a few instances only can be included in the category of sadism. In some cases force is employed only because the victim resists the act of violation, and here there is no question of sadism; but the rape is sadistic when the use of force is per se a sexual stimulus. Moreover, children are often endangered by "stabbers."

In the year 1899, there was much anxiety in the city of Cologne on account of such a stabber. Those injured were all schoolgirls, and ultimately no children were sent alone to school, but they were always accompanied by a servant or a relative. In 1901, there was a similar series of cases in Moscow, a number of half-grown girls being stabbed by a man with a dagger. In the year 1896, a stabber appeared in Berlin. He enticed schoolgirls into the vestibule of a house, under the pretence that he wanted to brush some mud from their clothing; then, drawing a knife, he would inflict on the child a long and deep incised wound. In the summer of 1901, the inhabitants of northern Berlin were terrorised by a man who stabbed one girl fatally, and wounded two others severely. A remarkable point about this case was that the stabber made three separate assaults in a single afternoon, at very brief intervals. Unless the offender is discovered, it is naturally impossible to ascertain whether he has acted under the influence of some ordinary mental disorder (such as mania or post-epileptic insanity), or if he is a sexual pervert. The act alone will not enable us to answer this question.

Boys also are liable to such attacks, as we learn from what happened in Breslau in the year 1889. A student of philosophy in that town enticed to his dwelling an eight-year-old boy whom he met in a public lavatory, and wounded the boy's penis with a sharp-pointed knife. It appeared that the offender had done the same thing before to other boys. Ultimately, having been examined by a committee of experts, he was on their recommendation adjudged to be insane. In the year 1869, Berlin was disturbed by the doings of a certain X. This man had made use of two boys for sexual purposes, and had inflicted on them horrible injuries: in one, he cut off the testicles, and inflicted other severe wounds, so that the boy died; in the other, he introduced a walking-stick through the anus, and pushed it roughly onwards until it had perforated the lung.

Far commoner than the acts of such stabbers are the cases in which the striking of children is to the sadist a source of sex-stimulation. Erotic literature is full of the description of such perversions. Thus, in a well-known pornographic eroticon, we find pictures of a girl who has to subserve the perverse lusts of a wealthy boyar (Russian territorial magnate), the latter mishandling the child most horribly with cane and knout. In the English erotic literature, it is remarkable how often and how fully the flagellation of children is described. Almost typical are the English educational works in which, with little variation, we find descriptions of the flogging of little girls in order to excite the perverse lusts of the schoolmistresses. Not very long ago, in a certain English newspaper, a special column was devoted to accounts of the chastisement of children, and especially of girls. Anyone who reads this column with care could not fail to recognise that for the most part these chastisements were the expression of perverse sexual sensibilities. The available material shows, indeed, that in England this sexually perverse whipping of children is no mere matter of imaginative literary expression, but that such perversities are a matter of actual experience. Such things are, however, by no means confined to England, as is shown by a large number of recorded observations.

In Paris, not long ago, the following case was noted. A woman entered into relations with the parents of girls of eleven and twelve years of age, in order to hire the children as the subjects of chastisement for perverse sexual purposes. The parents, who must have known for what their children were wanted, received payment. Apparently the woman did not do this for the satisfaction of any perversion of her own, but for her perverse husband or for other perverts, who watched the whippings through spy-holes. In Germany, some years ago, there was an important trial, in which I was called as an expert witness, of a man who had flogged his pupils (with one exception, they had all been boys) solely to obtain perverse sexual gratification.

Many of these cases obtain publicity through the columns of the daily press, although occasionally, in part from sensationalism, and in part from sheer ignorance, a case may be allotted to the category of sadism, which really has nothing to do with this perversion, or whose sadistic character is doubtful. This applies, for example, to the well-known Dippold case. Here, the sons of a wealthy Berlin family were mishandled by a private tutor to such an extent that one of the children died. Neither by the legal proceedings in this case, nor by any subsidiary evidence, was it established, in my opinion, that sexual motives existed for the maltreatment; and only when such motives exist have we any right to speak of sadism. As a rule, such cases are elucidated only when the mental life of the offender is very carefully analysed. Therefore, in a great many cases, while there may be grounds for suspecting the existence of sadism, adequate proof of this is not forthcoming. Some cases bearing on this matter will now be briefly recorded.

A furniture polisher, twenty-five years of age, induced two young fellows to enter his dwelling, and there, under the threat that if they resisted they would be severely punished by their parents, he made them submit to a thrashing with a cane. A similar case was reported in Paris some years ago. A man thirty-seven years of age, supposed to have formerly been a private tutor, took boarders into his house for love, and not because he made his living by doing so. He also had under his care an orphan boy, and it appeared that this child was grossly ill-treated. When the authorities entered the house, they found the boy entirely unclothed, but wrapped in rags;

he was fastened to the crossbars of the window, and quite exposed to the cold winter air. To prevent the child from crying out, a gag had been placed in his mouth. Of dubious nature, also, was a case which occurred at Berlin in the year 1906, in which a girl twelve years of age was enticed away by another girl, and taken to a man who, at the suggestion of the second girl, drew two teeth from the first. In the case reported from Salzwedel some years ago, it is possible that the offender was insane; but he may have been sadistically inclined. An eleven-year-old fifth-form boy was enticed away by a young man of twenty, who took the lad to a hotel, gagged him, beat him unmercifully with a walking cane, threatening him with a revolver to prevent his calling for help. The boy suffered also two severe contused wounds of the head. The offender himself put cold compresses on these. When the police who were in search of the boy broke into the room, the young man shot himself.

In the year 1891, the following case occurred in Berlin. A young man, not yet eighteen years old, had in three cases undressed boys, and performed improper acts on them. Then he misused and bound the boys. The youth, who had previously been convicted of theft, was on this occasion sentenced to ten years' imprisonment for an offence against (sexual) morality. At Liegnitz, a few years ago, a pupil-teacher was sent to prison for three months, because he had lured little boys to a remote field, and there had mishandled them by beating them with a walking-stick. The court held that these acts had been performed under the influence of the sexual impulse, resulting from a sadistic tendency. About two years ago, a teacher of the pianoforte committed suicide in Berlin, because he had been accused of ill-treating children, apparently owing to a sadistic tendency. The children were nine or ten years old; he had undressed them and then flogged them. The matter had, it seemed, been kept secret for a long time, until the parents of some of the children discovered traces of the ill-treatment, and this led to the charge being brought. A case which attracted considerable attention occurred in Berlin in the year 1896. A man, supposed to be a Russian prince, entered a well-known saddler's shop in the Potsdamerstrasse, asked to be shown some dogwhips, and, on the pretext of wishing to try their quality, persuaded some boys employed in the establishment to allow him to try the whips on their persons. The boys were handsomely paid for this, and the practice went on until the head of the firm intervened and forbade it. Whilst some regarded the matter as a joke, others expressed the suspicion that it was a case in which the rein had been given to sadistic tendencies. A similar case was that of the author, X., which occurred in Hamburg a few years ago. X. was acquainted with a woman named Y., who lived in Berlin. The latter's son, eleven years of age, was sent to reside with X. for educational purposes; and without proper cause, but under the pretext of educational necessities, this lad was severely mishandled by X. The boy was frequently taken from his bed, stripped naked, and then struck with a switch. The boy's mother stated that her boy had been put under the care of X. because the lad needed severe discipline, being untruthful and dishonest. Further charges were made against X. of various indecent acts against the boy. Teachers and others, who were acquainted with this boy, deposed that he was well behaved and not untruthful, and that he had in no way merited such punishments as had been inflicted on him. A very remarkable case was reported six years ago, from one of the minor German principalities. Here, children who had been sentenced to imprisonment were pardoned by the Prince, on condition that they submitted to a whipping; and the remarkable feature in the case was that not only did the Prince make a point of seeing the whipping, but himself in part administered it. In some of the reports of this case it was added that the children were stripped naked.

It is a not infrequent reproach against Catholic priests, monks, nuns, &c., that they make use of the children entrusted to their care for perverse, sadistic acts. I may recall the Graubund scandal of September 1906, in which girls and women were whipped by an acolyte until the blood ran; also an affair which occurred in Christiania about fourteen years ago, where, at a home kept by an unmarried woman, for children from the age of two years until their confirmation, a horrible and elaborate system of punishments was in use, whippings and other tortures being the order of the day. In many biographies and other works giving descriptions of life in the cloister, we find additional details: for instance, in the memoirs of the Countess Kaunitz, mother of the well-known statesman Kaunitz, we find an account of the severe whippings which were administered to her during her childhood spent in a nunnery.

All kinds of subterfuges are employed by the sexual pervert to make the punishment appear harmless and legitimate. Schoolmasters find this comparatively easy, inasmuch as they are able to allege misconduct such as would ordinarily be visited with a verbal reprimand, if not completely overlooked, as the reason for a whipping. Obviously, some of the excuses will be remarkable. In one case the flagellant asserted that he wished to write a work on education, and had therefore to ascertain how many strokes a child could endure. In a case which came under my own notice the offender stated that he wished to make the children courageous.

The expert who studies the advertisements in the newspapers will observe that they often subserve such perverse tendencies. "Educational" advertisements may be classified in three groups. Those of the first group are perfectly harmless (in appearance). To this class belong advertisements in which a teacher offers instruction to children. Since this is the ordinary form of serious advertisement, it attracts no special attention; there is nothing suspicious about it, and it is merely intended to lead to correspondence with those who have boys or girls to place as pupils. The advertiser hopes that in the course of instruction he will find opportunity for inflicting chastisement without giving rise to any suspicion. The second group has a definitely suspicious air, some catch-word being employed to manifest to initiates the existence of a perverse tendency; but there is nothing more than this to excite suspicion. Among such catch-words, are the words "energetic", "severe", "English instruction." In some cases an energetic governess desires children to instruct; in others it is some one else who desires an energetic instructress. It may be that the actual advertiser is on the lookout for the energetic instructress; here we have to do with masochism. But in other instances, the advertiser wants the energetic instructress for children, and the wording of the advertisement sometimes indicates that the advertiser's aim is to experience sexual excitement in watching the instructress chastise the children. Since these advertisements are intelligible only to initiates, they naturally receive answers from persons who have failed to understand their purport; but the sadist (male or female) and the masochist (male or female) is aware that the use of the word "energetic" refers to this sexual perversion. Of course, however, an advertisement in which an energetic tutor or governess is asked for, may he perfectly innocent. If an advertisement inserted in all good faith has really been open to a double meaning, the advertiser will sometimes be greatly astonished by the receipt of all sorts of perverse offers. A married woman of my acquaintance advertised for energetic supplementary instruction for her son, a rather naughty boy of ten; and received, in addition to many serious answers several answers from perverts, who stated that they would be delighted to be able to handle a boy in the sense she mentioned. In many cases, notwithstanding the use of the words "energetic" or "severe," we recognise from the general wording of the advertisement that it is seriously intended, and not issued with a perverse aim; but at other times we derive an opposite impression. When an "energetic instructress" advocates her "Anglo-American methods of education," hardly any room for doubt remains; and such advertisements as this belong to our third group.

I will now give some of the advertisements which I have been collecting for years, some belonging to the second, and some to the third group, in illustration of what has just been said. Certain of the advertisements which I have classed in the second group, were probably not issued with a perverse intent; this being partly shown by the context, although without this context they would have been suspicious.

The following advertisements belong to the second group: "Boy of seven to be placed under simple and scrupulous care, for the purposes of energetic education (premium paid)." "Boys and girls of a fair age received in a strict and severe boarding-school." "A strict, disciplinary master required to teach English at a preparatory school for the Army." The following advertisements are extremely suspicious: "A fairly well-educated gentleman offers energetic gratuitous supplementary instruction." "Severe education for boys and girls; energetic gentleman offers also free supplementary lessons." "Distinguished, experienced lady gives advice and help in difficult educational questions; defects of character, &c., treated with success." "Advertiser recommends himself for the severe chastisement of naughty children."

Many advertisements worded as above, or similarly, are, as was pointed out above, shown by the context to be seriously meant, and must not then be interpreted as perverse; but in the absence of such a context, the use of the catch-words so well known to sexual perverts would have rendered them highly suspicious. "Education of Boys, strict if necessary, diligence at school, school-work under continuous control, &c." This advertisement was probably not issued with perverse intent, since the advertiser's full name and address were given, and a number of additional details suggested that it was seriously meant. The same is true of the following advertisements: "Private tutor, elderly, experienced, severe instructor, holds classes, and also takes private pupils." "Daily supplementary lessons desired by a student in the fourth form of the Gymnasium [School] at X. An energetic and experienced governess wanted." "An experienced and energetic governess, thoroughly competent in the English language, very musical, desires morning or afternoon employment as teacher of children or adults." "Officer desires board with small family, preferably with authority over sons, with whom strict care would gladly be taken." "Some pupils under eleven years of age wanted to live with our own well-behaved children—no objection to those difficult to manage. Energetic assistance, strict individual instruction in the family, &c." The last few advertisements are appended in illustration, although the context (which is not in all cases given in its entirety) shows that they had no perverse intent.

Speaking generally, in view of the significance attached by sexual perverts to the words "energetic," "strict," "severe," "English methods," "discipline," &c., it will be wise, alike for those offering and for those seeking instruction, to exercise the utmost care when there is any possibility of mistake; as thus only is it possible to avoid being misled by the overtures of perverts.

Advertisements belonging to the third group, some examples of which will now be given, have of late become much rarer. Here are some: "Distinguished, energetic lady desires fairly old boys and girls for strict education." "Distinguished lady desires a child of fair age (girl by preference), to receive into the house for strict education and training." "Distinguished lady wishes to undertake the strict care and education of children of fair age, boys and girls, whose relatives have gone abroad." "Artist offers to teach French and English, strict and energetic." "Strict, energetic tutor desires children of fair age for strict education." "Energetic widow desires a boy of fair age and of good family, for strict education. Apply 'energetic,' Post-Office, No.——." "Girl, seven years old, received by energetic lady for strict education." "Tutor undertakes, gratuitously, strict education of growing children; especially suitable for cultured widow, who lacks herself the requisite energy. Unexceptionable references." "Pupils requiring energetic management, even if fairly old, received by a gentleman for strict education." "Half-grown girl received in strict board by a governess." The perverse character of these advertisements is rendered unmistakable by the fact that the catch-words are all italicised. "Naughty children; recommended for severe discipline; replies to 'Free.'" "Governess, from England, recommends her admirable boarding establishment for pupils of fair age. Apply 'Hearneshouse.'" No doubt is possible in this case, since "Hearneshouse" is the title of a sadistic novel. "Strict task-mistress wanted for a naughty girl of fourteen. Those replying to this advertisement should describe their methods of instruction." Here it is obvious that the advertiser hopes for sexual excitement from reading the descriptions of chastisement for which he asks. "English, strict method, offered by gentleman." "Highly cultured lady seeks position as English gouvernante. Delight William, Post Office, No.——." "Governess Housekeeper; cultured and distinguished lady wanted, good-looking, age twenty to twenty-eight, for the education of two motherless children, knowledge of English language required. Good presence requisite, and must be extremely energetic." Here it is possible that the advertiser really wants a housekeeper; but the advertisement is perverse in character. "Governess, youthful, energetic, very strict, either Englishwoman or Frenchwoman, wanted for spoiled children. Very good salary." "Energetic gentleman, severe disciplinarian, offers English instruction to boys and girls of fair age." No shadow of doubt is possible as to the perverse nature of this last advertisement. The same is true of the one that follows: "Gentleman offers strict instruction to older boys. Replies to 'English,' c/o Office of this paper."

An advertisement which appeared about four years ago in a Hamburg paper had a tragi-comic sequel. It ran as follows: "Difficult educational opportunity. Advertiser, residing in Hanover, with pretty daughter of twelve years, wishes to place her under strict discipline in the care of a widow with a daughter of similar age. Arrangements must be made to enable the advertiser herself to stay with the lady in Hamburg when visiting that town from time to time. In replying to the office of this paper, give a detailed account of the methods of punishment." A gentleman who suspected that this advertisement was issued by a sexual pervert, and was anxious about the future of the child, sent a reply in the simulated handwriting of a woman.

The answer he received showed that the child was, in fact, being subjected to perverse maltreatment, and in order to rescue the girl, after consultation with some friends, he communicated the facts to the Public Prosecutor. However, that official refused to interfere at this time. Then the advertisement appeared once more, and this time the offender was arrested. The gentleman thereupon wrote to the Public Prosecutor, blaming him for not having taken action on the first occasion. The Public Prosecutor regarded this as libellous, and actually brought an action for libel against the philanthropic gentleman. Happily the Public Prosecutor lost his case; but none the less, in view of what happened, a good citizen may well hesitate in future to take similar action in the public interest, if, for some trifling excess of zeal, he is to render himself liable to an action for libel.

As I said above, of late years, in Berlin at any rate, such advertisements appear less often; or those that do appear belong chiefly to the second group. Doubtless we owe this to the action of the authorities, and more especially to a paragraph of the Lex Heinze, of whose existence but few persons are aware, and of which, as my own note-books show, certain sexual perverts have only become aware to their sorrow through a legal prosecution. I refer to the paragraph by which the issue of advertisements for an immoral purpose is declared to be a punishable offence. The newspapers have now become cautious about the insertion of advertisements whose immoral purpose is plainly perceptible. Moreover, the perverts themselves who used to issue such advertisements, having through the activity of the authorities learned the significance of the paragraph in question, no longer advertise in unmistakable terms.

CHAPTER IX

SEXUAL EDUCATION

In view of the dangers to which children are exposed from the side of the sexual life, the question presses whether and how it is possible to prevent these dangers arising, or, if prevention has failed, to minimise them. To enable us to answer this question, the general question of sexual education will have to be considered. In so far as sexual manifestations in the child may arise from hereditary taint, the sociologist will endeavour to prevent them by hindering marriage or procreation on the part of those likely to give birth to such children (eugenics). Our present knowledge, however, does not enable us to say, when an individual exhibits some particular tendency to sexual aberration, whether this same tendency will appear as a concrete symptom in the descendants. Apart, indeed, from certain cases of very severe taint, we are hardly in a position even to predict with any high degree of probability that the offspring will exhibit morbid endowments. There are marriages which we expect to result in the birth of congenitally defective children, and in spite of this the offspring are healthy; and conversely, we sometimes meet with affections which we are in the habit of regarding as dependent upon hereditary transmission, and yet we fail, in these cases, to find any evidence of such affections in the progenitors. And, apart from these theoretical considerations, the physician's advice is not of much importance, for experience teaches us that in questions of marriage his advice is very rarely followed.

The less power we have to operate by control of the congenital factors, the more necessary shall we feel it to be to minimise the dangers threatening the child by influencing its environment. It is true that in this department, as in others, there is much diversity of opinion regarding the limits of educability. Some contend that we can mould the child like wax, a view which prevailed especially during the "period of enlightenment" in the eighteenth century; others maintain that organic development is predetermined at the time of procreation, and that subsequent influences can have no effect. Although we must be careful not to overestimate the power of education, it would be no less erroneous to assume that development is inalterably predetermined at the time of procreation This applies to the efficacy of educational influences in general, and to educational influences affecting the sexual life in particular. The following consideration must be given due weight. The power of the educator is limited, not merely by the child's hereditary dispositions, but also by the nature of its environment. Rudolf

Lehmann, in his work on Education and the Educator (Erziehung und Erzieher), rightly points out that Rousseau, in his Émile, when discussing the problems of education, neglects too much the influences of environment. If we wish our reasoning to furnish us with results of practical value, and not to remain confined to the purely theoretical plane, we must give due weight to this consideration. This applies with equal force to the matter of sexual education. We know that the sexual impulse may be excited by innumerable external stimuli. Such stimuli are continuously in operation, and the best educator has no power to exclude their influence. The mere association of the child with persons of the opposite sex provides such stimuli. But a separation of the sexes will not do away with them, as is proved, not only by the homosexual manifestations of the undifferentiated sexual impulse, but also by those that arise transiently, at any rate, when the members of one sex are completely segregated from those of the other—as in boarding-schools, on board ship, and in prisons. The educator cannot even count on being at all times able to safeguard the child from the sight of sexual acts. In the country, but also in the town, children have opportunities for this; not only when the members of a large family sleep in a single room, and the children can watch their parents and others in the act of sexual intercourse; but in various other ways. The mere kissing of affianced lovers must in this sense be regarded as a sexual act, and how is it possible so to bring up a child that it will never have an opportunity of seeing anything of the kind? If we go further, and recognise that through the association of ideas such a sexual stimulus may arise from witnessing the coupling of animals—of dogs, for instance, in the street—we shall understand how the educator's powers are limited by the milieu in which he has to work. We have, therefore, to recognise clearly from the first, that in the education of the child the complete exclusion of sexual stimuli is impossible.

Obviously, when the external noxious influences exceed a certain measure, we may endeavour to effect an improvement by measures of general hygiene, through the activities of the central government, the municipality, or the community at large. In this connexion, we think of better housing conditions, of the separation of children from night-lodgers, and the like measures. But, even here, we must guard against making Utopian demands, after the manner of many fanatics on the subject of social hygiene, whose proposals are often quite incompatible with the maintenance of human intercourse. Independently of such impracticable demands for future reforms, the educationalist of to-day seeks to protect the child from unduly frequent sexual excitement. But sometimes the result is other than he expects. Sport is recommended to divert the mind from sexual ideas, and yet I have known cases in which marked sexual excitement has been induced in this way. I am not now referring to mechanical stimulation through bicycling or horseback-riding, of which I shall speak later; but many a child has been sexually excited through playing tennis with a girl-companion, and many a boy has been sexually excited through rowing with another. Still, the fact that here and there a child may have been sexually excited in such a way, is no reason for condemning what is invaluable to the enormous majority of children.

This is all that need be said regarding the manner in which general influences may counteract the efforts of the educationalist. But experience shows that the good effects of education are also seriously impaired by individual factors, especially by congenital predisposition, or by a tendency acquired very early in life. Although we no longer assume that human impulses, emotions, and sentiments take their course quite independently of the influence of other psychical powers, such as the reason and the will, still, unprejudiced observation shows that the power of the reason and the will is less than many persons imagine. In very many cases we are able to see how difficult it is, in a child of ten or less, to exert any notable influence upon the impulses, the emotions, and the sentiments. This is no less true in the positive than it is in the negative aspect. In one child it may be just as difficult to induce a fondness for music or reading, as it is in another to break it of an inclination for romping or other games. The same is true of the emotions—fear, for instance. In many cases, logically planned efforts may be altogether out of relationship to the result. Above all, great weight must be laid upon the consideration that there is a tendency to overrate the effect of education in the form of precept as compared with the effect of example. A child may receive the best of instruction without result, if in its own environment it is continually seeing something precisely the opposite of that which it is being told. This applies with equal force to the sexual life, which can be influenced far more readily by example than by good teaching, if the latter, though daily repeated, conflicts with what the child sees every day in the conduct of its relatives and companions.

Although, for this reason, we must avoid forming an exaggerated idea of the utility of individual sexual education, this is not meant to imply that we should assume a perfectly passive attitude, and leave everything to the uncontrolled course of development, in order to allow the child, as the modern phrase goes, "to live its own life."

Before passing to consider details, we must consider the elementary bases of all matters connected with the education of children—namely, morality and custom. These two words are connected by their inner significance, and not merely by etymological meaning; but they represent different standards for passing judgment upon our actions. Certain things conflict with established custom, without its being permissible for us to speak of them as immoral. If at a social gathering for which evening dress is the rule, a gentleman turns up in light tweeds, he is guilty of a breach of custom, but not of an immoral action. If an officer in the army, having impregnated a young girl of the working class, marries her, his action is a moral one in the positive sense, but in spite of this he commits an offence against the customs of his class. Moreover, we have to remember that an act which is immoral or opposed to custom at a certain time and among a certain people, may at another time, or among another people, be neither the one nor the other. In such matters, opinions change; and this applies also to the case of actions connected with the sexual life. Herodotus relates that in Babylon the virgins had, for a money payment, and in honour of the Goddess of Love, to give themselves to a strange man; and similar customs are reported of other peoples of antiquity. In providing for the sexual education of the child, we have to take into account such changes of view; but we have also to consider the matter in relation to the present condition of our civilisation, for the child is to be a citizen of a real, not of an imaginary State.

Intimately related to custom and morality are certain psychical processes, especially the sentiment of shame. This is aroused by actions which are considered immoral by ourselves or by members of our environment, and by actions which conflict with established custom. The child detected in a lie is ashamed, either because the act is immoral, or more often because the act is by others regarded as immoral; for the opinion of others plays a great part in the causation of shame. The man who has forgotten to put on his necktie, and in that condition appears in public, is ashamed, because he has committed a breach of custom. This dependence of the sense of shame upon morality and custom is true above all in matters of sex. A girl who is undressing in a hotel room, and has forgotten to bolt the door, so that a strange man suddenly enters by mistake, is ashamed; equally ashamed is a girl who encounters an exhibitionist with his penis exposed. These examples suffice to show that the sentiment of shame, which is associated with great discomfort, is a safeguard against immorality and against breaches of custom.

Similar relations exist for the sense of disgust, which is allied to the sense of shame. Shame is felt in the performance of an action disgusting to others, if against one's will one is watched in the process. Defæcation is usually effected in some retired place: in the onlooker, defæcation arouses disgust; whilst by the person defæcating, if he knows that he is being observed, shame is felt. Normal sexual intercourse between a man and a woman, objectively regarded, is a no less unæsthetic act than pseudo-coitus between two men. None the less, in most persons, the sight of the former act arouses less disgust than that of the latter. This difference depends upon the fact that by most persons homosexual intercourse is also felt to be immoral. In this relationship between the sense of disgust and immorality, it is often impossible to determine what is primary and what is secondary. A mutual retroaction occurs: the sense of disgust is increased, because the act is regarded as immoral; and, on the other hand, a strong sense of disgust may increase the perception of immorality. The same mutual relationships with the ideas of morality are found in connexion with the sense of shame. Beyond question, the sentiments of shame and of disgust are closely connected with the ideas of custom and morality; for shame and disgust arise especially in connexion with matters which conflict with our ideas of morality. It will, therefore, readily be understood that in moral education it is of the greatest importance what are the processes in connexion with which the instructor seeks to arouse the sentiments of shame and disgust; and, on the other hand, it is obvious that the ideas of morality induced by education, favour the development, in certain specific relationships, of the sentiments of shame and disgust.

It is a disputed question whether the sentiments of shame and disgust are inborn. In this controversy, two matters are confused, between which it is necessary to distinguish: the general disposition to experience such sentiments, and the special disposition to react with these sentiments to specific occurrences. The fact is incontestable, that the general disposition to these sentiments is inborn. Inborn, also, is the association of specific bodily processes with the corresponding mental states: blushing, with the sentiment of shame; retching and vomiting, with the sentiment of disgust; these associations are certainly not chance products of education. The only point in doubt is, to what extent the tendency is inborn to experience these sentiments as a result of certain specific stimuli. By some it is assumed, that when we experience disgust at the sight of certain animals—a worm, for instance—such concrete reactions depend upon inborn dispositions; whereupon the further problem emerges, how did our ancestors acquire the disposition they have transmitted to us, their descendants. Others believe that influences operating after birth have led to the association with the sight or idea of the worm of the tendency to feel disgust. Very early in life, the child has seen others exhibit disgust at a worm; doubtless he has often been told how disgusting this animal is; and thus gradually the sentiment of disgust has become associated with the sight or the idea of the worm. With the sentiment of shame, similar conditions obtain. If a human being feels shame in connexion with certain matters, and therefore avoids them, this may depend upon influences operating in the individual life (imitation, education, suggestion, &c.), by which the feeling of shame has been associated with certain perceptions. On the other hand, it is possible that shame may be dependent upon a special inborn disposition. Certain processes in the animal world—for example, the fact that many animals deposit their excrement in hidden places, and the fact that bitches and other female animals sometimes behave in a way which is interpreted as the exhibition of shame—may be regarded as the result of an inborn disposition. But others refer to the slight degree in which little girls appear to feel shame, as an indication that this sentiment is acquired during the individual life. Undoubtedly, we sometimes find manifestations of shame in very early childhood. Sikorsky reports that his son exhibited typical shame at the early age of three and a half years. The boy was washing himself, having for this purpose taken off his coat and bared the upper part of the body. When his father unexpectedly entered the room, the boy was ashamed and startled, and said pleadingly, as he endeavoured to cover himself by crossing his hands over the breast, "Please don't come in, for I haven't got my shirt on." Sikorsky rightly points out that this position of the arms is typical of the sentiment of shame. Still, such cases are comparatively rare; and in contrast with them we may often note that older children, even girls of eight or a little more, will in play raise their petticoats so high that it is necessary to turn away if we wish to avoid seeing the genital organs, and often a word of reproof is needed from the mother or nurse to indicate to the child that it is doing something improper. The fact that in little children the sense of shame is so little developed, but that subsequently this sentiment becomes clearly manifest, has been used as an argument against the theory that it is inborn; but this argument cannot be accepted without reserve, for an inborn quality may not manifest itself until a certain definite age is reached—as we see clearly in the case of the sexual impulse—and this apart from the consideration that the development of an inborn quality may be inhibited by influences acting during the individual life. Whatever view we take of this problem, there can be no doubt as to the possibility of exerting a marked influence upon both qualities, the sentiment of disgust and the sentiment of shame, by means of influences operating during the lifetime of the individual. Thus, by education and habituation, it is possible to learn to repress disgust towards certain animals or certain excreta, as is done by the physician, and by nurses, male and female. The sentiment of disgust also depends largely upon general customs. The civilised European makes a mock of the fact that other races, certain oriental races, for instance, eat foods which to us are disgusting. A European invited as a guest at certain foreign banquots, is thoroughly disgusted when he sees food put into the mouth with the fingers instead of with knife and fork. And yet there is no great difference in respect of our own practice, when we put a piece of chocolate, a grape, or the like, into our own mouths. If, in Europe, we saw someone eating a pigeon in the same way as that in which we are accustomed to eat a crayfish, many persons would experience disgust. And yet, objectively considered, there is no reason to be less disgusted at the eating of crayfishes than when some other kind of animal is eaten in the same manner. Such modification of the sentiment of disgust by habit and custom applies also to sexual matters. A girl who experiences disgust at the sight of semen or the act of its ejaculation, may, through habituation, cease to feel such disgust.

Similarly with the sentiment of shame, we find that in some persons it is aroused by matters to which others are more or less completely indifferent—and this is true no less of the sexual sense of shame than of shame in general. We note the way in which habit or other influences may diminish or even entirely suppress the sentiment of sexual shame, from the fact that prostitutes willingly undress in the presence of a strange man without any sense of shame (although it must be admitted that some remnants of shame may remain even in many prostitutes). Finally, the experience of the marriage-bed shows how rapidly the sentiment of shame in respect of certain situations may disappear or largely diminish. Although a refined woman may long, and in some cases permanently, manifest a certain reserve towards her husband, still, there is an enormous degree of difference between the intensity of the sentiment of shame which a young bride experiences when undressing on her bridal night and that which she experiences in the like situation after a year of married life.

Other circumstances show that these sentiments are influenced, not merely by individual habituation, but also by the nature of general customs. A lady of the nobility, president, perhaps, of a Ladies' Society for the Promotion of Public Morals, may regard the short skirts of a music-hall dancer as the acme of impropriety, and yet will not hesitate for a moment to go into society in the evening in a low dress, with her breasts plainly visible to anyone standing by her when she is seated. The same lady would probably be furious at the suggestion that she should show herself to men in the dress of a ballet-dancer, but with a high corsage. And yet, experience shows that in other circumstances the short skirt is quite acceptable, inasmuch as when bicycling first obtained a vogue among the upper classes, ladies of high standing were to be seen in the streets with short skirts and visible calves. In Germany, and in many other countries, it was for long regarded as improper for men and women to bathe in common. The Americans, however, saw no impropriety in mixed bathing, and of late years even the Germans find it possible for the sexes to mix in bathing without any offence to the sense of shame. Here we have nothing more than the revival of an old custom, for in former centuries mixed bathing was practised in Germany.

From the examples just given, we see clearly the way in which the objects and situations with which are associated manifestations of shame and disgust, depend upon habituation and general custom. But just because this is so, both these sentiments are in the highest degree adapted to furnish protection against actions which are opposed to dominant custom, or are condemned by the prevailing moral code. By the sense of shame, the young girl is prevented from surrendering her person to any man who desires her. Shame interferes with the very preparations for the sexual act; for example, with the act of undressing in the presence of a man. The sentiment of disgust may also exert a protective influence, for disgust is aroused in women by the semen and its ejaculation, and by many other things connected with the sexual act.

All these considerations combine to show how important it is that proper care should be taken to promote in the child the proper development of the sentiments of shame and disgust, and also of the moral ideas. It need hardly be said, that the sentiments of shame and disgust are not the only psychical aids in the sexual education of children. There are others, such as the fear of disagreeable consequences, which deters human beings from many immoral actions, and often enough at the outset greatly furthers the development of moral ideas; also there is direct instruction, the influence of which will be considered later.

But in the moral education of children, and also in the disquisitions of adults upon morality, mistakes are made. In particular, no distinction is made whether anything is to be regarded as immoral per se, or whether it is only considored immoral in certain circumstances. This is shown very clearly in the formation of opinions, from the standpoint of sexual morality, regarding nakedness and the sexual life. Because, in particular situations, nakedness is immoral, the child is often taught to regard nakedness as being per se disgraceful. Similarly with the sexual life. Instead of aiming at its proper control, the idea instilled is that the mere mention of sexuality, and even its very existence, are things gravely immoral. The very same persons who teach the child to repeat the commandment, Honour thy father and thy mother, educate it also in such a way that it is forced to regard the act to which it owes its own existence as something which must have rendered its parents unclean. It has to be admitted that at times it is by no means easy, in these matters, to find the right way; its discovery demands, not interest merely, but also intelligence; it is, perhaps, an art. But often the right course is not so very difficult to find; and if we only exercise reasonable care in the repression of hypocrisy and of perverse moral ideas, we shall be able to educate the child in such a way that he will come to understand that exposure of his person is not a matter of pure indifference, and yet will not regard nakedness as something unclean. The little girl who draws her petticoats too high, will stop doing so when her mother forbids it. A child will not always ask the reason for such a prohibition; and if it does ask, all the mother need answer in this case, as in so many others in which the child is not yet competent to understand the reason, is that it will understand well enough when it is older. When the child is older, and when its understanding has enlarged, the mother need make no difficulty about explaining the true reason in a suitable manner.

In respect also of the sentiment of disgust, exaggerations must carefully be avoided. From a feeling of shame, and for fear of arousing disgust in others, many young girls refrain, when in the company of other persons, from retiring to satisfy the calls of nature. The physician knows that this may result not merely in discomfort, but in consequences by no means indifferent to health. In this respect also, a just mean must be the aim of education. The child has to be taught that, alike for æsthetic and for hygienic reasons, the evacuation of the excreta must be effected in a retired place. But it is necessary to avoid going to the extreme of producing in the child the impression that there is something disgusting in the faintest intimation of such a physical need, or of making it feel that there is something essentially shameful in the fulfilment of these natural functions. The same considerations apply also to the sentiment of disgust in relation to the sexual life. In this also overstatement must be avoided. The education of young girls aims to a large extent at inducing them to regard the sexual act, not merely as something of which they should be ashamed, but as something in itself disgusting. It is well known that quite a number of women are altogether unable to give themselves up to the sexual act in such a way as to derive from it real enjoyment and satisfaction. A part of the severe disillusionment following marriage, depends upon the lack of normal sexual sensibility in the wife; and it is by no means improbable that this state depends in some cases upon the education received in girlhood. If it is impressed on anyone from childhood upwards that a particular act is disgusting and shameful, ultimately inhibitions may arise, owing to which the natural impulse to the performance of that act, and its natural course and natural enjoyment, may be prevented. And although the widely prevalent lack of sexual sensibility in women has additional causes, nevertheless I regard it as probable that in some of the cases, at any rate, this insensibility directly results from educational influences. In this matter, too, we must guard against exaggeration. We must educate children, boys as well as girls, in the belief that to mishandle the genital organs is forbidden alike by divine and by human law. But we must not teach them to regard the sexual act as in itself disgusting; more especially in view of the fact that such an idea conflicts with the lofty ethical significance of the act to which we all owe our existence.

What has been said about nakedness, has bearings also upon the relationships of the education of children to the matter of the nude in art. No intelligent person will deny the importance to art of the representation of the nude. A clothed Venus is a thing with which the connoisseur would prefer to dispense. Although I am not myself an enthusiastic adherent of the movement started a few years back with a great flourish of trumpets for the introduction of art into the education of children—a movement which has already perceptibly slackened—I do not wish to deny the important bearings of art upon the education of the child. Children who are still comparatively young, have not as a rule much understanding of art. None the less, we must not withhold from the child possibilities of appreciating the beauties of the nude. Apart from this purely educational aim, we have to remember that it is impossible to preserve children completely from the sight of the nude in art. We might, of course, exclude them from our museums; but our own houses also often contain nude statuary, and books with illustrations of the nude figure; and nude statues are to be seen also in places of public resort. A demand for the removal of such nude figures is so stupid, that it hardly deserves serious discussion—outside of the columns of the comic papers. A classical education, too, gives so many opportunities for the sight or the mention of the nude—for instance, delineations of the gods of the ancient mythology that the demands of the "morality-fanatics" could be met only by cutting off the child from the most beautiful sources of culture. But now, let those who, in the lower classes of our schools, have seen in the text-books of mythology pictures of unclad gods and goddesses, seriously ask themselves whether in this connexion they ever experienced even the faintest uncleanness of thought! If in one among thousands of such children, the sight of such a picture is followed by an undesired result, we have further to remember that this fact does not give us the right to deprive thousands of other children of the spiritual nourishment requisite for their emotional and æsthetic development, and for their general culture. There is no need for any anxiety about this question of the nude in art; and we must avoid suggesting to children that there is anything peculiar about the nakedness of statuary. We are, indeed, justified in asking whether the replacement or concealment of the genital organs by a fig-leaf—a practice supposed to have been initiated by the influence of the Jesuits about the middle of the eighteenth century—is a sound one; or whether this is not the very way to lead to objectionable conversations between children. The child compares the work of art with its own body and with the bodies of others which it has seen, notes the difference at once, and is thereby incited to improper conversation.

Those who wish to prevent children seeing artistic representations of the nude are influenced by two very different motives, although by the morality-fanatics themselves these motives are not clearly distinguished. Sometimes we are told that the sight of the nude in art may awaken the child's sexual impulse, sometimes that morality forbids such representations of the nude. These two reasons must not be confused; for even if well-developed moral ideas may repress sexual acts, it does not follow that everything which is immoral is also sexually exciting. A great many pictures are immoral, and yet do not tend in the very least to induce sexual excitement—it suffices to mention illustrations of scatological scenes. Another source of error lies in the fact that things which appear sexual to the adult, may to the child be entirely devoid of sexual colouring. There is an amusing anecdote of a little girl who had been bathing with other children, and on her return home was asked whether boys had been bathing as well as girls; "I don't know," said the little one, "for they were all naked!" This story is based upon a profound insight into the nature of the child, for children in general do not regard nakedness as sexually important—though a few exceptions to this rule may be encountered. Just because the child is so often taught that nakedness is in itself immoral, we are apt also to teach it to experience sexual excitement at the sight of a nude statue; whereas if the child had simply been taught that nakedness at unsuitable times and places was wrong, no such reaction would ensue. I remember the time in which the strong agitation took place which led to the passing of the Lex Heinze; and I was acquainted with a gentleman—he was a patient of mine—who was a member of the party by which the new law was so strongly demanded. When one day he came to see me, bringing with him his little boy, the latter noticed in my waiting-room a nude statue of a woman, but which the little boy took for a man. The child, who was obviously attempting to repeat something he had often heard said, asked his father naïvely: "Papa, if that were a woman, it would be improper, wouldn't it?" This remark is at once natural and characteristic; the child would never have felt the possibility that the statue was in any way improper, unless his education had led him to regard nakedness as disgraceful, or as immoral and improper. There is no doubt that our clothing is intimately connected with the development of the sentiment of shame and with the formation of our ideas of morality. But the more we learn so to form the mind of the child that it will not regard nakedness as being per se immoral, the sooner shall we be able, not only to instil into children truly moral ideas, but also to safeguard them against the risks of premature sexual excitement.

The considerations just stated apply mutatis mutandis to the question of what children should be allowed to read. Although we should give to children neither obscene or erotic books, still, we should not withhold from them every poem which deals with love. If such were our rule, we should have to forbid the most beautiful works in our literature, and also our folk-tales. Read, for example, Grimm's tales, and you will find many passages which our morality-fanatics would reject as improper; for instance, the story of the Sleeping Beauty in the Wood, and many others, telling of beauty, love, and kisses. The same remark applies to the folk-songs. There are persons, indeed, who would like to edit such songs and stories especially for the use of children. The case will be remembered in which the song, In einem kühlen Grunde, was so modified for the use of children that they were told, not of the "beloved maiden" who dwelt there, but of an "uncle" instead! Now, either the child that hears this song for the first time has as yet no understanding of the idea of love, and in that case there will be no danger in singing in its original form this song whose full beauty will not until later become manifest to the child; or else it has some understanding, and then the replacement of the girl by an uncle will certainly do nothing to safeguard the child's morality, but will merely corrupt its taste. The assumption that by hearing such a song, the awakening of sexuality can possibly be antedated, is almost ridiculous; and little or no proof has been offered that anything of the sort ever occurs. One who in such a song sees the least suspicion of immorality, and who thinks that the hearing of it entails danger to a child, not only betrays the corruption of his own taste, but lays himself open to the countercharge that his own moral endowments are somewhat defective. Similar conditions apply to the theatre, and to the other factors in the mental development of children, and of human beings in general. It is quite impossible to isolate children from every intimation of the erotic or the sexual. Let us remember the wide diffusion of the newspapers of our day. We cannot prevent children from reading newspapers; a statement that applies not to large towns merely, but to small towns and to the country districts as well. I speak here, not only of newspapers which are known to be sensational, but of others as well. The more serious periodicals are to-day often inclined to devote a good deal of space to many sexual occurrences; they even err in transforming many non-sexual matters into sexual ones, giving them a superfluous erotic background. They miss no chance of converting an ordinary murder into a lust-murder; of describing a common assault as the outcome of sadism; and of writing of any woman of whom mention has to be made in connexion with some public occurrence, as a young lady of surpassing beauty. But apart from all this, the newspapers are to-day so full of sexual matters (the question of sexual enlightenment, the prevention of the venereal diseases, the suppression of prostitution, the protection of motherhood, &c.), that with the best will in the world it is impossible to keep children from reading about such things. Nor can this be regarded as unfortunate, so long as these questions are treated in a moderate manner.

It is altogether different as regards erotic and obscene books and pictures. Unfortunately such products obtain a wide currency in schools, in part as printed pornographica, and in part passed from hand to hand in the written form. Thus, from a number of girls' schools come reports of the circulation of thoroughly obscene writings among girls from twelve to fourteen years of age. Especial favourites are descriptions of the wedding-night, mostly in manuscript form; also an obscene version of the story of Faust and Gretchen; and quite a number of other improper poems pass from hand to hand in girls' schools. In boys' schools, the circulating matter consists rather of obscene printed books and pictures. It is evident that the advertisements in many newspapers indicate the chief source of such articles. There is a trade in obscene pictures advertised under the harmless title of "Parisian Landscapes." For the most part these advertisements originate in Paris; to a lesser extent they come from Hungary, Austria, Italy, and Spain. The German traders in such commodities do not venture to advertise their wares in the German newspapers; nor is there any evidence in foreign newspapers of such advertisements proceeding from Germany. Through the meritorious activity of the Volksbund zur Bekämpfung des Schmutzes in Wort und Bild (The Popular League for the Suppression of Obscene Writings and Pictures), these advertisements have of late almost disappeared from our newspapers. But it can hardly be doubted that formerly immeasurable harm was done to children in this way. This is shown by the fact that half-grown boys often buy such things and circulate them among their school-fellows, all the more in view of the comparatively low price at which they can be obtained. The wide diffusion of the evil is proved by the frequency with which such things are confiscated in boys' schools, and with which obscene photographs are found even in girls' schools. For the suppression of such pornographica in recent days we have certainly in great part to thank the League above named, whose efforts for good must not be confounded with the obscurantist aims of the pious and hypocritical individuals to whom every nude statue is an improper object.

The frequency with which such pornographica are circulated in schools is subject to very great variations; but in the production of these differences, certain factors which are sometimes given great weight, really play a comparatively small part. Thus, it is commonly supposed that there is a great difference in this respect between large towns and small; but in the schools of small towns, pornographic writings and pictures are at least as common as in those of large towns; and, indeed, the addresses to which pornographic photographs are despatched from Paris are usually in the small towns. Thus the determining influence is not the difference between the large town and the small; and the character of the school depends, not only upon the moral level of its pupils, but above all upon the moral level and the personal influence of the head of the school and the assistant teachers. I know certain schools, and some of these in large towns, in which hardly a single improper word is spoken by the pupils, and where no sexual improprieties take place among the children, even though it has to be assumed that many of them indulge, at any rate from time to time, in solitary masturbation. But, on the whole, the spirit of such schools is an admirable one, in contrast to others, in which extremely loose manners prevail. Above all, therefore, we must avoid thinking that we state the truth of this matter by using the catch-word of "the corruption of the great towns."

It cannot be contested that the diffusion of these things among children involves serious dangers alike to their morals and to their health. Speaking generally, upon adults pornographic objects have rather a repellent than a sexually exciting effect. In the case of children in whom no sexual sensibility has as yet developed, they exercise no sexual stimulation, but may later give rise to ill effects. But it is to ripening children and young persons, who do not yet understand the sexual life, but to whom it is first displayed in this form, that such pornographic objects are especially dangerous. Thus we find that many offenders against sexual morality show children obscene pictures, in order to excite them sexually, and render them compliant. Such sexual excitement is per se bad for the child's health; but the moral dangers are even more important.

Children who have become familiar with such obscene objects may perhaps suffer in consequence from an inadequate development or even from a complete inhibition of the higher psychical elements of the sexual life. The grave injury inflicted on children by these pornographica cannot possibly be doubted. What has been said above should, however, suffice to show that the nude in art has no necessary connexion with this danger from pornographic objects; although unfortunately, for business reasons, many persons hypocritically attempt to justify by false reference to the interests of art, drawings of the nude really intended to furnish erotic stimulus.

The much-discussed question of the common education of the sexes (coeducation) is related to the mental hygiene of the sexual life of the child. I shall deal with this question only in so far as it bears upon our subject; and shall not consider whether other reasons, such as the different endowments of the sexes, are decisively opposed to coeducation. But coeducation has been opposed also for reasons of sexual education, on two grounds: that it leads to a premature awakening of the sexual life, and that it gives rise to immoral practices between the children.

It is true that when boys and girls associate freely together the first sexual feelings of boys are directed towards girls. But a separation of boys and girls at school would here be of little use. Not only would some other person of the female sex be apt to take the place of a girl school-fellow, some person the boy often sees, it may be a grown woman, it may be a child (a school-friend of the boy's sister or of the family, a girl-cousin, or some girl employed about the house); but in many cases, if the sexes are separated in youth, both in boys and in girls the sexual impulse, when it awakens, may perhaps be directed towards a member of the same sex.

A further problem is that of the sexual practices which may result from the sexual impulse. It is an indisputable fact that many boys, when the contrectation impulse is intermingled with the detumescence impulse, readily take to sexual practices with others. Examples of this constantly occur in boarding-schools, and in all other kinds of educational institutions; even in day-schools, where tho children live apart from one another, we may observe that occasionally they begin sexual practices very early in life (mutual masturbation, and intimate physical contact, especially contact involving the genital organs). We must always bear in mind the possibility that coeducation may lead to the more frequent occurrence of such practices between boys and girls. But we must avoid over-estimating this danger. In the first place, there are many institutions, higher schools and others, attended only by pupils of one sex, in which mutual sexual practices never take place, and in which neither boys nor girls, even though sexual inclinations arise in them, ever effect sexual intimacies with other children. Although mutual masturbation is fairly common in schools, it cannot be regarded as the general rule. Further, it may be pointed out that when boys and girls are educated in common, the girls' natural instincts of self-defence will in many cases lead them to repel improper sexual advances. This is proved by the actual experience of coeducation. Finck gives reports regarding coeducation in the schools of the western states of the American Union, and informs us that there every girl has her beau of fourteen to seventeen years of age. Notwithstanding the fact that these are boys of a fair age, undesirable consequences have not been observed. This view is substantiated by the reports made to me personally by American men and women, in whose truthfulness and judgment I have complete confidence. During a lengthy American tour, and on other occasions, I have elaborately questioned American physicians, ministers of religion, school-teachers, and fathers and mothers of families, regarding this matter. Their universal opinion was that no such undesirable results of coeducation were ever observed. Indeed, I received numerous assurances regarding the customary sexual abstinence of American young men who had been educated in common with American girls. In many of these circles, a young man known to indulge in sexual intercourse, whether with a prostitute or in a so-called "intimacy," was immediately ostracised; and this shows that as far as the question of sexual chastity is concerned, the results of the coeducation of the sexes are at least not more unfavourable than those of the separate education of the sexes. I am well aware that many doubt the harmlessness of these conditions in America, and declare the account given of them hypocritical. My own information, however, leads me to contest this for numerous cases. Of course we have to remember that the population of the United States of America is an extremely composite one, made up of numerous nationalities, whose customs differ as much as do those of the different social strata. The above remarks refer chiefly to the old Anglo-American circles. It is indisputable that even in these circles certain changes have recently taken place. The Americans refer this to their more extensive relations with Europe, in consequence of which European customs and opinions, by which sexual abstinence is not demanded of young men, have been gradually introduced into those circles of American life in which formerly other views obtained.

But even if we believe that in isolated instances coeducation may lead to unfortunate results in the way of sexual practice, we have to remember the objections which may be adduced from the standpoint of sexual education against the separate education of the sexes. Especially we have to think of the fact that by the separation of the sexes during childhood we may favour the development of homosexuality. Apart from this consideration, I believe that in girls the capacity for self-protection arises much earlier in life when frequent association of boys and girls is permitted—a method of education which in Europe of late, at any rate outside the school, has become far more common than in former days, and one which is greatly favoured by the joint playing of games and other joint sports.

If the question be asked whether the sexual life awakens earlier in children who mix freely with those of the opposite sex, or in those whose companionship is confined to members of their own sex, we find it difficult to detect any notable difference in this respect. As regards boys in boarding-schools, the information available certainly suffices to lead us to this conclusion; and from such information as I have received from girls' schools, and from the behaviour of schoolgirls (some of these quite young), I infer that no notable difference in the age at which sexual sensibility first makes its appearance, results from the coeducation or the separate education of the sexes.

One condition has to be imposed, if coeducation is not to entail any dangers. The child must not be allowed to regard such education as experimental, and as possibly dangerous. If the child were to be enlightened with all sorts of warnings, dangers might ensue. It is necessary that the child should regard coeducation as something perfectly natural. In this connexion, the matter assumes a different aspect, according as coeducation is undertaken from the outset, or only after the children are already half-grown. From the latter course, perils might sometimes arise, as Gertrud Bäumer rightly insists. From the earliest days of childhood onwards, coeducation should appear to the child as a matter of course; only if this is not the case, may the practice prove dangerous from the sexual standpoint, and especially from the standpoint of sexual morality.

Here, of course, I make no attempt to offer a decisive opinion one way or the other upon the disputed question of coeducation of the sexes. My sole aim has been to show that certain of the objections commonly made to coeducation, on the grounds with which we are especially concerned in this book, do not bear examination.

Better reasons can be found for objecting to some other modes of association on the part of children of the two sexes. The most important of these are common dancing lessons and children's balls. These are not so recent a development as is often assumed. More than a century ago, Pockels, the distinguished psychologist and educationalist, objected strongly to dancing parties for children, which commonly lasted, he tells us, from five o'clock in the afternoon till midnight, and sometimes even on into the small hours of the morning. Beyond question, the association of children in dances can by no means be regarded as more innocuous than coeducation, all the more in view of the fact that the children at such dances are often fairly old—towards the end of the second period of childhood, or in the early years of the period of youth. For my own part, the danger of children's balls appears to me to affect, not so much the sphere of sexual morality, as that of hygiene and general morality. As regards the danger to health, I have known parents who were always complaining of the way in which their children were overworked at school, and yet saw nothing wrong in these same children going to dancing lessons on two evenings every week.

In conclusion, I will report a case which proves that when children are inclined to sexual practices, they will find sufficient opportunity, even in the absence of coeducation. This was the case of a boy of eight and a girl of seven years, who stripped quite naked and got into bed together; from the fact that spots of blood were found on the bed-clothing, it appeared that very definite sexual malpractice had taken place. The girl's sexual history was followed up for three years after this. She showed herself much inclined to make sexual advances towards adults, pressing herself up against them in a way which innocent persons interpreted as manifesting the caressive inclinations of the child.

Having given this illustrative case, I must not omit to state that similar incidents may, of course, occur from time to time in connexion with the coeducation of children. But we must avoid the error of attributing to external chance-influences, such as coeducation, occurrences which are dependent upon the very nature of human beings; for such things happen whatever method of education be adopted. Naturally, the difference between the sexes must not be ignored; but in children the existence of sexual differentiation must not be incessantly and anxiously emphasised. Brothers and sisters, when they have reached a certain age, should certainly not be placed naked together in a bath. But this is to be avoided, not for fear lest thereby sexual excitement might result in the children, but because to do so would be in opposition to the customs of our time, and it is precisely by such contrasts with generally accepted customs, that the attention of children is aroused. Further, we may approve of the fact that in consequence of the movement for child-protection (Kinderschutz), the misuse of children in various ways—in the theatre, for example—has undergone a notable diminution. But in this matter also, the decisive factor is not exclusively the interest of sexual morality, but rather the rights of the children themselves. The same consideration applies, in part, to an earlier movement. In France, in the year 1848, the appearance of children on the stage was legally prohibited, one reason alleged for this enactment being the moral dangers resulting from the mixing of the sexes in such conditions, but reference was also made more particularly to the need for the better protection of the physical and mental powers of the children.

I come now to the description of certain other mental influences necessary for the child. A very important point is that we should use our utmost endeavours to divert the child from the sexual impulse. The more the awakening of this impulse threatens to force itself upon the child's attention, the more necessary is it to bring into play the measured activity of other faculties and interests. We think here as much of methods of æsthetic culture, reading, and the theatre, as of bodily sports and games. At the same time, it must be our aim to cultivate the general strength of the will, since this is needed alike for the control of the sexual impulse, and for the overcoming of other temptations and passions. The general moral education of the child, the formation of its character, and the encouragement of a pursuit of ideal aims, are all also of the greatest possible importance in relation to sexual education. Nothing is better adapted to ensure personal happiness and a high moral standard, than the inculcation of idealism, which must on no account be confused with aloofness from the everyday affairs of the world.

By many persons, an especial stress is laid upon the value of religious education, for the purpose of directing in proper paths the sexual life of the child, and of giving help in the mastery of its temptations. But notwithstanding the fact that I value most highly a genuinely religious education, I feel that for the purposes just mentioned we cannot place much reliance upon that which in our schools of to-day passes by the name of religious education. I have been personally acquainted with too many persons brought up on "strictly religious" lines, adherents of the most diverse creeds, but chiefly Protestants, Catholics, and Jews, whose religious education has been of remarkably little use to them in this respect. Among children, I have known some who masturbated immoderately, and yet their progress in their religious studies was extraordinary. I have known of serious epidemics of masturbation, in some cases of mutual masturbation, in boarding-schools in which the day's work was always begun with prayers and hymns. Quite recently, another case has been reported to me, of a so-called exemplary school, where the educational methods had a strong religious trend, and yet seduction to mutual masturbation played a great part. In spite of these experiences, I do not dispute the fact that even in association with the modern methods of religious instruction—but not always in consequence of these—many have been withheld from masturbatory and other sexual acts. These cases fall into three groups. The first group consists of cases in which the sexual impulse is very weak, so that very little is requisite to prevent the occurrence of sexual practices. To the second group belong the cases of those who are kept in check by the fear of God's anger, which will be visited, they are taught in their lessons on religion, upon all unrighteous acts. The third group is comprised of those rare natures who are really profoundly inspired by religious ethical sentiments, and in whom even the ordinary unpractical methods of religious instruction have not been able to inhibit the development of genuinely religious feelings. These three groups may readily be recognised among adults as well as among children. But when I compare the number of the children and young persons making up these three groups with the number of those to whom religious instruction has been quite useless, I feel justified in a certain scepticism. I do not pretend to assert that those who have received religious instruction have become more immoral than the others; but I am certainly entitled to contest the assertion that religious instruction induces a loftier sexual morality. Indeed, a further limitation is needed here, and one to the discredit of religious instruction. A portion, even, of those persons comprising the exceptional cases just enumerated, have not thereby attained to spiritual peace. Tormented, and at times almost mastered, by the sexual impulse, they struggle unceasingly under the influence of terror lest they should commit a deadly sin by yielding to this impulse. The mental condition of such persons—I speak chiefly of

young men—is in some cases such that a doctor may well doubt if he be not justified in advising them to indulge in illegitimate sexual intercourse. I have myself never given such advice in these cases, nor do I intend to give it in similar cases in the future. I refrain from doing so on ethical grounds, which I have discussed in great detail in connexion with the sexual question in my work on Medical Ethics. The physician has no right to advise his patient to the performance of an act which is regarded by the latter as a deadly sin. But all the more because I have felt unable to give such advice, do I feel it my duty to insist here upon the seamy side of the education by which this state of mind is induced.

My view that what is commonly called religious education does not as a rule help the subject to master the sexual impulse, has been forced upon me by the numerous confessions entrusted to me by persons who have received such an education. Very recently, I was shown a diary in which a young man, obviously very religious and pious, to whom God was the source of all hope, and who thanked God for His grace on every page, refers again and again to the fact that he has found himself unable to overcome the lower forms of sensuality. He writes: "In resisting this powerful sensual impulse, religion was of some help, but unfortunately not very much. When I was only twelve years of age, the impulse towards the lower forms of sensuality made its appearance, and speedily attained great intensity. Again and again I believed myself to be strong enough to withstand it, only to pass from a weak and inefficient resistance, to a profound fall." And later he writes: "But the lower sensuality persisted, however much and however often I resisted it. My imagination continually produced the horrible pictures. And though in desperate rage I clenched my teeth to drive them away, they always left traces in my soul, and from time to time I fell. How I have struggled, how I have fought! How often with tears have I sought God's protection and help, praising God with holy zeal and faith. In my room I knelt, praying for grace and strength. I write this, not for self-glorification, but to show you, dear reader, how terrible, how gigantic is the struggle for virtue."

Notwithstanding all that I have written, I do not for a moment dispute the fact that a religious education may effect admirable results, both in respect of sexual matters, and of others. Indeed, I am firmly convinced of this. But the religious education competent to do this does not consist merely of learning Bible texts by heart; nor is its chief aim the inculcation of precepts which are to-day impossible of fulfilment—as the child sees at every turn in the conduct of the members of its own environment. I refer to the religious education which has an internal reality, and arises spontaneously out of the demands of morality. I do not mean the sort of education which regards it as almost a disgrace that we come naked into the world; not the religious education which regards man as soiled by the fact that he is born from his mother's womb; nor that which considers every sexual act as essentially sinful, and asceticism as man's salvation. It is not religious education of such a kind that will have any good effect in the matter of sexual education; but that religious education only which is in complete accord with our ideas of morality, and which is based, not so much upon the historical and material contents of the Bible, as upon the internal and everlasting truths of religion.

The sexual dangers of the Bible have often been pointed out. But this work would be incomplete, if I omitted making a fresh reference to the matter. In the Bible, sexual processes are repeatedly mentioned. In the mind of the child a conflict inevitably arises when, on the one hand, he finds that everything of a sexual nature is diligently concealed from him, and, on the other, in the Holy Book which is put before him as the basis of his moral instruction, he finds that so much attention is paid to sexual things. It is not the actual accounts of sexual things in the Bible which constitute the danger, but the contrast between the plain speaking of the Bible in these matters, and the general affectation of secrecy outside its pages. An additional point of importance is the fact that in the Bible sexual topics are handled in a way which is by no means always delicate. I may recall the frequency with which the idea of the whore is employed for purposes of comparison; and I may refer also to the occasional use of strongly erotic language, as, for example, in the Song of Solomon. A further danger lies in the fact that the Bible contains descriptions of customs which are no longer in harmony with modern ideas; it suffices to mention the accounts of polygamy in the Old Testament. Unless the distinction between what is historical and what is truly religious is carefully explained to the child, the latter's moral ideas will very readily become confused.

In this connexion, I must also refer to the Catholic confessional, about which of late years a good deal has been written. I may recall the disquisitions on the moral teaching of Liguori. The father confessors have to read books in which are discussed the questions of casuistry with which they have to deal, in order to learn what authoritative decisions have been given regarding the concrete cases on which they are asked to pass judgment. In these books, sexual misconduct plays a leading part. This is also true of the confessional manuals written to assist the penitents in the discovery of their sins, in which sexual errors also find a place. Opinions as to the wisdom of giving such manuals to penitents are certainly very divergent. When we read the authoritative decisions, for the use of confessors, pronounced by Catholic theologians upon sexual faults, we are sometimes astonished at the practical insight displayed in these decisions; the opinions expressed must, indeed, often appear dubious to the strict moralist, and yet they are occasionally marvellously well adapted to the practical requirements of the case. In many instances, however, even this cannot be admitted; and however right from the practical point of view the decisions may sometimes be, we must not overlook the dangers of the confessional. Cases have been personally known to me in which, at the confessional, penitents have been cross-questioned in such a way about sexual details that unfavourable consequences were, in my opinion, extremely likely to ensue. This statement applies with equal force to the case of children, who have to go to confession as soon as they arrive at the "age of reason." No one will dispute the assertion that the father-confessors gather much experience in the exercise of their profession, and that most of them possess sufficient tact to avoid asking improper questions. But to assert this of all of them would be to rush to the other extreme; and for the same reason that in the latter part of this chapter I shall express myself as opposed, at any rate in part, to sexual instruction in schools, do I think that to ask such questions of children as are sometimes asked in confession, may in certain circumstances lead to very undesirable results. When the child penitent describes to the confessor sexual faults (masturbation, &c.), however well intentioned the words of the confessor may be, it is impossible that they should be so individually adapted as is really necessary in such cases; and the detailed discussion of these matters which sometimes follows is open to grave objection. In what I have just said, it is far from my intention to attack one of the sacraments of the Catholic Church; but the matter is one to which it was necessary to allude, and I will merely add that the error must be avoided of taking as a basis for criticism much that is written with a party bias against the Catholic Church, and much also of the mockery of the confessional which abounds in erotic literature. For example, when Michelet asserts that, in matters concerning love and the sexual life, a French girl of fifteen is as far advanced as an English girl of eighteen, and when he refers this to the effect of a Catholic education in accelerating the process of human development, it is necessary to observe that these far-reaching generalisations are not supported by any jot of proof.

In the earlier parts of this chapter, I have discussed certain questions belonging to the psychical sphere in their bearings upon sexual education. I have now to refer to two specialised methods of treatment: first of all, the one which has initiated the whole of the newer psychotherapy, namely, hypnotism; and, secondly, the psycho-analytic method. Hypnotism has been employed against all kinds of sexual processes, both in adults and in children. As far as children are concerned, it is masturbation, in especial, for the prevention of which hypnotic suggestion has been tried. When the child is old enough to be hypnotised, good results will occasionally be obtained; but in many other cases the desired end can unquestionably be attained without the induction of the hypnotic state, either by suggestion in the waking state, or else by the other methods to be described in the present chapter.

Here are brief notes of a case in which hypnotic suggestion was employed with beneficial results.

Case 17.—X., a boy eleven years of age, was diligent at school. For some time past he had withdrawn from the companionship of all his school-fellows, and his parents had noticed that he was continually in the company of a schoolgirl two years older than himself. He availed himself of every opportunity to play with this girl. When they sat together at table, it was noticed that they endeavoured to secure physical contact by bringing their knees together. In addition, they were often seen kissing one another. It was obvious that the two had a mutual inclination each for the other. If anyone gave the boy a present of money, he shared it with the girl. The two wrote letters to one another, and some of these letters fell into the parents' hands. Thereafter the two were watched, so that this exchange of letters became impossible. At first, the matter was not regarded seriously; on the contrary, the two were teased about it, especially the boy. The latter became very unhappy, and for a time it was believed that the intimacy had been broken off. In reality, the rupture was apparent merely, and was simulated to escape the teasing. In secret, they continued to meet. Whereas regarding the girl few details were at my disposal, I had a good deal of information about the boy. It was astonishing how many excuses he made to deceive his relatives. Sometimes he was supposed to be writing his home-lessons, sometimes to be at a gymnastic lesson or at church, when in reality he was with his girl friend. It had been observed before that the boy occasionally played with his genital organs. Since a complete separation from the girl gave rise in the boy to a state of profound depression, followed by his paying attentions to a somewhat older girl living in his house, his parents now sought my advice. The boy proved to be extremely susceptible to hypnotism and to hypnotic suggestion, and it was remarkable how rapidly a complete change in his demeanour was effected. Since then I have seen the boy occasionally, the last time being when he was about fifteen and a half years of age. There had been no return of the sexual tendencies previously observed. Quite recently, indeed, he had been known to masturbate occasionally; and it was for this reason that he was again brought to consult me. But for four years previously, notwithstanding the fact that he had been very carefully watched, no improper conduct had been detected. Undoubtedly, the recent practice of masturbation would have escaped notice, had not the parents been made very anxious by the earlier experiences. No special treatment was now undertaken, since it appeared that there was nothing more amiss than is observed in average boys of his age; symptoms which in most cases disappear spontaneously, and without treatment.

A short account must also be given here of the method of Breuer and Freud, or the psycho-analytic method. It is true that this method is applicable to adults only, but its aim is to relieve the ill effects of sexual experiences during childhood. I have before pointed out that in Freud's view four neuroses always result from previous sexual experiences; and two of these, hysteria and compulsion-neuroses (Zwangsneurose) are considered by him to depend upon sexual experiences during childhood. Freud, who originally worked out this method in co-operation with Breuer, but subsequently further developed it by himself, assumes that the hysterical symptoms which result from the noxious influences of sexual experiences during childhood, are always permanently allayed if we succeed in making the subject once more actively conscious of them, and enable the emotions thereby again aroused in the mind of the patient to obtain an efficient outlet (sie zum abreagieren zu bringen). If we are able, either with or without the aid of hypnotism, to reawaken the effect which was originally experienced as a result of the sexual trauma, the hysterical symptoms will be permanently relieved. Originally, he endeavoured to reawaken the memory of the sexual trauma by means of the induction of profound hypnosis. Later, however, he was able to do this, without the aid of hypnotism, by conversing with the patient, and by awaking his memory by means of questions. This method, to which formerly Freud gave the name of the cathartic method, but which is now generally known as the psycho-analytic method, has to some extent been further developed by Freud's pupils. Freud's view is that by means of psycho-analysis he is enabled, from the sphere of the unconscious, or rather of the subconscious, to restore to the supra-consciousness the lost sexual experiences of childhood or of later life; and by this means to effect a permanent cure of the most diverse diseases. No detailed criticism of this method of treatment will here be attempted, but my views on the matter will to some extent have become apparent from what has been said in earlier parts of this book. The value of Freud's work appears to me to consist chiefly in this, that he has insisted more definitely than other writers upon the reality of subconscious processes. But I believe that the general sexual etiology which he assumes to exist can from no point of view be regarded as sound, even with the limitation which he later imposed upon his own doctrine, namely, that it is not the sexual experience itself, but the reaction against this experience, which is etiologically significant. Recently, I have several times tried to treat by the psycho-analytic method some of the cases for which that method is supposed to be suitable, and as a result of my experience I have been forced more and more to the conclusion that, notwithstanding all the other advantages of the psycho-analytic method, the importance of the factor of sexual experiences in the causation of disease has been greatly over-estimated by Freud. Moreover, I believe that the cures effected by Freud (as to the permanence of which, in view of the insufficiency of the published materials, no decisive opinion can as yet be given), are explicable in another way. A large proportion of the good results are certainly fully explicable as the results of suggestion. The patient's confidence in his physician, and the fact that the treatment requires much time and patience, are two such powerful factors of suggestion, that provisionally it is necessary to regard it as possible that suggestion explains the whole matter.

There are, of course, many other psychological influences to which attention must also be directed. One of the most important of these is the avoidance of psychical contagion. A boy who is sexually premature, or in whom some other striking sexual manifestations have occurred, may exercise an extremely harmful influence upon other children. We must endeavour to remove such a boy from the companionship of others, and in this country this often can be effected through the instrumentality of the Law of Guardianship (Fürsorgegesetz). But it will by no means always be easy to find the guilty person. It is extremely common for such an abnormal child to set the tone for the others; and such a child may be making remarkable progress in study, although its sexual and moral level is a very low one. A number of other measures will be inferred from what has been said in the section on etiology. These are social rather than medical problems. We must avoid letting children have the chance of seeing others engaged in sexual intercourse; they must not live in too close and intimate an association with other children; they must not grow up in the society of prostitutes; children who are past infancy should not share a common bed. As regards school-life, it is supposed to be a matter of great importance that there should be separate closets for the two sexes. I am myself doubtful if this last matter is one of much moment.

In any case, we can interfere for the special protection of children who have been exposed to peculiar risks, and have for this reason been led astray sexually. I have seen children who have been taught sexual misconduct, either by a nursemaid or by other children, and have practised such misconduct for a time; but in whom a complete cure has resulted from separation from the seducer. In some cases, of course, it will be necessary to do more than this, and to subject the child to some special treatment; and in rare instances, in which the sphere of the sexual is already markedly developed, it may be necessary that this treatment should be institutional. But such cases are certainly very uncommon. A matter of importance is that the parents or other persons responsible for the care and guidance of the child, should understand the psychical management of children; for example, that they should not fall into the common error of regarding the love-affairs of children as a joke, and that they should not, by this attitude, actually encourage the children in their course of conduct.

One part of sexual education is made up by the question of the purposive sexual enlightenment of children—a matter much discussed at the present day. I have shown, that this question is not, as many suppose, a new one. Those who have written on the subject of sexual enlightenment use this term with somewhat various meanings. As regards the extension of the term, it may be applied to either (or both) of two fields, which we may term the objective and the subjective aspects of the sexual life. To the objective side belong the physiological processes by means of which is effected the reproduction of organisms, whether plants, animals, or human beings. In explanation of these it is necessary to describe the reproductive organs, and the processes of conjugation, fertilisation, and fructification, as they have long been customarily taught in the botany class; and the nourishment of the nursing infant from the breast of the mother may also be described. To the subjective side, belong the relationships of the sexual processes to the individual organism, the good and the bad effects of the sexual impulse, &c. In this connexion, reference will be made to the dangers of masturbation, sexual excesses, pregnancy, venereal infection, and so on. By many writers, these two fields are not distinguished each from the other with sufficient clearness. The question, whether children should be taught about the methods of reproduction in plants, animals, and human beings, must not be confused with the question whether they should be taught about masturbation or the venereal diseases. It is possible to teach children that self-abuse is a harmful practice, without giving them any account of the physiological processes of reproduction; and, conversely, these processes may be described, without any special reference to the bearings of the matter on the individual life. Of course, the two fields are interconnected; and some writers suggest that in teaching children and young persons a proper respect for the genital organs, such teaching should be based upon a knowledge of the subsequent function of these organs in the work of reproduction. The individual processes cannot at once be referred to one field or the other; involuntary sexual orgasm, menstruation, the puberal development, inasmuch as they exhibit both a subjective and an objective aspect, belong to both fields. This is also true of the sexual act itself, in connexion with which, moreover, the principal difficulties of sexual enlightenment arise.

Having thus considered the general significance of sexual enlightenment, we have next to ask what are the grounds on which such enlightenment is thought to be desirable. These will have become partly apparent from what has been said regarding the importance of the sexual life of the child; but this does not exhaust the matter, for the sexual enlightenment of the child may also comprise instruction concerning the entire subsequent development of the sexual life. The reasons for sexual enlightenment may be classified under various heads; the chief of these are reasons of health, of social life, of law, morality, education, and the intellectual development.

To consider first the matter of intellectual development, we have here to think, not so much of a limitation of the intellectual growth in consequence of the sexual thoughts of the child, as of the fact that instruction in the nature of sexual processes, at least as far as the objective field is concerned, promotes the general culture. The degree to which even adults are ignorant about such matters, is hardly credible. There are persons who believe that every egg laid by a hen will develop into a chicken if incubated by the mother, or if kept for the proper time in an artificial incubator; there are persons who do not know what the hard roe and soft roe of fishes are, who do not understand the nature of the spawning process, and are, in fact, quite uninstructed concerning the process of reproduction in fishes. I have conversed with adults who did not know wherein a wether differs from a ram, or a bullock from a bull; and who were even ignorant, as regards great groups of the animal kingdom, whether they reproduced their kind by means of eggs or living young. But on such matters as these, every cultured person should be sufficiently informed, and should not be capable of being shamed by the superior knowledge of an uneducated child from the country. On one occasion, I even saw a married woman, actually twenty-eight years of age, who had been examined by a gynecologist, and for whom the latter had recommended the operative division of the hymen; but the lady confused this operation with oöphorectomy, and it was by no means an easy matter to make her understand the difference between the two. It will readily be understood that every grown man and woman ought ultimately to be fully informed concerning all such matters. In part, such instruction will take place at school, and more especially in the case of processes in the vegetable and lower animal world; these things will be explained in connexion with instruction in natural history and biology. But information about the human reproductive organs cannot be given in the school, unless to children of a considerable age; for these matters, direct personal instruction at home is more suitable.

Apart from the demands of general culture there are other reasons why sexual enlightenment is desirable. These chiefly concern the subjective aspects of the sexual life, whilst the objective processes serve principally for preparatory instruction.

First of all, grounds of health have to be considered. It may be desirable to enlighten the child regarding the dangers of masturbation, those of ordinary illegitimate sexual intercourse, and those of sexual excesses. No detailed discussion of these points is here necessary, since they have been dealt with before at considerable length. Here I will merely point out that this aspect of enlightenment affects the entire future of the child and the family it will one day have. The first consideration here is the danger of venereal infection, and it is this danger, in close association with the other prophylactic efforts of our time, which has given rise to the recent movement in favour of sexual enlightenment. In this connexion the dangers may be explained that threaten the male from gonorrhoeal infection, not only in his own person, but also in the persons of his future wife and children. The wife may be infected by the husband, and the visual powers of the new-born child may also be endangered. Ophthalmia of the new-born, which often leads to blindness, commonly depends upon conjunctival infection received during the act of parturition. Here it may be added that still-births and abortion and miscarriage may result from syphilitic infection either of the mother or of the embryo. Or the child may be born alive, but suffering from syphilitic infection. Even when no actual infection of the offspring results, syphilis favours the occurrence of a general degeneration of the progeny. If we desire to safeguard human beings against such dangers as these, we shall feel it necessary to enlighten them before it is too late; and in view of the fact that from a single act of intercourse infection may result by which the health may be permanently injured, such enlightenment is no less necessary for girls than for boys.

I need not describe the dangers to health resulting from masturbation and sexual excesses, for these have previously been considered in detail; but it is necessary to allude to the exaggerated statements which are sometimes encountered regarding the dangers of masturbation, especially in popular works on the subject, so that the physician may be on his guard about this matter. A child who during and after the act of masturbation has a keen sense of wrong-doing, and consequently suffers much from self-reproach, may, if the fear is superadded of having done serious permanent injury to health, be affected with grave hypochondriacal manifestations. Many instances of this have come under my notice, in young men and young women of sixteen or thereabouts. Even when the practice of masturbation has long been discontinued, and the patient is quite grown up, such symptoms may arise, owing to the persistence of the fear of disastrous results, and the auto-suggestive influence of this fear. Nowhere is more tact required by the physician than in his dealings with those who masturbate or have masturbated. There is even a real danger that a moral lecture may cause a shock to the system; in the case of some young men it may sometimes be better to acquiesce in masturbation, rather than to alarm them by talking about the disastrous consequences of the indulgence. I refer to those unfortunate creatures who suffer from severe hyperæsthesia of the sexual impulse, and who for social reasons are not in a position to satisfy the impulse in any other way than by masturbation, or who refrain from illicit intercourse in the well-grounded fear of venereal infection. The physician who has seen a number of such cases, who has learned how they continually relapse into the practice of masturbation, notwithstanding all their good resolutions and their conviction that masturbation is at once dangerous and immoral, will be likely to feel that it is better, not indeed to recommend masturbation, but from time to time tacitly to permit it. To do in these cases what it is well to do in certain others, namely, to describe the bad effects of masturbation, may give rise to grave conditions of depression, and even to suicide. Certainly, in such cases, we must carefully avoid alarming the patients too seriously about the consequences of masturbation.

In undertaking the sexual enlightenment of the child, those phenomena of the sexual life should not be forgotten which are shown by experience to arouse in the ripening child, now curiosity, and now anxiety—and the chief among these are involuntary sexual orgasm and menstruation. Imagine the state of mind of the girl who has never heard a word about menstruation, and awakens one morning with blood flowing from the genital organs; or that of the boy, who has his first nocturnal seminal emission, without having received any information as to its significance. Similar considerations apply to some of the other signs of puberty; and especially to the growth of the pubic hair, which has made many a child extremely anxious. Although, by the time this age is reached, a child has commonly been sufficiently informed about these things by his playfellows, we meet with instances in which nothing of the kind has occurred.

Hitherto I have been considering the hygienic grounds for effecting sexual enlightenment; but there are also important ethical reasons for such enlightenment. It is not possible in our life to speak the truth always and unconditionally; but this fact does not give us the right to lie to children without good cause. Especially dangerous is it to relate to children fables about the stork or the cabbage-garden, at a time when they have long been enlightened about sex from other sources. I recall the case of a girl seven years of age, whose mother was still in the habit of telling her that babies were brought by the storks; but this child was accustomed to join with other girls and boys in playing at "father, mother, and midwife," wherein they displayed a comparatively exact knowledge of the processes of reproduction and birth. We are not surprised when a woman tells us that as a child her confidence in her mother was seriously shaken from the moment when she was enlightened by others concerning the sexual life, and she recognised that what her mother had told her about the matter was quite untrue. I do not mean to imply that stories of the stork and cabbage-garden variety are to be altogether excluded. It would be as reasonable to prohibit all kinds of fairy tales. Some tell us that we should tell children fairy stories only so long as they regard the whole of life as a fairy tale. But in view of the vivid imagination of childhood, no such sharp distinction is practicable. Let the reader recall his own childhood. Does the child regard the fairy tale as a lie, even after he has began to doubt if the world of fairy stories has any actual existence? Certainly not. Similarly with regard to the stork fable. I consider that the complete suppression of this fable, unless we replace it with some like poetical fancy, can do nothing but harm to the child's nature. All that we must ask is that such a story shall not for too long be put before the child as fact. When the child's development has gone far enough, it will be well to dispense with the stork story. This is suggested by considerations both of prudence and of morals, and the like considerations urge us to describe to the child, tactfully and at the proper time, the true nature of the reproductive processes.

Such a course is desirable, if merely for the reason that when a child is sexually enlightened by other children, this is usually effected in so coarse a manner as very readily to undermine the bases of respect for the sexual life of humanity. A child who has been instructed regarding this grave and important matter by his parents and in a proper manner, is in a position to reject offers of a coarse method of enlightenment; but by the customary—too long customary—plan, as far as children are concerned, of altogether ignoring the sexual life, children are deprived of the power of repelling obscene methods of enlightenment.

The legal dangers are additional reasons for undertaking the sexual enlightenment of the child. I pointed out that, in certain circumstances, a boy of thirteen who undertook sexual practices with a girl of twelve was committing a punishable offence. But sexual enlightenment is desirable, not merely for those of this age, but also for those who are somewhat older. A large number of people are completely ignorant of our penal code in these relationships. I recall the case of a sexually perverse young man of twenty who on a number of occasions performed the following acts with boys of about thirteen years of age. He would go to a public bath, induce a boy of thirteen or so to enter his dressing cubicle, and, as if in joke, tie the boy's hands together. In reality, as he did this, he experienced sexual excitement to the point of ejaculation.

This latter occurred especially when he touched the boy's body—not his genital organs. He had absolutely no idea that such acts were punishable with imprisonment, in accordance with the third paragraph of Section 176 of the Criminal Code; and it gave him a terrible shock when I explained to him that he had rendered himself liable to imprisonment. Some persons even believe that they may handle children's genital organs, for the purpose of exciting themselves sexually, without rendering themselves liable to punishment. It is obvious that on these grounds also enlightenment on sexual matters may be extremely desirable.

Finally, there are certain social and economic reasons for sexual enlightenment. These reasons are closely connected with those bearing upon health, but they may in part be separated from the latter. No one will deny that illegitimate sexual intercourse may entail grave social consequences. For women these dangers are much greater than they are for men; but for men, even, they are by no means inconsiderable. As far as women are concerned, the danger of extra-marital impregnation occupies the first place. The importance of this of course varies greatly in various regions and in different social strata. In the servant-class in the country, for instance, pre-marital sexual intercourse, and even pre-marital motherhood, is far from having the seriousness which attaches to these things among the old peasant families firmly rooted to the soil. Among the servant-class in towns, the matter has a more serious aspect than among the same class in the country. On the other hand, in many artistic circles in the Metropolis, pre-marital intercourse, even on the part of women, is regarded far more indifferently than in other strata of society. None the less, for a girl of the upper ranks, extra-marital pregnancy is for the most part tantamount to social annihilation. Even here exceptions occur, and we shall find good families of the aristocracy and the upper bourgeoisie in which a woman who has given birth to an illegitimate child, or even one who is manifestly a cocotte, will be socially recognised, provided she has attained some great position, such as that of a great artist, for instance. In such cases we may even find that women who on other occasions are unable adequately to express their hatred and contempt for prostitutes and similar unfortunate beings, will yet be proud of their friendship with such a woman, and will boast of it in public. But such opportunities of social recovery are open to very few; most women of the upper classes sink rapidly and far in the social scale as soon as it is publicly known that they have experience of illegitimate intercourse. For this reason, such consequences must be taken into the reckoning. The objection need not be raised that the sexual enlightenment would not safeguard a girl, since, when she gives herself to a man, a girl knows well enough that children are the result of sexual intercourse. The objection is unsound, if we only have a right understanding of what we mean by sexual enlightenment, and if at the same time we do not neglect the general sexual education. Enlightenment should not be limited to merely making the person concerned aware of the consequences of sexual acts; it should, as it were, become ingrained in the flesh and blood, so as to influence the actions, even unconsciously. A girl brought up in this way will defend herself instinctively against the wiles of a seducer. But only by such an education, by one which is not confined to the mere imparting of information, can we produce in the girl greater powers of self-protection and a more enduring self-consciousness, and so save her from the far too common fate of behaving like a stupid unripe creature, and believing all the asseverations of the first man who makes love to her—asseverations which the man himself, in the moment of passion, very probably believes. Let me, then, repeat that all that appertains to the sexual enlightenment must became part of the flesh and blood of the subject; only from this can we expect good results, whereas a sexual education which consists merely in the acquirement of information, is altogether valueless. But by a true sexual enlightenment, in the sense above defined, it is probable that many a girl may be safeguarded from prostitution; and many a child, boys as well as girls, may be better protected against the attempts of pædophiles. And these considerations apply, not merely to childhood, but also to subsequent life—especially as regards girls. How many girls enter upon marriage quite ignorant and altogether inexperienced. They commit themselves to the keeping of a man of whom they know hardly anything at all. The parents are often satisfied with the most meagre information. It is considered improper to ask for detailed information regarding the husband's past life, and hence it often happens that a girl is delivered up to an unscrupulous man suffering from venereal infection, simply because she has never been adequately informed regarding the serious step she is undertaking, regarding the completely new mode of life upon which she is so suddenly entering. We thus see that there are ample grounds for explaining to a girl in good time precisely what she will undertake in entering the married state.

A question of importance is at what age the sexual enlightenment can most wisely be effected. Some advise that enlightenment should begin with our answers to the first questions the child propounds upon the subject; others contend that it is better to wait till it is somewhat older than this. There is truth in both these views; but the matter and manner of our communications must be appropriate to the age of the child with which we are dealing. When a young man is being sent to the university, it is wise to instruct him concerning the dangers of venereal infection; but to inform him that human beings come into the world as the result of an act of sexual intercourse would be altogether superfluous. Conversely, if a child asks its parents where its little brother has come from, we do not need to say anything about syphilis and gonorrhoea; but none the less we can give such a child an account suitable for one of its age of the way in which human beings come into the world. Speaking generally, it may be said that the biology and physiology of reproduction—that is to say, the objective processes—may be described at a comparatively early age; but that cautions regarding masturbation should not, in average cases, be given before the age of thirteen or fourteen; and that instruction about the risks of venereal infection should be deferred until even later than this. In the case of boys, in so far as enlightenment in the school is concerned, information about venereal infection may, for practical reasons, best be given about the time the boys are preparing to leave for a higher school. In the case of girls, for whom a caution against risks of impregnation and against prostitution are especially in question, we have also, as far as sexual enlightenment in the school is under consideration, to recommend the time when they are about to leave school. But if we prefer that sexual enlightenment, or at any rate a part of such enlightenment, should be effected at home rather than in the school (a course which I regard as essentially preferable), it will be impossible to lay down a fixed rule as to the age at which this should take place. To a lively girl of twelve or thirteen years, a great deal can be said far better by the mother, than can be said to a girl considerably older, say at fifteen, by the school physician, schoolmaster, or schoolmistress. Speaking generally, in the case of girls, the enlightenment may well begin at a somewhat earlier age than in the case of boys—at any rate as regards the subjective processes of the sexual life.

On the whole, it may be regarded as definitely established that the child may well receive information about the objective processes at a very early age, and this long before the time commonly regarded as marking the commencement of puberty. But as regards the subjective processes, it is better that there should be some delay. It may, indeed, be asked whether it would not be preferable that in the case also of the subjective processes, the child should be instructed before they actually make their appearance in the child's own consciousness, to render possible the adoption on the child's part of a more objective attitude towards these phenomena. But in reality such a course offers no advantages. The child is quite unable to understand the dangers of the sexual life, as long as it has no actual experience of sexual feelings. For this reason, it is better to accept the view of those who contend that, as far as the subjective processes of the sexual life are concerned, we should wait till near the end of the second period of childhood before beginning the enlightenment. But we must not forget what has previously been pointed out, that the puberal development may begin at a time when nothing of the sort is apparent to the eye of the observer; and we must also bear in mind that the first seminal emission and the first menstruation are by no means so important, as marks of the puberal development, as is commonly believed. For the fulfilment of the aims of the sexual enlightenment, however, it does not so much matter when the first physical manifestations of the puberal development make their appearance, but when the first sexual feelings and sentiments, which must be distinguished from the unconscious and purely physical symptoms, are experienced. The important matter is, not whether follicles have already matured in the ovary, but what influence such a process has exercised upon the mental life of the child. For this reason, in our study of the individual case, we must have some knowledge of the psyche of the child with which we are concerned.

A matter also within the scope of our subject is the question by whom the sexual enlightenment may best be effected. This question is connected with the questions for what reason and at what age enlightenment should take place. As regards these points, it lies between the school and the home. Some writers contend that so far as possible every thing, others, that, at any rate, a great deal, should be imparted at school. The latter view is also my own.

In so far as the enlightenment has to do with purely biological processes, and especially in so far as it relates to processes in the vegetable and lower animal world, it can be effected in the school, and in the first years of the second period of childhood; but of course the giving of such instruction at school does not prevent a father who goes out walking with his son, or a mother with her daughter, from seizing opportunities of giving information about the sexual processes of plant-life. At school, education regarding such biological processes will form a part of the lessons in botany and zoology; or will be imparted in the class on general biology, if such a class exists. Instruction in hygiene, such as is often advised, has little to do with the matters we are now considering; and at any rate could merely involve an elementary account of such processes. The school may even be the best place for sexual enlightenment regarding the sexual life of human beings, at least in the case of the older pupils. There is no adequate reason for objecting to boys about to leave school being warned by a schoolmaster or a physician about the dangers of venereal disease; and at the same time a plea may be put forward against the view that it is incumbent upon every young man to prove his strength by the maximum indulgence in sexual intercourse.

But the matter is very different as regards the enlightenment concerning the subjective processes of the sexual life of those who are still quite young. It is impossible to approve of the suggestion that a girl of twelve or a boy of fourteen should receive instruction in school as to the dangers of masturbation. Enlightenment of this sort must be given in a purely individual manner, and for this reason the school is here out of the question. It may be objected to this that we now and again encounter a schoolmaster who is able to establish between himself and his pupils a relationship of complete personal confidence, and that such a man is just as well able as the father to instruct his boys about these matters; mutatis mutandis, the same considerations apply to the exceptional schoolmistress as compared with the mother. But although it must be admitted that such cases really exist, they are—and this is no fault of master or mistress—such rare exceptions, that it is out of the question to base upon their existence a general rule that enlightenment upon these particular points should be given in the school. Enlightenment regarding the earliest manifestations of the sexual life, whether about the feelings or about the peripheral processes, demands such a degree of individualisation, that a schoolmaster or a schoolmistress, who has to teach from thirty to fifty pupils at once, or even a larger number than this, is quite unable to undertake anything of the kind. Such enlightenment can be properly effected only by an individual confidant, and by one who makes the fullest possible allowance for the child's own individuality. Such a confidant is most suitable, if only for the reason that enlightenment on these questions can best be effected, above all in the case of little children, as far as possible in response to spontaneous inquiries, or at least when an opportunity is afforded by some chance occurrence. The express manufacture of an opportunity, such as would be necessary in the school, might entail very unfortunate consequences; and even if, in response to a wide demand of our day, instruction in hygiene is given in school, either by a schoolmaster or a medical man, the anticipation of such topics might have undesirable results. In the German Medical Congress of the year 1908, it was evident that even the advocates of hygienic instruction in the school were not all prepared to answer with an unqualified affirmative the question whether the school was the best place for effecting sexual enlightenment; and a resolution proposed by Scheyer was adopted, to the effect "that this Congress considers that the question of the school taking part in the work of sexual enlightenment is one which it would at present be premature to discuss."

Those who are inclined to assume to-day that we have left the older authorities far in the rear, would do well sometimes to study the works they despise. Basedow in his Elementarbuch für die Jugend und für ihre Lehrer und Freunde (Handbook for Young Persons, their Teachers, and their Friends), gives some ideas as to how a mother may best enlighten her children regarding sex-differences. Looking at a chest of drawers, one of the children says to the mother that the purpose of clothing is to protect the body from cold and heat, and to cover the private parts. The mother replies that the last-named use of clothing is indeed very important, and that it is very naughty to allow these parts of the body to be seen, unless in cases of the greatest need. But the child goes on to say that an additional use of clothing is to help us to know one person from another, and to distinguish the female sex from the male; and her little brother remarks that he knows of no difference between the sexes other than that shown by the clothing: "If I were dressed like my sister, I should be a girl." "No, no, my child," answers the mother, "as time goes on, a girl's form becomes very different from that of a young man. In men, a beard grows; but not in women. Men cannot give birth to a child, nor can they suckle a child; they can only procreate children, or become fathers. For this reason, even from the time they are born, their bodies are different from those of little girls. And not only are their bodies different; their inclinations are different also; &c. &c." Although we may be disinclined to accept everything that Basedow and other early educationalists have said about such matters, none the less, in these old writings the modern educationalist will find much that is suggestive.

Of late years, now that the school physician has gained a higher position, the suggestion is sometimes made that it is by him that the sexual enlightenment may best be undertaken. As far as children of a fair age are concerned, and in the matter of imparting warnings against the dangers of venereal infection, I share this view. But as regards enlightenment as to the personal sexual life in the case of a child of thirteen or so, I am compelled to differ. My reasons will be obvious from what has been said before. The principal reason is that the enlightenment ought to be effected by someone who enjoys the child's personal confidence. Undoubtedly there are certain school physicians who fulfil this condition; and to such persons this task may, of course, be entrusted. The very fact that they enjoy the children's confidence suffices to show that they possess certain special qualifications for such a task, and further, that they have the faculty of coming to a real understanding with children. But the fact that a man is appointed to the position of school physician, does not by itself prove that he possesses to an adequate degree the fine perceptions and the tact that are needed in effecting the sexual enlightenment; nor does it prove that he is the person best fitted to enlighten the children with whom he has to deal. In this difficult matter, we cannot be too careful in formulating any general rule. The person who is to effect the sexual enlightenment must possess, not merely a theoretical knowledge of the processes of sex, but also the faculty of making these processes intelligible at the right moment and in the right way. But how is the school physician or the schoolmaster to know, in individual cases, the degree to which the sexual life has developed? He must have definitely abandoned the old view that either the child's age in years or the external physical signs of puberty can be regarded as indicating with any degree of precision the progress of psychosexual puberty. But since this latter, the psychosexual development, should most often guide us in the choice of the right moment for effecting the sexual enlightenment, we are compelled to depend upon an individual consideration of the child, such as will be possible only to a person who is fully in its confidence. We learn from everyday experience that even very near relatives, if they have failed to penetrate the child's intimate psyche, may have utterly erroneous conceptions of its mental life. They completely ignore the extent to which the sexual imaginative activity has already developed; they know nothing as to whether the originally obscure sensibility of the child has now become focussed in a particular direction, so that its feelings are stimulated by definite individuals; they are ignorant of the degree to which the child's genital organs have become subject to the peripheral changes characteristic of sex. In the fourth chapter of this work I have discussed the wide individual differences which children exhibit in these various respects; and a mere reference to the matter here should suffice to show that the most careful and detailed individual examination of the child-soul is indispensable, and that the observance of a mechanical routine in the process of sexual enlightenment would be even worse than no enlightenment at all.

It is a question of great importance, who, outside the school, is the person best fitted to undertake the sexual enlightenment; and I have repeatedly expressed my preference for the selection of the mother. But a mother who is unable to superintend the general education of her children, because she is compelled to spend most of her time away from home engaged in earning a livelihood, is not fitted to undertake the sexual enlightenment of her children; equally unfitted for this is the mother who leaves the education of her children in the hands of hired assistants, whilst herself occupied in attending public meetings, perhaps on behalf of the woman's movement, of the education of children, of the promotion of the sexual enlightenment, of rational dress, or the like, whilst her children at home are abandoned to moral corruption; and the same considerations apply to the mother whose nights are so much occupied in dancing and feasting, that the greater part of her days have to be spent in bed. Fortunately, however, there are many mothers who have very different conceptions of their duties to home and children. We find such mothers very often among the class of skilled artisans, but also among the cultured middle class, although among these latter the desire to ape the manners of the so-called upper classes is unfortunately far too general. I have seen cases in which the mother was still the confidant of her sons after they had entered the period of early manhood; and thus I have known a mother who in the case of a son of sixteen and even of eighteen years, was in a position to allay the grave anxiety awakened by the first occurrence of nocturnal emissions. But where the mother is not the confidant, some other person must take this place, as, for instance, a governess or a near relative. In the case of boys, the father is often the person best able to undertake the sexual enlightenment; or it may be a physician who enjoys the lad's confidence, and especially a family physician in the old and excellent sense of the term; in other cases it may be an elder brother, or an old family friend. Much good in such cases may be done by a friend, older, indeed, than the child who is to receive enlightenment; and yet not so much older as to make the child feel that a mutual understanding is hardly possible. In any case, next to the possession of a cultivated intelligence by the person who undertakes to effect the sexual enlightenment, the point of greatest importance is that this latter person should receive the full confidence of the child. Only when the child has such perfect trust, will it accept as true what it is told, and not suspect that, as has so often been the case, it is being put off with hypocritical phrases— for children recognise the hypocritical character of much of what they are told about sexual matters at an age far earlier than most elders are willing to believe. But another reason why the person who undertakes the enlightenment must be one who has the child's fullest confidence, is that in that case only can the child be expected to be absolutely straightforward. A very frequent mistake in dealing with children is to mistrust them needlessly. Let us suppose that a child has been discovered to masturbate, and that it is spoken to very earnestly in order to break it off the habit. I have known cases in which, although everything pointed to the fact that the child had abandoned its bad habit, yet, when it denied masturbating any longer, it was accused of lying. A child will naturally never give its confidence again to one who has once unjustly reproached it in this manner. On the other hand, a child is far more likely to acknowledge its faults to one in whom it has perfect confidence. The child's confidence can be gained only by an individual confidant. In the presence of such a confidant, a child loses all sense of false shame, and this is an indispensable precondition for effecting a really valuable enlightenment. Where no individual is forthcoming who fulfils the requirements just specified, it is usually better to dispense with the enlightenment; and above all, in this matter, a mechanical routine must be avoided.

I will now briefly report a case in which a younger brother made a confidant of his elder brother, and will show how unwise it would be to lay down any general rule as to who is the person best fitted to undertake the sexual enlightenment of a child.

Case 18.—One day a student of medicine came to me to ask my advice about his younger brother, a lad of thirteen. This latter, an intelligent boy, was attending the upper third class of the higher school. The boy confessed to his brother that he masturbated to excess, and that he found that scenes of cruelty especially aroused sexual stimulation. I asked the student to bring his young brother to see me, and the latter made on me a very favourable impression, especially in the matter of his frankness. He spoke to me quite openly, and attended most carefully to all my advice. I explained to him truthfully that his future was endangered, not only by the masturbation, but also by the perverse ideas; I told him that the danger of a combination of masturbation with perverse ideas was especially serious; and I assured him that he was still at an age when it remained possible for him to develop into a normal man. Some years later, I saw the young man once more. His subsequent development had been excellent, and he was almost free from perverse sexual sensibility.

In this case it would have been utterly wrong to insist on the lad's being enlightened by his father, his mother, his guardian, or his schoolmaster. The particular circumstances of the life often point out the right way. In this instance, it was his older brother in whom the lad had complete confidence. Now, if the elder brother had consulted the parents in this difficulty, such a course would not merely have destroyed the younger's confidence in his elder brother's silence and discretion, but would have undermined the lad's confidence in general. Especially towards the parents, but also towards other relatives, a feeling of shame commonly exists—perhaps a mistaken feeling, but one with which we have to reckon. Often it is the parents' own fault, when they fail to gain the confidence of their children.

The question has also been mooted whether the sexual enlightenment of girls should not be entrusted to some companion of the same sex, more especially in cases in which the mother is for one reason or another unfitted for this task. This view is altogether erroneous. Sex has comparatively little to do with the question. For example, Heidenhain, whose practical experience in these matters is most extensive, has shown that the enlightenment of girls may be effected most admirably by a male physician endowed with the requisite qualities. The thing that matters is not the sex of the person who effects the enlightenment, but the manner in which the enlightenment is effected.

To sum up. The sexual enlightenment of the child is advisable. The biological processes of sex in the vegetable and lower animal world may be taught in school as early as the second period of childhood. A warning against the dangers of venereal infection may be given at school to the senior pupils shortly before they leave, or at some similar suitable opportunity. But for effecting enlightenment regarding the processes of the individual sexual life, the school is unsuitable; this matter can best be undertaken by some private person, and above all by the mother. Choice of the time for this last phase of the sexual enlightenment must be guided, in part by the questions of the child, in part by the child's physical maturity, but more especially by the indications of psychosexual development.

Deliberately I avoid discussing the question as to the precise words and phrases with which the child's enlightenment is to be effected. Moreover, this question is subordinate to another, namely, to what extent instruction in natural science has prepared the way, in the child's mind, for such enlightenment. Both in Germany and in Austria, schemata have been drawn up for systematic preparation of this kind. Speaking generally, we may draw the following conclusions. We have to distinguish according to the age of the child with which we have to deal. Where we have to caution a young man about to leave one of the higher schools, about the dangers of venereal infection, our difficulties are inconsiderable. But where we have to do with a girl of eight, who has asked her mother where her baby brother has come from; or with a boy of fourteen, whom we wish to protect because he has taken to sexual malpractices with his school-fellows, our difficulties are great. In such cases, tact, which cannot always be taught, and a desire for the best interests of the child, must show us the right path. It is obvious that each case will require individual consideration and treatment. An intelligent mother, who constitutes half the child's world and more, can describe these matters to her child, can even describe the sexual act, whose existence most persons prefer to conceal from children. It is by no means impossible to present even this act to the child's mind in a tactful way. It can be done in a poetical manner, and yet without departing from the strict truth. The same considerations apply to the act of birth. In a book dealing with this subject, a mother is asked by her child where children come from, and she answers as follows: "You see, little one, how fruit grows upon a tree; in just the same way, little children grow within the body of the mother." Beyond question, there is no justification for the assumption that sexual enlightenment can be effected only in a repulsive manner; and this view depends merely upon the fact that through a perversion of moral ideas certain persons regard as unclean things which are essentially clean. Everything depends upon the person who effects the enlightenment, upon finding a suitable opportunity, and upon choosing words and phrases adapted to the child's intelligence. Success will often follow upon replying in an illuminating way to some chance question of the child. In other cases, there may be indications for making the enlightenment part of a festival occasion—a method described in an old book, in which the father effects the enlightenment of his children to the accompaniment of public prayers. The description shows a truly religious spirit, and a genuine love for children; it shows, further, that natural processes may be described truthfully to children without wounding in any way their sense of shame. There is no ground whatever for the belief that to a fairly advanced child a serious person cannot suitably describe all the natural processes of the human body, including sexual intercourse. The child to whom these things are described in a well-considered way, will receive no kind of injury to its moral sentiments; nor will such a description, once more, if it is couched in well-chosen words, provoke in the child any tendency to laughter. The secrecy with which the sexual life is surrounded, confused by many with the sentiment of shame, often gives rise to the belief that the child has the same feelings about the sexual life as the adult. But the unspoiled child has absolutely no feeling that the sexual life is in any way unclean; and for this very reason, no great difficulty arises in the sexual enlightenment of such an unspoiled child—an enlightenment which includes a description of the sexual act. I have myself on several occasions been asked by parents with a proper care for the future morality and health of their children, to undertake the necessary enlightenment of these latter. I am absolutely convinced that when the child has complete trust in the person who effects the enlightenment, the explanation of everything is fully possible. In this book, I have more than once proved that a description of sexual intercourse, appealing as it does rather to the intellectual side of the child's mind, need have no bad influence at all upon its emotional life; and in the further course of this chapter I shall have to speak of the matter once again. I may add here that there are books written specially for the purpose of assisting parents in the instruction of their children in these matters.

From what I have written it will have been obvious that I regard the sexual enlightenment of the child as very desirable; but it does not follow from this that I regard it as something that must be undertaken. Not everything is practicable which may seem desirable. We must not forget that there are dangers associated with the sexual enlightenment. It will not be right simply to ignore a reason often alleged against the desirability of sexual enlightenment, namely, that in this way it is possible that the child's thoughts will be turned in the sexual direction. This is unquestionably possible, and the danger can only be avoided by great adroitness. But when we remember that such adroitness is not found everywhere, we shall have to admit, however much we may wish that the sexual enlightenment of children should invariably be effected, that it will often be necessary to dispense with it, because the person suitable to undertake the enlightenment of a particular child is not forthcoming.

If the right person is not to be found, the idea of the sexual enlightenment must be abandoned. However unsympathetic and even dangerous the manner in which, as a rule, children mutually enlighten one another about sexual matters, even more serious dangers may attach to the enlightenment of a child by an adult unsuited for this difficult task. Inept enlightenment may entail extremely serious consequences, and more especially it is likely to bring about the particular evil results that we are most eager to avoid, that is to say, it may direct the attention of the child to its own sexual inclinations. We have also to take into account the fact that there are persons who cannot discuss sexual topics without themselves becoming sexually excited; and we cannot afford to ignore the danger that among those who undertake to effect the sexual enlightenment of children there may be persons who will gladly seize every opportunity of speaking to the children upon sexual matters, intoxicating themselves the while with their own sexual imaginings. The grave danger of allowing an unsuitable person to undertake the sexual enlightenment is obvious from the existence of those persons who teach that homosexual inclinations occurring in children indicate that they are permanently homosexual—a view which, as has been shown, is utterly erroneous. But let us suppose that one who holds such a doctrine is the person who has undertaken the sexual enlightenment of a child, and we can hardly doubt what the result will be, namely, to foster homosexuality. The greatest possible care must therefore be exercised in the selection of the person who is to undertake the sexual enlightenment.

Nor must we expect too much from the sexual enlightenment. Although to adults the way in which one schoolboy instructs another about matters of sex may appear to be extremely unpleasant, yet, as a matter of practical experience, this method has not had the disastrous results that some believe to attach to it. Unquestionably, the Germans and other civilised races have done much very important work, not only in the intellectual field, but also in that of ethics and in that of social life. Still we have learned that disadvantages are entailed by the rough-and-ready methods of sexual enlightenment hitherto commonly practised. Will these ill-effects disappear with the realisation of the modern efforts for a purposive and deliberate sexual enlightenment? Even though the modern ideas on the subject are to be preferred, it must not be supposed that their adoption will immediately result in the disappearance of all the unfavourable aspects of the sexual life. We shall not thereby transform children into little angels; and I doubt very much if the new methods of enlightenment will have much effect in diminishing the frequency of masturbation among children. I am led to this conviction by my experience that at the time when the process of sexual ripening begins, a child does not usually possess an adequate sense of the dangers of such malpractices. I am certainly afraid that nothing we can do will greatly lessen the prevalence of masturbation among children. I would rather venture to hope for a diminution in the prevalence of venereal diseases, as a result of the newer methods of sexual enlightenment; but even here there will be many cases in which passion will gain the victory over all possible prudential considerations. The same remarks apply also to pregnancy, and to the other consequences of the sexual life.

I am, moreover, sceptical because the very persons to whom to-day we have to look to effect the sexual enlightenment of children, are themselves to a great extent also in need of enlightenment; and in respect of many of the questions about which the child has to be enlightened, no general harmony of scientific opinion can as yet be said to obtain. Take, for example, the question whether masturbation during the period of sexual development is or is not a physiological act; or the question whether sexual abstinence can do any harm to the health. It is true that such differences in scientific opinion are not so extensive as gravely to affect the question of the sexual enlightenment of the child. In the matter of sexual abstinence, for example, the majority of physicians are to-day agreed upon the view that such abstinence in general does no harm; and that those, if any, whose health may be unfavourably influenced by sexual abstinence, constitute at most a very small minority. In my own view, the persons who may suffer from this cause are those affected with hyperæsthesia of the sexual impulse, and in whom the impulse is dominant to such a degree that it interferes with all their alternative activities. But it is certainly only an extremely small percentage of persons about whom, among medical men able to speak authoritatively, that there is any difference of opinion.

A more serious matter is the extent to which erroneous views about sexual questions still prevail among the populace. A father who starts with the false assumption that his son must inevitably have intercourse with so many prostitutes and must seduce so many girls—in a word, a father who regards sexual abstinence as unmanly, or as necessarily dangerous to health (and fathers who hold such opinions are no rarity)—such a father must himself be sexually enlightened before we give him the right to enlighten his son. Those also themselves greatly need enlightenment who, for instance, advise a young bridegroom who has always lived a chaste life to visit a prostitute before marriage, in order to prove his sexual potency. As if potency in intercourse with an experienced prostitute, skilled in all the tricks of her trade, were a proof that the bridegroom will prove sexually potent in intercourse with a chaste woman; or as if, on the other hand, the fact that a man proves impotent when he attempts intercourse with a prostitute whose embraces are repulsive to him, were in any sense whatever a proof that the same man will fail to effect intercourse with the woman he loves. Thus, many full-grown men are in need of enlightenment about this matter of sexual potency, and especially need information regarding the extent of the individual variations in this matter. We hear of young men who believe themselves to be ill, simply because they are not sexually potent to a degree that enables them to effect complete sexual intercourse several times in brief succession. Their error often depends upon the fact that they have been told by other young men that normal sexual potency enables a man to have repeated intercourse at intervals of a few minutes. As regards the informants, it may be that, having had such exceptional potency on one or two occasions, they really believe it to bo a normal requisite of full manhood; more often, however, the mistake originates from a young man taking at its face value the boasting of one of his comrades who has lied freely about his own "virile potency." I have known similar things happen in the case of women, among whom boasting about the intensity of the voluptuous sensations experienced during sexual intercourse is by no means uncommon. There are a great many women in whom voluptuous sensations during intercourse are entirely lacking, and in whom even sexual desire may be in abeyance. Sometimes this is a matter of no great importance. But wives whose women-friends have boasted to such an extent of the intensity of the voluptuous sensations experienced in sexual intercourse, are apt to overestimate the importance of the lack of such voluptuous pleasure in their own experience of the sexual act; and it is therefore desirable that women should know the true facts of the case. We have further to remember that many of the disillusionments of marriage depend upon the fact that before marriage girls have allowed their imaginations to run riot concerning the intensity of enjoyment they will experience in sexual intercourse; all the greater is their disillusionment if they are among those who fail, after all, to experience sexual pleasure to the full.

In conclusion, I may refer to another instance of the way in which the importance of the sexual enlightenment is apt to be over-estimated, namely, as regards the effect of the enlightenment in furnishing protection against the venereal diseases. It is by this very error attaching to so much of what is said about the sexual enlightenment, that attention is readily diverted from a far more important field. Namely, in moral questions, a child is far more easily influenced by good example, than by any amount of good instruction by word of mouth. Example arouses a stimulus towards imitative action, whilst, in countless cases, the listener has no inclination whatever to do what he is merely told. This applies even to very little children, who adopt for themselves the practices they observe in their elders to a far greater extent than is commonly believed—although, as Bleuler has shown, in this imitativeness the conceptual life may play a comparatively small part. If, therefore, from the first the principal stress is laid on giving a good example, the subsequent sexual enlightenment would be rendered far easier, and its success to a large extent assured. In a pure household, it is not so necessary that a child should be fully enlightened; or rather, the child's enlightenment will be extremely easy. Conversely in the case of an impure household. Unless the greatest care is taken that children shall never be exposed to the contagion of bad example, how readily may it happen, that the child, after it has received the sexual enlightenment, and has been cautioned against any kind of obscene talk, is allowed to watch all sorts of improper acts and to listen to obscenities! Such mischances may occur, not only, as self-satisfied parents are apt to imagine, through the misconduct of servants or strangers, but often the members of the child's own family may be the persons at fault. Adults believe that a child hears nothing, when in reality it is paying careful attention to that which is not intended for childish ears, and to that which gives the lie to what the child has just been told in the form of the sexual enlightenment. And this may happen without the grown-up persons having made any indiscreet connected speeches in the child's presence. Various slight indications, gestures, a stolen laugh, &c., may be interpreted by the child after its own fashion, which is often one directly conflicting with the sense of the lesson previously given. How easily may it happen that a boy is taught that the seduction of a girl is a wicked thing, or a girl is told that she must never be so ignorant or so stupid as to become the victim of a seducer, and yet a few minutes later the child may overhear the instructor relating the heroic deeds of a cousin, who has seduced so and so many girls of the lower orders!

Thus the importance of the sexual enlightenment must on no account be over-estimated. Rather should the words of the old proverb always be kept in mind: "As the old birds sing, so will the young birds chirp." Those who guide their own conduct in accordance with this principle, will find the sexual enlightenment of their children an easy matter; but in other houses, the theoretical enlightenment may be effected as carefully as you please, and yet it will do but little good. It is evident that the earlier movement in favour of the sexual enlightenment, to which I referred, failed because the expectations of its advocates were pitched too high, and because the emotional life of the child was ignored—an error rightly pointed out by Thalhofer. I have no doubt that in a few decades the efforts of our own day on behalf of the sexual enlightenment, in so far as they lay the principal stress upon the theoretical enlightenment, and expect its enforcement to initiate the golden age, will arouse similar feelings of amusement to those with which we ourselves now contemplate the failures of the past.

The above is all I have to say about the psychical aids to the sexual enlightenment of the child, I turn now to consider the hygienic measures—those with a direct effect upon the body. Speaking generally, these are identical with those which are recommended for the treatment of masturbation.

When the child awakes in the morning, it should not be permitted to lie in bed too long, above all, not in a hot feather-bed. To send children to bed, or to keep them in bed all day, as a punishment, as a means of depriving them of liberty, is, from this point of view, a practice which must unreservedly be condemned. Very dangerous, from this outlook, is also the rule common in boarding-schools and similar places, in accordance with which the children are sent to bed at a fixed time, and are not in any circumstances allowed to leave their beds before a fixed time in the morning. Everything must be done strictly according to the rules. Now although we may admit that no such institution can be carried on without some discipline, yet it is necessary to point out that when there is a rule in a boarding-school that no inmate shall get out of bed before seven o'clock in the morning, children that are wide awake and lively at an earlier hour are exceedingly likely to take to masturbation. The dangers attendant upon prolonged lying in bed arises from a combination of mental and physical influences. Among the physical influences, the warmth of the bed is the most important; among the mental influences, we have to consider the lack of occupation, and the ease with which the genital organs are handled.

We have further to take steps to allay as far as possible all kinds of local irritation of the genital organs. Among these may be mentioned: phimosis and skin-eruptions of the genital region, which latter may lead to scratching, and so give rise to masturbation, even apart from the fact that the itching itself may favour the occurrence of voluptuous sensations. In addition, we have to think of the clothing. I pointed out before that breeches which pressed on the perineum sometimes led to the practice of masturbation. Hence this article of dress, breeches, knickerbockers, or trousers, should be made loose and comfortable. With regard to the proposal to do away with breeches altogether in the case of children, a recommendation which, as previously explained, has been made by several authorities, I cannot think that we should gain much thereby, for, to be effective, this measure would have to be continued up to a comparatively advanced age, and would thus involve a complete remodelling of our customary dress. It may be doubted however, if attention to this point will do much to prevent premature sexual stimulation; for the danger is not so great as has sometimes been suggested. Still, a careful mother will take care that the tailor does not cut her little boy's breeches so as to fit too closely: for though this may please the parental eye, it is undoubtedly dangerous to the child. I have previously referred to the dangers attendant upon climbing the pole in the gymnasium; and here will merely add that a number of teachers of gymnastics regard pole-climbing as an exercise of very great value, whilst they believe that the danger of sexual stimulation in climbing results from the use of too thin a pole, and does not occur in climbing a thick pole, or in climbing a rope. It has been suggested, in this connexion, that the rocking-horse should be eliminated from the list of permissible toys. Objections have also been made, on the ground of the possibility of improper sexual stimulation, against bicycling and horseback-riding; but I think these objections are largely unfounded, for, as far as bicycling is concerned, a well-shaped saddle cannot improperly stimulate the genital organs; and just as little does such stimulation occur in horseback exercise unless when the lower part of the trunk is pressed forward against the front peak of the saddle, as in halting, or in passing from a faster to a slower pace. Of course, for horseback exercise, the breeches must be properly cut, as otherwise they may exercise injurious pressure on the genital organs when the rider is in the saddle. Intestinal stimulation may also give rise to reflex excitation of the genital organs; for example, intestinal worms may initiate such reflex disturbance. Mantegazza lays especial stress upon stimulation of the rectum, being of opinion that stimulation of this region is very likely to lead to the development of pæderastic inclinations. There are no grounds for such an assumption; but it is quite true that stimulation of the anal or gluteal region will very readily irradiate to the sphere of the genitals. For all these reasons, constipation, and more especially the accumulation of large scybalous masses in the rectum, are above all to be avoided.

In cases of obstinate inclination to masturbate, all kinds of local measures have been recommended to prevent manipulation and artificial stimulation of the penis or the vulva. But speaking generally, no great reliance can be placed in any of these local measures. Moreover, casual local stimulation, especially towards the end of the second period of childhood, has no very profound etiological significance. The chief stimuli giving rise to reflex excitement of the genital organs are of an organic nature, and are therefore but little influenced by external measures. Besides, the fact that among races who never wear breeches, the boys masturbate freely, and perhaps even more freely than do boys in Europe, proves that such external stimuli as the pressure exercised by breeches on the genital organs play no decisive part in the causation of masturbation.

I purposely refrain from further reference here to such measures as a methodical "hardening" by hydrotherapeutic procedures, and the like. In special text-books, whether upon masturbation, or upon hydrotherapeutics, ample information will be found about these matters.

The suggestion has also been made that from the sexual outlook the diet of children is a matter worthy of the most earnest attention. Nothing should be given to the child which may exert a sexually stimulating effect; especially we must avoid giving heavy foods late in the evening. More detailed directions are also given as to the use of particular kinds of food, some of which may be consecrated by tradition, and yet seem to have but small reasonable foundation. To this category belong the prohibition or limitation of flesh-foods, and the prohibition of asparagus, celery, and other articles of diet. There is no proof that such things have a stimulating influence upon the sexual impulse, either in children or in adults. We might more readily incline to believe that certain spices may have such an influence; but even as regards these, no great anxiety need be felt. As regards alcohol, many maintain it has an exciting influence upon the sexual life, and thus gives rise to all kinds of excesses. This is true of a good many cases, but the rule is by no means so general as is commonly assumed. I recall that in my own student days we often classified the students into two groups, the alcoholic and the sexual; those of the former group spent their money upon alcohol, those of the latter group upon women. My own experience of these days certainly leads me to dispute the assertion that those addicted to alcohol are generally more inclined than others to indiscriminate sexual intercourse. But this reservation is necessary, that at that time actual abstainers were almost unknown among the students, and we classified in the alcoholic group those who consumed very large quantities of alcohol; whilst the members of the sexual group certainly also consumed alcohol, though not very much. Beyond question, the common belief that there is an association between the free use of alcohol and sexual excesses is one which lacks foundation. This view is to too great an extent based upon criminal statistics, and upon the records of the perversions to which the sexual perverts among alcoholics have been inclined. But think of the countless normal persons in whom the enjoyment of alcohol induces no tendency to sexual excesses; and, on the other hand, abstainers from alcohol have been personally known to me whom no one could venture to call moderate in their sexual relations. But although I make all these reservations with regard to the effects of the use of alcohol by adults, I am in full accord with the view that the use of alcohol should be prohibited to children. Alcohol cannot do any good to children, and the possibility that in individual instances it may stimulate the sexual imagination, is one which cannot be denied. But this fact does not justify us in advising against the moderate use of alcohol by adults.

Passing to consider the general mode of life, we certainly agree with Hufeland, who, in his Makrobiotik, recommends vigorous bodily activity. He contends that children who go to bed at night healthily tired out, will not be likely to think of masturbation. In the present age of sports and games it will not be found difficult to fulfil this indication; and we see as a matter of fact that a great deal of trouble is taken to give children every opportunity of keeping in active movement. Even in our large towns, in which, owing to the lack of a sufficiency of open spaces, great difficulties have arisen in this respect, much has of late been done to improve matters. For many years past in England special efforts have been made to provide such playgrounds for children and adults.

I take this opportunity of drawing attention to a method recommended by Féré for the cure of masturbation, which I have myself found of good use in several cases, but which appears to be almost entirely unknown. It is that the child addicted to masturbation during the night hours should be watched by a trustworthy person; every time the child puts its hand to its genital organs, or endeavours to stimulate these organs mechanically in some other way, the attendant must immediately intervene, and draw the hands from beneath the bed-clothing. This plan may be adopted whether the child masturbates while asleep or while awake. But good can be expected from the method above all in those cases in which the child masturbates during sleep, and in which it commonly wakes up directly it is interfered with. In most cases the children treated in this way soon give up the practice of masturbation, even though the evil is of long standing. But it will be advisable to continue to supervise the child for some time after a cure has apparently been effected, lest what may have become a nervous automatism should be resumed after a brief intermission. The chief difficulty in the practical application of this method lies in the choice of a trustworthy person to watch the child. As a rule, the mother will be the most suitable, but now and again we shall find a hired nurse to whom this extremely difficult task may safely be entrusted. In a number of cases with which I have had to deal, I have recommended the mother to undertake the duty herself, because she seemed to me the most trustworthy person available. But it is a very regrettable fact that many mothers are altogether unwilling to make the necessary sacrifice for their child's good; and most of them are quite ready to believe that some woman whom they can hire for a few shillings a night will perform the duty which they themselves as mothers have renounced. Such lack of proper feeling is especially common among those who belong to what are termed the upper classes of society—to the aristocracy whether of birth or of wealth—whereas among the middle classes I have found mothers far more ready to make the necessary sacrifices.

In sexual education, the sexual perversions must receive especial attention. I must first of all refer again to two matters, of which some account has previously been given: the influencing of congenital inborn tendencies; and the undifferentiated sexual impulse. As regards the former, we have to take the following data into consideration. The fact that the indications lead us to believe that a particular sexual perversion is inborn, need not induce us to think there is no hope of counteracting this perversion by well-planned educational influences. I have already written at considerable length about the undifferentiated sexual impulse, and have shown that perverse manifestations during the period of the undifferentiated sexual impulse do not prove that a permanent perversion has developed. But everything possible should be done to guard against the further development of any such perverse mode of sexual sensibility, including sexual qualities in the wider sense of the term. We know, for example, that many homosexual men have a tendency to dress in girls' clothing, and many homosexual women to go about in men's clothing, and, in both cases, to adopt the inclinations and occupations of the opposite sex. During the period of the undifferentiated sexual impulse, we must not attach too much importance to the appearance of inclinations of this kind; but it would be equally erroneous to ignore them altogether. Boys who adopt a girlish behaviour, should not be encouraged in doing so by treating the matter as a joke. If a boy frequently dresses up as a girl, or a girl as a boy, and if we observe between two boys, or between two girls, an unduly intimate friendship at an age which corresponds to the period of the undifferentiated sexual impulse, it will be as well to modify the children's education accordingly. A girl with such inclinations should, for example, be thrown as much as possible into the society of lads of an appropriate age. In the case of those who are still quite young, there is no doubt that by the proper measures we can in part check the development of perverse manifestations, and in part completely repress them; notwithstanding the fact that interested agitators, whose principal aim is to secure the repeal of Section 175 of the German Imperial Criminal Code, maintain the contrary, and assert that homosexual tendencies appearing in the child necessarily indicate the future development of permanent homosexuality. Parents, tutors, schoolmasters, and physicians, must not allow themselves to be led astray by these agitators, who falsify the data of science. In the interest of truth, in the interest of the children endangered by these perversions, and in the interest of civilisation, these misstatements must be contradicted.

The chief danger associated with the appearance of sexual perversions lies in the fact that the child thus affected, whether boy or girl, endeavours again and ever again to revive these pleasurably-toned sensations; and above all in the fact that as soon as the genital organs are sufficiently mature, the boy or girl obtains sexual gratification by masturbating simultaneously with the imaginative contemplation of perverse ideas. Such perverse psychical onanism, accompanied or unaccompanied by physical masturbatory acts, is eminently adapted to favour the development of the perversion. Obviously, the actual performance of the corresponding perverse sexual act will be just as dangerous as is perversely associated masturbation. Thus, a boy who is homosexually inclined may masturbate while allowing his imagination to run riot upon homosexual ideas; or he may take to homosexual acts with one or more other male persons. Every sort of gratification that is associated with perverse images, is dangerous; and no less dangerous is the spontaneous cultivation of such perverse sexual images.

A very real and serious danger to children is to be found in my opinion in the risk of the progressive cultivation of homosexuality, if they become victims of a pædophile. The adult homosexual will sometimes conceal a perverse inclination directed towards children under the cloak of friendship or of an educational interest. I have previously referred to the danger that the child, at a time of life when its own sexual impulse is still undifferentiated, may sometimes reciprocate such a feeling. When I recall the light-heartedness with which homosexual males have acknowledged to me their experiences of sexual intercourse with apprentice-boys, and with pupils attending the higher forms of our secondary schools, and when I think of the readiness with which homosexual women seek opportunities of sexual intercourse with immature or partially mature girls, it seems to me that there are good grounds for the utterance of an urgent warning. My experiences in this department further lead me to believe that if Section 175 of the German Imperial Criminal Code is to be repealed, a further alteration in the Code will also be indispensable, namely, that the Age of Protection (Schutzalter—equivalent to the Age of Consent in the English Criminal Law Amendment Act) should be raised to the completion of the eighteenth year, and that the protection should apply, not merely to the actions now specified in Section 175 as "unnatural vice," but to all acts of sexual impropriety in the widest sense of the term. Recently this proposal has been approved by a resolution of the Reichstag.

There are certain additional points about which it is unnecessary to write here, for the reason that these have all been considered in some appropriate connexion earlier in this book. For example, I have insisted upon the importance of anyone who possesses children's confidence taking steps for the removal of corrupted children from the environment of uncorrupted ones.

Where we have reason to believe, in the case of a particular child, that a perverse mode of sexual sensibility is developing, we shall occasionally find it preferable rather to attempt to hinder the growth of the perversion, than to try to check the general manifestations of the sexual impulse. Thus, in the case of a boy of fourteen, who is continually affected with homosexual imaginings, we shall find it far more difficult to repress sexual manifestations altogether, than to divert the homosexual sensibility into heterosexual channels. If a boy affected in this way be thrown much into the society of girls, or conversely, a girl into the society of boys (at dances, games of lawn-tennis, &c.), the subsequent effect is likely to be good, because the sexual pervert, even if his perverse tendency be congenital, can nevertheless be educated out of his perversion. It should hardly be necessary to state expressly, that when I speak of finding for the homosexual associates of the opposite sex, I am not thinking of suggesting intimate sexual intercourse. Apart from moral considerations, we could not, in the cases under consideration, expect any benefit to accrue on medical grounds; my reference was to a purely platonic association.

No one need suggest that all these recommendations are superfluous, for the reason that, according to my own previous account of the matter, the undifferentiated condition of the sexual impulse is spontaneously replaced by the normal heterosexual impulse. For, first of all, the signs that give rise to anxiety may not be manifestations of the undifferentiated sexual impulse, but may be the first manifestations of a developing congenital perversion; and, secondly, it is by no means improbable that, even in the entire absence of any congenital tendency to sexual perversion, unfavourable external conditions may lead to the further development of the perverse manifestations of the undifferentiated period. I may refer in this connexion to what was said previously.

It is necessary to refer at length to one additional educational method which plays a very important part in sexual development, namely, punishment. The sexual perversions known by the names of sadism and masochism have of late attracted much attention from students of the sexual life. In sadism, sexual excitement occurs in association with the infliction of ill-treatment, humiliation, or pain upon others; in masochism the sexual excitement results from the experience of such ill-treatment, humiliation, or pain by the masochist in person. But in sadism, it is not essential that the sadist should himself play the active part; very often, the maltreatment by a second person of a third suffices to cause sexual excitement in the sadist who looks on. Masochistic and sadistic modes of sensibility are frequently associated in the same individual. As far as the relationship of these perversions to punishment is concerned, we learn from many adult masochists and sadists that their first experience of sexual excitement occurred when as children they received a whipping, or saw another child whipped— at school, for instance. The oft-quoted case of Rousseau has previously been mentioned in this work. It is thus evident that the subject of the punishment of children needs to be considered, not merely from the general educational point of view, but also from the special outlook of sexual education. The principal question is whether as a result of corporal punishment, either personally experienced or witnessed, an enduring sexual perversion may be induced in a child; and this problem must be carefully distinguished from another problem, which, however, is also of very great importance, namely, that of the sexual excitement which may be experienced by the person who inflicts the punishment. The significance of the materials available to guide us to a conclusion upon these questions, is not, however, perfectly clear in all cases. I may refer to what was said previously; and will here merely add that the question whether the infliction of corporal punishment really originates a perversion in the sufferer, or whether it merely awakens to activity a pre-existent tendency, and one which, in the absence of this particular exciting cause, would almost certainly have been awakened by some other and unavoidable cause, some influence acting from without—this is a question to which conflicting answers have been given.

But corporal punishment entails other dangers, in addition to the risk of the origination or the awakening of a sexual perversion. Certain children, having experienced sexual stimulation as a result of such punishment, will endeavour to secure its repetition. I have known cases in which sexual perverts have deliberately misconducted themselves in school, in order to be punished, and thus to enjoy voluptuous sensations. Finally, there is a third danger to be taken into account, and this is a danger of whose reality I have been convinced by the direct confessions of schoolmasters and schoolmistresses, that they have struck their pupils for the purpose of thereby enjoying sexual stimulation. Even if no such admissions had ever been made to me, I should have regarded it as by no means improbable that such incidents should from time to time occur. Let no reader draw the inference that whenever a master chastises a naughty boy, he acts always under the influence of a sadistic inclination; I do not even consider that sadistic inclinations are a frequent cause of the infliction of corporal chastisement. The danger of such sweeping generalisations is obvious, especially in view of the fact that to-day many children, even, know what sadism is. Hence a schoolboy who has been punished might readily attribute sadistic motives to his master; and might even make a definite accusation of this kind.

When we come to ask what practical conclusions may be drawn from our recognition of the relationships between corporal punishment and sexual perversions, the first point that occurs to our minds is to consider whether the corporal punishments which may possibly give rise to such perverse stimulations are in fact absolutely indispensable. Although in this matter I find myself in opposition to a great many physicians and to not a few educationalists, I remain of the opinion that we cannot propose to do away altogether with corporal punishments in our schools; at any rate, such punishment remains, I consider, essential, so long as certain other reforms are still wanting. Among the reforms which are indispensable preliminaries to the complete abolition of corporal punishment, is one giving a greater power to expel insolent and undisciplined boys. Not until such a power is granted can corporal punishments be abolished from our schools. For a flogging is oftentimes the only punishment of which a rough and ill-conditioned boy is afraid. Moreover, and altogether apart from this consideration, the discipline of our schools is to-day endangered in various ways: for instance, by public disquisitions about overwork in schools; by the conduct of many parents, who prejudice their children against the schools in a most indiscreet manner; and by attacks in the newspapers on the schoolmasters—attacks which are often unfair and inconsiderate. Further, the recent widely advertised public pronouncements against the right of the schoolmaster to inflict corporal punishment, are hardly calculated to strengthen the discipline of our schools, or to assist the masters in the performance of what must be at best extremely difficult duties. So long, therefore, as we lack the safeguard to discipline that would be provided by extensive powers of expelling undesirables, I consider that corporal punishment is essential to the discipline of our schools.

Unquestionably it would be a good thing if we could entirely dispense with the use of corporal punishments, or at least dispense with them in all cases in which there might be any possibility of their doing harm, as by giving rise to sexual stimulation. But unfortunately we have no means of ascertaining beforehand what are the cases in which corporal punishment is likely to do harm. There is no possibility of withholding the right to inflict corporal punishment from those masters in especial who might use it to gratify their own sexual passions—if only for the reason that we have no means of finding out who these persons are. For it is not the masters with free views about sexual questions who are especially open to suspicion from the point of view we are now considering; nor is it the masters who are morally defective or irreligious. Indeed, I am acquainted with some extremely pious schoolmasters who, according to their own admissions to me, have experienced sexual excitement when chastising children; and some of these have in other respects had admirable characters. Cases recorded, not merely in erotic literature, but also in historical literature, show that religion affords no safeguard against such temptations; we learn, for instance, that in the cloister, monks and nuns have utilised their right to inflict punishment in order to procure sexual excitement. For these reasons, it is inadmissible to infer, because a schoolmaster is a religious man, that therefore he is the one to whom the right to inflict corporal punishment may safely be entrusted.

The danger of an excessive use of powers of administering corporal punishment, and more especially the danger of awakening the sexuality of children prematurely and with perverse associations, may be minimised by the proper treatment of schoolmasters. We must not treat our schoolmasters in such a way that behind them they always feel the presence of the inspector, compelling them to force the pupils through the prescribed, but excessive tasks. Nor must the schoolmaster's own work be excessive, for nervous overstrain will very readily lead to outbreaks of violence. It seems also desirable that the right of administering corporal punishment should not be entrusted to masters who are still quite young, for a certain experience is needed to guide them to a reasonable moderation. What I have said of schoolmasters applies, mutatis mutandis, to schoolmistresses and governesses. There are many reasons for the belief that the danger that the right to inflict corporal punishment may be utilised to procure erotic excitement for the person exercising that right, is considerably greater in women than it is in men. Even if we take no notice of erotic literature, in which sadism in women manifested by the mishandling of children is so frequent a motif, we shall find quite a number of experiences of actual life which compel us to admit the frequency of such perverse sensibilities in women. Among various records bearing upon this matter, I may remind readers of those of the upper class women of ancient Rome, and of the horrible punishments they inflicted upon their female slaves; and also of American women of the slave-owning class, in the South before the war, who sometimes flogged young male slaves in the most terrible way.

Whether this matter is regarded as one of great or of small importance, it is as well to inquire whether it is not possible that the necessary disciplinary punishment should be inflicted in such a way as to reduce to a minimum any dangers from the sexual point of view. Now, we learn from experience, that when a perversion is traced back to its origination in a chastisement endured during childhood, this chastisement was as a rule the customary whipping of the buttocks. Far less frequently, and indeed hardly ever, are we told that any other form of punishment has initiated a sexual perversion. This may, of course, depend merely upon the fact that other modes of punishment are far less common. But there are many reasons for supposing that stimulation of the buttock is especially apt to induce sexual excitement. It is possible, also, that another factor is in operation here, namely, the fact that the child undergoing punishment is commonly placed across the elder's knees in such a way that pressure upon the child's genital organs is almost unavoidable. Moreover, when we bear in mind the fact that other methods of chastisement may involve dangers to health (boxing the ears, for instance, may threaten the integrity of the sense of hearing), the question which is the best method of corporal punishment becomes a very serious one. I have myself elsewhere expressed the opinion that as far as the possible effects on health are concerned, and especially from the point of view of sexual hygiene, blows upon the palm of the hand perhaps constitute the least dangerous form of corporal punishment. But I by no means suppose that even here danger is altogether excluded, or that no sexual stimulation can possibly ensue from such chastisement. For the local physical stimulation is not the only matter we have to consider in connexion with a whipping upon the buttocks. In quite a number of cases in which we are told that some experience during childhood has been the initiating cause of subsequent masochism or sadism, there has been no question of purely physical causation, as by a whipping upon the buttocks. I may recall the case in which sexual perversion appeared to have developed out of witnessing the slaughter of animals, so that the only stimulus acting upon this child belonged to the psychical sphere. The cases, also, in which a child refers the origin of his perversion to having looked on at a whipping (in school, for instance) show that such perversions are not only aroused by mechanical stimuli, but may depend also upon psychological factors. For these reasons I consider that we are not justified in assuming, if whipping upon the buttocks were altogether done away with, and if blows upon the palm of the hand became the only permissible form of corporal punishment, that permanent sexual perversions would then become impossible. With further reference to what I have said above about discipline in schools, I may add that the kernel of the problem is this: is the probability that corporal punishment will lead to permanent sexual perversion, or will induce sexual excitement, sufficiently great, to render it necessary that corporal punishment should be completely abolished from our schools, so long as our schoolmasters possess no other adequate means of making certain of their pupils observe the discipline of the school? It is unconditionally necessary that the discipline of our schools should be maintained; and those who are unreservedly opposed to corporal punishment in all its forms should make it their business to see that some other adequate means are provided for the maintenance of school-discipline. However strongly we may feel that it is essential that there should be no abuse by schoolmasters of their right to administer corporal punishment, none the less, even in this "Century of the Child," we need safeguards also against the abuse of sentimentality.

In this chapter I have attempted to deal with a few only of the problems of sexual education. To discuss the subject exhaustively would have been impossible within the limits of this book; nor have I endeavoured to take into consideration the enormous mass of literature relating to the modern movement in favour of the sexual enlightenment. I have made no reference to the fact that it has recently been recommended that every girl should spend a year of service [Dienstjahr—analogous to the term of military service obligatory on all males in Germany] in hospitals, asylums, &c., whereby she would gain enlightenment concerning many things which will be of value to her in her subsequent married life. All such proposals are so much matters of detail, that I have thought it inadvisable to discuss them here.

The most important requirement of all is certainly a good educator—a word used here in the widest possible signification. The best of all educators for the child should be its own mother; although we may agree with the assertion recently made by Eschle and others, that the father has important duties to fulfil as instructor, even during the child's first year of life. Nevertheless, the father, even if his professional training gives him especial skill in these directions, is not really likely to do very much in the educational way for his infant offspring. It is to the mother, above all, that the care of infants and young children is of necessity entrusted. We have, however, to remember that a large proportion of mothers, especially those belonging to the ranks of the proletariat, take part in the work of breadwinning for the family, and are thus prevented from giving as much attention to their children as might be wished. But in the families of the well-to-do there is often no question of the mother herself playing the principal part in the education of her children, since it is customary for her to depute so many of her maternal duties to hired substitutes. It has recently been maintained that it is to the Woman's Movement that we owe the fact that the question of the sexual enlightenment has now become a live one; but this is certainly an overstatement, though it is not to be denied that women have had some influence in this direction. But if the women who play a prominent part in the Woman's Movement would do more than they have done as yet to impress upon the women of the well-to-do classes an understanding of their duties towards their children, they would certainly be doing excellent work. No paid substitute can adequately replace for the child the benefits it will derive if its mother herself does all that she could and should do. A mother who seriously devotes herself to the care of her child, need have no anxiety about the risks of its being misused by others for sexual purposes. Such a mother keeps herself fully acquainted with her child's sentiments. She is in a position to choose the best moment for effecting the child's sexual enlightenment, and she can best judge when the use of the stork story is no longer justified. Of such a mother, a child far more readily makes a confidant. Moreover, if the mother devotes a great deal of time and pains to the personal care of her child, this has, in the case of a boy, the great advantage of inculcating a greater respect for the female sex in general than is apt to be found in boys to-day. I consider this last-mentioned point to be one of the utmost importance in relation to the sexual enlightenment, for only in such a way can the boy when grown to manhood be led instinctively to refrain from the seduction of girls—with all the misery which such a course usually involves for the victims. Similarly, a young man brought up to respect women will refrain from making a mock of pregnancy, whether "legitimate" or "illegitimate." When we see a young woman bearing a new life in her womb, owing her position it may be to all the subtle arts of the seducer, and note how cruelly she is treated by the law and what scorn and contempt are poured upon her by society and by the individual, we cannot fail to welcome most heartily the movement for the Protection of Motherhood (Mutterschutzbewegung) which has recently made such progress in Germany. When children are properly educated, there is reason to hope that sexual matters will be less often treated in an obscene spirit than is the case to-day. Nor need we fear, when such education becomes the rule, that every allusion to sexual things may involve dangers to the child. Precisely because the sexual life will then be known to the child in a natural way, will there be less reason to dread the deliberate cultivation by children of sexual topics of conversation. When at school the love adventures of Mars and Venus are the subject of the lesson, in children thus educated no unclean thoughts need arise. It must never be forgotten, however, that when the imagination has been perverted, opportunities for unclean thoughts recur with extraordinary frequency; and indeed by no means whatever can such opportunities be altogether avoided. Since this is so, we must strengthen the child against the dangers it will inevitably encounter, and must be careful not to pervert its imagination by a false prudery.

Of course we must avoid leading the child to dwell too much upon sexual topics, and fortunately human beings have numerous other interests. The sphere of the sexual must be regarded as a fraction merely of the general educational field. The inculcation of true ideas of morality, and of a sense of honour not confined to externals but one by which the entire being is permeated—these will be the safest essentials of a good sexual and general education.

~PROVIDING EVERYTHING THAT MAKES LIFE
PLEASANT~
M.G.V.T

OTHER BOOKS OF INTEREST TO YOU:
AMIELS JOURNAL
TRENCH ON THE STUDY OF WORDS
ISRAEL IN BRITAIN
AND MORE

GO TO MGVT.CO.UK
TO FIND OUT MORE

GOD BLESS